IMPOSSIBLE GOD

Impossible God introduces Derrida's theology for a new generation interested in Derrida's writings and in the future of theology, and clarifies Derrida's theology for those already familiar with his writings. Derrida's theological concerns are now widely recognised but *Impossible God* shows how Derrida's theology takes its shape from his earliest writings on Edmund Husserl and from explorations into Husserl's unpublished manuscripts on time and theology. Rayment-Pickard argues that Derrida goes beyond the nihilism of the 'death of God' and the denials of negative theology to affirm a theology of God's 'impossibility'. Derrida's 'impossible God' is not another God of the philosophers but a powerful deity capable of wakening us into faith, ethical responsibility and love.

Showing how central theology has been to Derrida's philosophy since the beginning of his career, *Impossible God* presents an accessible study of a neglected area of Derrida's writing which students of philosophy and theology will find invaluable.

Transcending Boundaries in Philosophy and Theology

Series Editors:
Martin Warner, University of Warwick, UK
Keith Vanhoozer, Trinity International University, USA

Transcending Boundaries in Philosophy and Theology is an interdisciplinary series exploring new opportunities in the dialogue between philosophy and theology that go beyond more traditional 'faith and reason' debates and take account of the contemporary reshaping of intellectual boundaries. For much of the modern era, the relation of philosophy and theology has been conceived in terms of antagonism or subordination but recent intellectual developments hold out considerable potential for a renewed dialogue in which philosophy and theology have common cause for revisioning their respective identities, reconceiving their relationship, and combining their resources. This series explores constructively for the 21st century the resources available for engaging with those forms of enquiry, experience and sensibility that theology has historically sought to address. Drawing together new writing and research from leading international scholars in the field, this high profile research series will offer an important contribution to contemporary research across the interdisciplinary perspectives relating theology and philosophy.

Also in this series:

Divine Knowledge
A Kierkegaardian Perspective on Christian Education
David Willows

Kierkegaard, Language and the Reality of God
Steven Shakespeare

Impossible God

Derrida's Theology

HUGH RAYMENT-PICKARD

Only *pure absence* – not the absence of this or that,
but the absence of everything in which all presence is announced –
can *inspire*.

(WD, p. 8)

ASHGATE

Published by
Ashgate Publishing Limited
Gower House
Croft Road
Aldershot
Hants GU11 3HR
England

Ashgate Publishing Company
Suite 420
101 Cherry Street
Burlington, VT 05401-4405

Ashgate website: http://www.ashgate.com

British Library Cataloguing in Publication Data
Rayment-Pickard, Hugh
    Impossible God : Derrida's theology. - (Transcending
    boundaries in philosophy and theology)
    1. Derrida, Jacques, 1930 -- Contributions in theology
    2. Theology, Doctrinal
    I.Title
    194

Library of Congress Cataloging-in-Publication Data
Rayment-Pickard, Hugh.
    Impossible God : Derrida's theology / Hugh Rayment-Pickard.
        p. cm. -- (Transcending boundaries in philosophy and theology)
    Includes bibliographical references (p.) and index.
    ISBN 0-7546-0597-3 (alk. paper)
        1. Derrida, Jacques--Religion. 2. Deconstruction. 3. Theology--Methodology. I. Title.
    II. Series

    BT83.8 .R39 2003
    210′.92--dc21   2002026233

ISBN 0 7546 0597 3

Typeset by IML Typographers, Birkenhead, Merseyside, and
printed in Great Britain by MPG Books Ltd, Bodmin, Cornwall

Contents

Abbreviations

Texts by Jacques Derrida

A   *Aporias*, tr. Thomas Dutoit, Stanford University Press, Stanford, 1993.

Adi   *Adieu to Emmanuel Levinas*, Stanford University Press, Stanford, 1999.

AF   *The Archaeology of the Frivolous: Reading Condillac*, tr. John P. Leavey Jr, University of Nebraska Press, Lincoln, 1987.

C   *Cinders,* tr. Ned Nukacher, University of Nebraska Press, Lincoln, 1991.

Cir   'Circumfession', in *Jacques Derrida*, tr. Geoffrey Bennington, University of Chicago Press, Chicago, 1993.

D   *Dissemination*, tr. Barbara Johnson, Athlone Press, London, 1981.

Dem   *Demeure: Fiction and Testimony*, Stanford University Press, Stanford, 2000.

EH   *Edmund Husserl's Origin of Geometry: An Introduction*, tr. John P. Leavey Jr, University of Nebraska Press, Lincoln, 1989.

EO   *The Ear of the Other: Otobiography, Transference, Translation: Texts and Discussions with Jacques Derrida*, tr. Peggy Kamuf and Avital Ronell, ed. Christie V. McDonald, University of Nebraska Press, Lincoln, 1988.

FK   'Faith and Knowledge', in J. Derrida and G. Vattimo, eds, *Religion*, Polity, Oxford, 1998.

G   *Glas*, tr. John P. Leavey Jr. and Richard Rand, University of Nebraska Press, Lincoln, 1986.

Ges   'Geschlecht', tr. R. Berezdivin, in P. Kamuf, ed., *A Derrida Reader,* Harvester Wheatsheaf, London, 1991.

Ges II 'Geschlecht II', in J. Sallis, ed., *Deconstruction and Philosophy: The Texts of Jacques Derrida*, University of Chicago Press, Chicago, 1987.

Ges IV 'Heidegger's Ear', in J. Sallis, ed., *Reading Heidegger*, Indiana University Press, Bloomington, 1993.

GD   *The Gift of Death*, tr. David Wills, University of Chicago Press, Chicago, 1995.

GT   *Given Time I: Counterfeit Money*, tr. Peggy Kamuf, University of Chicago Press, Chicago, 1992.

H 'How to Avoid Speaking: Denials', in Toby Foshay and Harold Coward, eds, *Derrida and Negative Theology*, State University of New York Press, Albany, 1992.

Hos 'Hospitality, Justice and Responsibility', in R. Kearney and M. Dooley, eds, *Questioning Ethics. Contemporary Debates in Philosophy,* Routledge, London, 1998.

LG 'The Law of Genre', in D. Attridge, ed., *Acts of Literature*, Routledge, London, 1992.

LI *Limited Inc abc...*, ed. Gerald Graff, Northwestern University Press, Evanston, 1988.

LO 'Living On: Border Lines', in G. Hartman, ed., *Deconstruction and Criticism*, Routledge and Kegan Paul, London, 1979.

M *Margins of Philosophy*, tr. Alan Bass, University of Chicago Press, Chicago, 1982.

Mem *Mémoires for Paul de Man*, tr. Cecile Lindsay, Jonathan Culler, Eduardo Cadava, Kevin Newmark and Peggy Kamuf, Columbia University Press, New York, 1989 (revised edition).

OG *Of Grammatology*, tr. Gayatri Spivak, Johns Hopkins University Press, Baltimore, 1976.

ON *On The Name*, ed. Thomas Dutoit, Stanford University Press, Stanford, 1993.

OS *Of Spirit: Heidegger and the Question*, tr. Geoffrey Bennington and Rachel Bowlby, University of Chicago Press, Chicago, 1989.

PC *The Post Card: From Socrates to Freud and Beyond*, tr. Alan Bass, University of Chicago Press, Chicago, 1987.

Par *Parages*, Editions Galilée, Paris, 1986.

PF *The Politics of Friendship*, tr. George Collins, Verso, London, 1997.

Poi *Points ... Interviews 1974–1994*, tr. P. Kamuf et al., Stanford University Press, Stanford,1995.

Pos *Positions*, tr. Alan Bass, University of Chicago Press, Chicago, 1981.

Pro *Le problème de la genèse dans la philosophie de Husserl*, Presses Universitaires de France, Paris, 1990.

Psy *Psyché: Inventions de l'autre*, Editions Galilée, Paris, 1987.

RD 'Remarks on Deconstruction and Pragmatism', in S. Critchley et al., eds, *Deconstruction and Pragmatism*, Routledge, London, 1996.

S *Signéponge/Signsponge* [bilingual edition], tr. Richard Rand, Columbia University Press, New York, 1984.

SM *Specters of Marx: the State of the Debt, the Work of Mourning and the New International*, tr. Peggy Kamuf, Routledge, New York, 1994.

SP *Speech and Phenomena and other Essays on Husserl's Theory of*

	Signs, tr. David B. Allison, Northwestern University Press, Evanston, 1973.
TP	*The Truth in Painting*, tr. G. Bennington and Ian McLeod, University of Chicago Press, Chicago, 1987.
TS	'I have a Taste for the Secret', in J. Derrida and M. Ferraris, *A Taste for the Secret*, Polity, Oxford, 2001.
TT	'The Time of Thesis: Punctuations', in Alan Montefiore, ed., *Philosophy in France Today*, Cambridge University Press, Cambridge, 1983.
UG	'Ulysses Gramophone: Hear Say Yes in Joyce', tr. Tina Kendall and Shari Benstock, in Derek Attridge, ed., *Acts of Literature*, Routledge, London, 1992.
WD	*Writing and Difference*, tr. Alan Bass, Routledge and Kegan Paul, London, 1978.

Texts by Edmund Husserl

CE	*The Crisis of the European Sciences and Transcendental Phenomenology*, tr. David Carr, Northwestern University Press, Evanston, 1970.
CM	*Cartesian Meditations*, tr. Dorian Cairns, Martinus Nijhoff, Dordrecht, 1960.
EJ	*Experience and Judgement*, tr. J. Churchill and Karl Ameriks, Northwestern University Press, Evanston, 1973.
IdI	*Ideas – General Introduction to Pure Phenomenology*, tr. W.R. Boyce Gibson, George Allen and Unwin, New York, 1931.
IdII	*Ideas Pertaining to a Pure Phenomenology and to a Phenomenological Philosophy (Second Book)*, tr. R. Rojcewicz and A. Schuwer, Kluwer, Dordrecht, 1989.
PI	*On the Phenomenology of the Consciousness of Internal Time (1893–1917)*, tr. J.B. Brough, Kluwer, Dordrecht, 1991.
PL	*The Paris Lectures*, tr. P. Koestenbaum, Martinus Nijhoff, The Hague, 1975.

Texts by Martin Heidegger

BP	*Beiträge zur Philosophie (vom Ereignis)*, Gesamtausgabe Band 65, III Abteilung: Unveröffentliche Abhandlungen, Vittorio Klostermann, Frankfurt, 1989.
BT	*Being and Time*, tr. Edward Robinson and John Macquarrie, Harper and Row, New York, 1982.
HC	*History of The Concept of Time*, tr. Theodore Kisiel, Indiana University Press, Bloomington, 1992.

IM   *Introduction to Metaphysics*, tr. Ralph Manheim, Yale University
        Press, New Haven, 1987.
OL   *On The Way To Language*, tr. Peter Hertz, Harper and Row, New
        York, 1971.
QB   *The Question of Being*, tr. William Kluback and Jean T. Wilde,
        Twayne, New York, 1958.
QT   *The Question Concerning Technology and Other Essays*, tr. W.
        Lovitt, Harper and Row, New York, 1977.
PT   *Poetry, Language, Thought*, tr. Albert Hofstadter, Harper and Row,
        New York, 1971.

Acknowledgements

I am grateful to Professor Rudolf Bernet, of the Husserl Archive at the Catholic University of Leuven in Belgium, for permission to study Husserl's unpublished manuscripts and to quote from them. I am also indebted to Mrs I. Lombaerts and Roland Breeur on the staff at the Husserl Archive for their kind assistance both on my visit to the Archive and afterwards in checking quotations against the original transcripts. Professor Simon Critchley kindly gave me a copy of an unpublished version of an article by Derrida, 'La phénoménologie et la clôture de la métaphysique'. Dr R. Burns, Dr Imelda Whelehan, Revd Dr Alan Everett, Martin Pickard, Dr Jill Lloyd, Michael Peppiat, Dr George Pattison, Dr Rachel Carr and the Reverend Dr Giles Fraser at various times read all or part of the text and made invaluable comments. I am also grateful to Elizabeth Teague for her suggestions during copy-editing and to Sarah Lloyd at Ashgate for her guidance and support.

I owe a special and enduring debt to Don Cupitt, whose writings first inspired me to study theology and whose friendship and encouragement have remained a constant support.

My deepest gratitude goes to my wife Liz, without whose unfailing love I could do nothing worthwhile, and to my children Henry and Alexandra.

HR-P

Note

Citations in the text for works by Derrida, Husserl and Heidegger are given in abbreviated form in parentheses (see list of abbreviations p. vii). Wherever possible, references refer the reader back to an English translation. Where English translations are not available, the translations given are my own. Dates given next to the titles of works named in the text are the dates of first publication. Unpublished texts by Husserl are quoted using the reference system in place at the Husserl Archive. The titles of particular manuscripts can be found in the Bibliography.

For Liz, Henry and Alexandra

Chapter 1

Death, Impossibility, Theology: the Theme of Derrida's Philosophy

Truth is not a value one can renounce.
(TS, p. 10)

... one thinks one is seeing themes in the very spot where the nontheme, that which cannot become a theme, the very thing that has no meaning, is ceaselessly re-marking itself – that is, disappearing.
(D, p. 251)

Simplicity and Complexity

'I would like to write to you so simply, so simply, so simply', writes Derrida in *The Post Card* (PC, p. 11). Those who have ever tried reading one of Derrida's books may emit a hollow laugh at this moment. Not only is Derrida's writing far from simple, it has become legendary for its complexity and difficulty. Many potential readers must have been discouraged and put off at the outset. Others have found in Derrida's difficult style a ready-made excuse for dismissing his writings without taking them seriously at all. Clearly such summary dismissals will not lead to an understanding of Derrida's work; rather we must ask the question of the meaning of Derrida's complexity: what does the *difficulty* of Derrida's writing reveal about his philosophical ideas? What *function* does this difficulty serve?

Some have treated Derrida's complexity with cynicism. There's a joke about two students at the end of one of Derrida's lectures. One says to the other, 'That lecture must have been brilliant ... I didn't understand a word of it!' Another joke runs: 'If Derrida makes sense, you haven't understood him.' Among British academics particularly, Derrida's complexity is often taken to be pretentious, an attempt to substitute the convoluted for the profound. The philosopher Barry Smith, writing to *The Times* on behalf of a number of his colleagues, wrote that Derrida's works 'employ a written style that defies comprehension. When the effort is made to penetrate it, it becomes clear that, where coherent assertions are being made at all, these are either false or trivial.'

For others – particularly the enthusiasts of deconstruction in departments of literary studies – Derrida's complexity is taken to be a poetic virtue, a sign that his texts are rich in meaning and nuance. Indeed Derrida has numerous imitators eager to outdo him in literary invention. Peggy Kamuf's 'Introduction' to *A Derrida Reader* is set out as a conversation which is, she says, 'not exactly a dialogue' but a 'typographical' interchange, 'the back and forth of more than one "voice" requiring the convention of blank intervals across the page. These, in turn, could be thought of as the slats of a venetian blind, or a jalousie, which partially obstructs the view.' This introduction is at least as difficult to understand as anything that follows in the anthology.

For us, in this volume, the question of Derrida's complexity is a valuable point of entry into his philosophy. If we can understand why Derrida's texts are so difficult, we will begin to understand what his philosophy is attempting to achieve. But first of all we need to filter out a number of general reasons for the difficulty of his texts. This will enable us to identify the important and essential reason for Derrida's complex writing.

In part, Derrida is 'difficult' because he assumes an audience of professional philosophers who can comfortably understand his constant reference to the philosophical tradition. This is further complicated by his meticulous textual approach. Generally speaking Derrida likes to make detailed readings of specific texts. This demands not only a general philosophical knowledge, but also a good grasp of the texts under discussion. For example, a really thorough reading of Derrida's *Speech and Phenomena* requires us also to have ready to hand a copy of Husserl's *Logical Investigations*. Reading Derrida is demanding work and the difficulty of this task is not simply the result of wilful obscurantism.

A further general complication is Derrida's use of specially designed terms and concepts. Most philosophers are striving to say something new, and this often leads to the creation of neologisms. Neologisms are particularly necessary when philosophers attempt to make a break with tradition and are forced to abandon or alter the traditional vocabulary of philosophy. This was certainly true of both Husserl and Heidegger, Derrida's precursors. Husserl developed a bewildering lexicon of terms to describe the various aspects and procedures of his phenomenological method. Heidegger not only created one set of concepts at the beginning of his career with *Being and Time*, but went on to create a further range of terms to express his later philosophy of language. In similar fashion Derrida has coined terms like 'the trace', 'arche-writing', 'dissemination' – and most famously *'différance'* – to create a language for his philosophy of deconstruction.

Beyond these incidental obstacles, we encounter the complexity that arises specifically because of the philosophical task that Derrida sets himself. We may separate this complexity into two closely interrelated aspects: a structural complexity that arises because of the way Derrida believes language functions; and a conceptual complexity that arises as he tries to indicate the unstable, paradoxical and impossible character of all foundational ideas and realities. These two aspects properly belong together, but it is useful to consider them separately for a moment.

The structural complexity of language results from the instability of language itself, which never permits a merely 'simple' expression of ideas. Derrida is not saying that language lacks structure, but that the structures of language are fluid and without definite centres or fixed boundaries. Rudolphe Gasché has coined the term 'structural infinity' to describe this condition (see p. 14 below). Derrida tries to be faithful to the structural infinity of language by acknowledging the plurivocal character of words and the dynamic interrelations of elements within a text. But more than this, he tries to exploit the structural characteristics of language to produce a philosophical effect. In fact this is precisely how deconstruction works, by exposing or laying bare the structural complexity of language, a complexity which constantly frustrates 'simple' claims to truth, meaning or reality.

Yet in laying bare the conditions of language, Derrida is also trying to say or show something about 'truth' and 'reality'. Here we enter an area of extreme paradox. The deconstruction of language as the medium for the expression of truth would seem to deny Derrida any basis for articulating a definite message. On many occasions he says that it is 'impossible' to say what deconstruction is or what it means. However, even to say that it is 'impossible' is to say *something*. Indeed Derrida writes a great deal *about* deconstruction and the difficulty of saying anything about it. So there is within his writing the need to *speak about* what deconstruction does, to *show* the outcome of his philosophical efforts. His need to-speak-about-the-difficulty-of-speaking forces Derrida to adopt a complex and twisted philosophical language.

The attempt to say the unsayable takes Derrida to a zone of fundamental questioning, where philosophical language doubles and redoubles back upon itself. What Derrida tries to show is that language itself always assumes its 'other', that which cannot properly be named or thought. If he is right, this would mean that the possibility of truth depends upon the possibility of non-truth: the possibility of God depends upon God's impossibility. At points in his writing Derrida uses the symbol of the cross, an *X* or chiasmus, the image of a self-erasing sign, to indicate the self-cancelling nature of all claims to truth.

Not only do Derrida's investigations push language to its breaking-point; they push philosophy to its limits. But is philosophy at the limits still philosophy? Or has it been taken to the point where it becomes theology? Or is this perhaps the moment where we pass over the extreme boundaries of both philosophy and theology into a pre-philosophical, pre-theological area of inquiry that properly belongs to neither discipline? Some people would indeed argue that this dimension of self-questioning is so primitive that it is prior to any particular academic or cultural discipline. Others would claim that such questioning must belong to philosophy, as the science of sciences, the grand inquisitor of all claims to truth. Still others would make the (arguably) more unsettling claim that this zone is necessarily theological, since the claims of theology are always foundational, indeed must always be foundational, as the question of God must, by definition, always be the first and last in any inquiry into origins. To say that there was something prior to God would be to say that God was not God.

Deconstruction and Truth

One of the things that is often casually said about Derrida is that he wants to overturn the idea of truth in favour of complete relativism. This 'myth' about Derrida is extremely misleading. He certainly challenges a particular *metaphysics* of Truth, truth with a capital T, but his whole philosophy is undertaken in the name of *another way* of thinking about truth, a truth *that takes account of* the undecidability of language, in fact the truth *of* the undecidability of language. As Derrida puts it,

> the disappearance of truth as presence, the withdrawal of the present origin of presence, is the condition of all (manifestations of) truth. Nontruth is the truth. Nonpresence is presence. Difference, the disappearance of any originary presence, is at *once* the condition of possibility *and* the condition of the impossibility of truth. (D, p. 168)

Derrida has expressed exasperation at those who have depicted him as a frivolous non-cognitivist with no concern for truth or contexts. Writing in *Limited Inc.*, he says: 'Once again (and this probably makes a thousand times I have had to repeat this, but when will it finally be heard, and why this resistance?) as I understand it the text ... does not suspend reference – to history, to the world, to reality' (LI, p. 137). Later he writes:

> Since the deconstructionist is supposed not to believe in truth, stability, or the unity of meaning, in intention or 'meaning-to-say', how can he demand of us that we read *him* with pertinence, precision, rigour? How can he demand that his own text be interpreted correctly? How can he accuse anyone else of having misunderstood, simplified, deformed it, etc? ... The answer is simple enough: this definition of the deconstructionist is *false* (that's right: false, not true) and feeble; it supposes a bad (that's right: bad, not good) and feeble reading of texts, first of all mine, which therefore must finally be read or reread. Then perhaps it will be understood that the value of truth (and all those values associated with it) is never contested or destroyed in my writings, but only reinscribed in more powerful, larger, more stratified contexts. (Ibid., p. 146)

So the deconstruction of a metaphysics of truth does not close off the possibility of truth understood in another way, understood contextually. This context is the field of language, a language that forbids totalization or the possibility of an organizing centre or 'logos'. The deconstruction of the metaphysics of truth means 'that every referent, all reality has the structure of a differential trace, and that one cannot refer to this "real" except in an interpretive experience' (ibid., p. 148).

We may ask what a commitment to truth can mean, when truth is subject to the play of the 'differential trace' and is therefore relative to other components in the ever-changing context of a 'structural infinity'. Part of Derrida's reply is that since truth is determined 'within interpretive contexts that ... are relatively stable, sometimes apparently unshakeable, it should be possible to invoke rules of competence, criteria of discussion and of consensus, good faith, lucidity, rigour, criticism, and pedagogy' (ibid., p. 146). So truth is contingent, but not *all that* contingent. The other part of his reply is to say that we must maintain *faith* in the truth.[1] Derrida has described this faith in another way saying that we must be 'the friends of truth' (PF, p. 43).

We could say that Derrida, finding the metaphysical concept of truth inadequate, is in fact engaged in rescuing the true concept of truth, truth *as* truth, faithful in the fullest and widest sense to the unstable, plural, historically determined, many-layered experience of human reality. This would mean that the undecidability of truth, the *impossibility* of truth, is *more true* than the metaphysical idea of truth as determinate and stable. The problem for Derrida – as we have been seeing – is how to say such things when the language used to express them disintegrates into paradox. One of the central challenges for Derrida is how to tackle the question of truth when one is forced all the time to make truth claims *in the very process* of pointing out their ultimate impossibility.

Restricted and General Theology

The questions of truth and its possibility are, for Derrida, essentially 'theological' questions. Yet how and why the question of 'truth' *per se* is a theological issue is not immediately obvious. To grasp what Derrida is saying, it is helpful to distinguish two applications of the term 'theology'. First, 'theology' may be used to label discourses about God. Theology in this sense – let us call it 'restricted theology' – is only one of Derrida's many philosophical interests. Second, 'theology' may be used to name the conditions of possibility of 'all the metaphysical determinations of truth' (OG, p. 10), whether God is explicitly invoked or not. Theology in this second sense – let us call it 'general theology' – is not merely one topic among others but is *the* core topic and organizing theme behind Derrida's entire project.

The relationship between the general and restricted orders of theology is explored by Derrida in his essay on negative theology, 'How to Avoid Speaking: Denials' (which is discussed in Chapter 5). Here he discusses Plato (who distinguishes between the manifest world and its formal conditions) and Heidegger (whose 'ontological difference' distinguishes between existing 'beings' and their existential ground of 'Being').[2] Derrida also raises the issue in *The Politics of Friendship*, and in an essay on 'Faith and Knowledge', where he describes the distinction between the two theologies as the difference between 'revelation' and 'revealability'; between 'manifestation' and 'manifestability'; between 'the science of God and the science of divinity'; between 'the experience of faith' and 'the experience of sacredness' (PF, p. 19). 'The event of revelation would reveal not only this or that – God, for example – but revealability itself' (PF, p. 18).

General theology embraces the belief, the explicit or implicit assertion, or the structural affirmation, that there is a central, or underlying, or over-arching, or essential, or inherent meaning to things. So a belief in God would be one example of general theology, and Derrida does write specifically about theism, faith and religion. But what we are calling 'general theology' here goes far beyond theism and formal religion: it extends to the conditions of possibility of the entire range of possible affirmations of the absolute. A belief in reason or absolute reality, in the certainty of the self or of human consciousness, in the logic of history or national identity, in the fixed meaning of words or the definitive interpretation of a work of art, in ideas of 'humanism' or 'human rights' – all this for Derrida is also 'theological', in the sense that foundational truth is being asserted.

Restricted theologies are instances of general theology which occur in different forms at different historical moments. There can be any number of restricted theologies, but there can only be one general theology, since general theology is the category which includes all restricted theologies, along with all other metaphysical systems. Derrida makes the distinction most clearly in an explanatory footnote to one of the opening pages of *Of Grammatology*.

> [Theological] prejudices are nothing but the most clear-sighted and best circumscribed, historically determined manifestation of a constitutive and permanent presupposition essential to the history of the West, therefore to metaphysics in its entirety, even when it professes to be atheist. (OG, p. 4 n. 3)

Here Derrida distinguishes between explicit 'restricted' theological prejudices, which are 'historically determined', and a 'general' theological presupposition which underlies the whole of Western culture.

Paradoxes abound in the distinction between restricted and general theology. Discourses about God appear to be at once 'restricted' *and* 'general' since most theologies invoke God *both* in the 'restricted' sense as a theological object *and* in the 'general' sense as the presupposition of all theological discourse. Derrida alludes to this tension in a footnote to his essay on the theology of Emmanuel Levinas, 'Violence and Metaphysics', when he picks himself up on the use of the phrase 'for example, God' (WD, p. 143 and n. 78). If God is both 'restricted' and 'general' he becomes an example or instance of himself, which is an apparently impossible state of affairs. This complexity notwithstanding – and it is not going to be possible to avoid complexity in a consideration of Derrida – the distinction does useful work in a reading of Derrida's treatment of theology.

One of Derrida's aims, particularly in his early career, is to deconstruct general theology. He attempts this by trying to outdo general theology at its own game, showing that general theology is a restricted example of a still deeper condition: the undecidability of meaning which Derrida calls *différance*. 'The "theological" is a determined moment' in the operation of language (OG, p. 47). Either one may call this the undoing or 'closure' of theology – as Derrida's non-theistic interpreters do; or one may say that this is general theology *par excellence*, theology in a more pure, more total and irreducible form.

Derrida himself appears to say both things. In his essay 'Différance' he repeatedly denies that *différance* is a theological concept, since *différance* defines itself *against* the presuppositions of the general theology of the West.

> *Différance* is not only irreducible to any ontological or theological – ontotheological – reappropriation, but as the very opening space in which ontotheology – philosophy – produces its system and its history, it includes ontotheology, inscribing it and exceeding it without return. (M, p. 6)

This can be read in two ways: on the one hand, Derrida is saying that *différance* cannot be understood as a concept within any theology, since *différance* is what makes possible all discourses including those of theology. On the other hand, he is himself using *différance* to make a general theological claim for the absolute primordiality of linguistic undecidability. It could be said that Derrida manoeuvres metaphysics into the position of a secondary restricted theology, precisely in order to instate *différance* as a first-order general theology. The fact that he does this without explicitly making any theological claims does not matter, since, as he points out himself, general theology operates 'even when it professes to be atheist'.

Logocentrism: Theology and Language

In his analysis of general theological presuppositions, Derrida uses a variety of terms: 'metaphysics'; 'the metaphysics of presence' (his own term) or 'ontotheology' (a term borrowed from Heidegger); 'phonocentrism' (for the theological prioritization of meaning in speech); and the 'transcendental signified' (God or a God-substitute). The most significant term, however, is 'logocentrism': the theological assertion of a logos or self-present truth. These terms are not just ideas, but are tools to root out the general-theological operation of the logos in Western philosophy.[3]

Derrida's philosophy has been the task of unmasking the logos in Western consciousness, showing us where it has been hidden and how it has operated, how general theology determines what and how we think, even when our thinking is apparently non- or anti-theological. In Derrida's estimation, the tradition of Western thought has been predominantly 'centrist' in that it likes organizing concepts around central themes or ideas: as a rule, it dislikes plurality, alterity, ambiguity, contradiction. It likes firm limits, set boundaries to areas of thought. It dislikes meanings that cannot be contained, which spill over. It likes things to be clear, to be seen in their proper light, to be known for what they are. It dislikes what is hidden, or repressed, or concealed, or distorted, or invisible. It enjoys what Derrida calls 'the metaphysics of light': a clarity of vision and a security of knowledge. It 'abhors a vacuum': darkness, absence, death, anything that cannot be given a place in a system.

One of Derrida's key arguments is that logocentrism is not just one attitude among others, but is a fundamental feature of the way we think. In his exploration of general-theological structures, presuppositions and attitudes, Derrida develops the argument first articulated vividly by Nietzsche that theology is written into the *grammar* of the Western mind, and entangled in its very structures of thought. As Derrida puts it (rather dramatically), 'the sign and divinity have the same place and time of birth. The age of the sign is essentially theological. Perhaps it will never *end*. Its historical *closure* is, however, outlined' (OG, p. 14). So any investigation of theology will require thought to be turned back upon thought, and language back upon language.

The unmasking of the theological presuppositions of the West, then, requires first and foremost an analysis of the way we use language. Given the alleged complicity between 'sign' and 'divinity', Derrida looks at the theological structures that exist in our understanding of, and our faith in, the way language works to generate meaning. The theology of the logos depends upon the ability of language to say things, to capture meanings and pass them between persons and across time. The presence of the logos, of ultimate meaning and reality, sustains the whole order of meaning in language. Derrida tries to show how the security of meaning in language depends upon a hierarchy of speech over writing (or, as he calls it, 'phonocentrism'). The spoken word is presumed to be nearer to the mind and the meaning of the speaker. The written word, as a record of speech, 'the signifier of the signifier', is further away from the originally intended meaning. This, argues Derrida, is general theology or logocentrism in its most virulent form. To expose this theology, Derrida turns the hierarchy on its head, claiming that writing is prior to speech.

Derrida's prioritization of writing over speech depends upon a very particular understanding of the term 'writing'. Although this term includes the physical inscription of signs, Derrida also uses the word to name the 'secondary' condition in which such signs find themselves. 'We tend to say "writing" ... to designate not only the physical gestures of literal pictographic or ideographic inscription, but also the totality of what makes it possible ... Thus we say "writing" for all that gives rise to inscription in general' (OG, p. 9). 'Writing' – or, as Derrida sometimes calls it, 'arche-writing' – is the state of being 'the sign of a sign', the condition of language as a fluid system dependent upon internal self-reference and differential relationships. By inverting the speech–writing hierarchy, Derrida is asserting the primacy of secondariness and linguistic uncertainty.

The challenge, therefore, that Derrida presents to general theology is the suggestion that our universe of meanings is not governed by an organizing logos at all but by a radical uncertainty and instability of meaning. The quest for the very beginnings or foundations of meaning does not take us nearer and nearer to an original meaning and logic, instead our search takes us ever deeper into the plurality and complexity of language. The origin is not a stable, unified theological *identity*, but an irreducible *difference*.

The form of Derrida's challenge to general theology is a strategy of subversion called 'deconstruction', the turning of logocentric thinking back upon itself. He tries to show the impossibility of theology because language disseminates meaning in an excessive and plural way. Meaning will simply not allow itself to be contained or defined. The effort to keep meanings ordered, centralized and coherent can never succeed.

On the face of it, this could be seen as an outright rejection of theology. But this is far from the case. Derrida's quest to describe the foundational character of meaning as difference is a mirror version, in parallax as it were, of the theological endeavour to uncover the logos. In other words, in order for Derrida to deconstruct theology, he must make a theological gesture of his own. Thus even as he argues for the 'impossibility' of theology, he implicitly recommends the idea of the impossibility of God as an alternative theology. This paradox of affirming in one way precisely what one has sought to negate in another is one of the reflexive effects of language that deconstruction seeks to exploit. So deconstruction becomes subject, or falls victim to its own procedures – as indeed it must since it takes place within the language of Western philosophy. Deconstruction becomes theological despite itself.

The task of launching an analysis of this theology will not be at all straight-forward. Derrida does not set out his theology in a conventional way; indeed the idea of setting out fixed, definitive positions is one that he avoids. Rather, he writes 'deconstructions' of other thinkers in the attempt to show, generally by example rather than precept, that all philosophy (and theology) is a form of writing and as such has its limits and possibilities determined by the pre-given conditions of language.

Given the emphasis that Derrida places upon linguistic instability and the impossibility of perfect communication, some commentators have argued that it is not possible to read Derrida's philosophy in a coherent or thematic way. The question of whether it is indeed possible to make an organized reading of 'what Derrida says' is an issue that must now be tackled.

The Possibility of Thematic Criticism

In certain philosophical and literary quarters, it has been argued that Derrida's deconstruction of logocentrism had changed the basic rules of philosophy. It became accepted among some of his readers that Derrida's writing was a one-off, *sui generis*, that he had broken the mould of philosophy, that his writings did not belong to any hitherto existing genre, and that it was not possible to use existing critical tools or standards to evaluate his work. All existing philosophical protocols had allegedly been 'deconstructed' by him. Derrida's writings were no longer philosophy as such, but post-philosophy occupying the ruins of old-fashioned Western thinking. In such circumstances, any conventional critical treatment of Derrida would be pointless, since he had already 'deconstructed' in advance the presuppositions of any philosophical critique. Faced with this, 'criticism' of Derrida would have to be replaced by 'readings' of his writings. One could follow Derrida's texts, admire them, marvel at them, but *evaluating* them appeared to have been made impossible. With talk like this, it is easy to see how a mystique gathered around Derrida and deconstruction. Derrida's writings were read more like scripture than philosophy, and his expositors assumed the mantle of priestly scribes whose role was to expound the mystery of deconstruction. At the centre of this mystique was the belief that Derrida wasn't saying anything at all in his writings, but merely dismantling the philosophical claims of others. Apparently with no 'position' of his own, Derrida gave detractors and admirers alike nothing to get hold of.

A sophisticated exponent of such a 'non-cognitivist' view is the American philosopher Richard Rorty. Rorty argues that Derrida started out writing philosophy but that he later took a 'literary' turn and produced texts that do not fit 'within any conceptual scheme previously used to evaluate novels or philosophical treatises'.[4] Speaking of one of Derrida's texts (The 'Envois' section of *The Post Card* which is set out as a series of letters), Rorty argues that there can be no 'result' or 'conclusion , 'no "upshot" – nothing to carry away … once one has finished reading it'. For Rorty, Derrida's 'literary' texts are pure playfulness, private-language games that defy public classification either as 'philosophy' or 'literature'. These writings do not 'demonstrate' anything, and they do not offer a 'philosophical theory'.

Rorty's view has, broadly speaking, been the received opinion of those critics who see Derrida as an essentially 'literary philosopher' who, to use Rorty's analogy, does for philosophy what Proust did for the novel, and who situates his texts in a twilight between private language and public discourse, subverting the protocols of existing genres, and rendering conventional criticism impotent. In the wider academic world this viewpoint takes the form of the belief that there is a 'special problem' facing the critic of Derrida's texts.

Although Rorty is an admirer of Derrida, others (such as Jürgen Habermas) use the same 'textualist' reading of Derrida to argue that his philosophy is 'mystification'. In *The Philosophical Discourse of Modernity* Habermas sees Derrida in the flow of the second of two traditions that descend from Nietzsche. The first tradition emerges from Nietzsche's desire to express the individual's will to power by uncovering the cultural superstructure which deadens and restricts the natural forces of life. This tradition is pursued in particular by Bataille and Foucault. The second tradition, to which Heidegger and Derrida belong, grows out of Nietzsche's critique of metaphysics. The leap from Nietzsche to Heidegger and thence to Derrida is not direct. Husserl and Saussure, although not directly within the tradition itself, provide stepping stones along the way. Heidegger is able to pursue Nietzsche's critique of metaphysics by turning Husserl's phenomenology from epistemology to ontology, placing rationalism in the service of temporal human existence and asserting the 'unconcealedness' of Being before propositional truth. Heidegger, in Habermas's view, tries to take a step beyond Husserl, into the philosophy of language, but fails because he cannot successfully describe the medium of language itself. Derrida, however, uses Saussurean insights to arrive at a general concept of language as 'writing'. This enables Derrida to pass around Heidegger's Being into the more ethereal realm of the sign. For Habermas, though, this apparent advance on Heidegger is really a step backwards into a mystical–transcendental foundationalism which does not 'shake [itself] loose of the intentions of first philosophy'.[5] Echoing Adorno's critique of Heidegger's 'jargon of authenticity', Habermas attacks Derrida's 'mystification' and his 'empty, formula-like avowal of some indeterminate authority'. Derrida is seen to merge philosophy with literature and supersede logic with rhetoric. In Habermas's estimation Derrida's non-cognitivist approach fails to complete the Nietzschean/Heideggerian aspiration of 'overcoming metaphysics', and merely leaves us stranded in a bleak awareness of the paradoxes of metaphysics.

By contrast, in the opposing camp, two critics in particular have been prominent in emphasizing the thematic and structural *coherence* in Derrida's philosophy. Rodolphe Gasché has argued powerfully that Derrida's writing needs to be rescued from monopolization by anti-cognitivist 'literary criticism' and returned to its proper place in 'philosophy'. Gasché maintains that Derrida's deconstructive programme 'reveals to even a superficial examination, a well-ordered procedure, a step-by-step type of argument based on an acute awareness of level-distinctions, a marked thoroughness and regularity'.[6] In order to understand Derrida's writing, Gasché urges the reader to return to 'the most essential *topoi* ... of philosophy since its incipience'. Christopher Norris has also argued passionately against Rorty's 'textualist' view. Norris, like Gasché, sets Derrida firmly in the 'Enlightenment tradition' of Western philosophy. Derrida is seen to raise certain highly subversive questions about the constitution and presuppositions of that tradition. However, he is not, in Norris's estimation, a prophet of the 'end of philosophy' who heralds a new age of thoroughgoing relativism and absolute free play of meaning. Norris argues that Derrida does not deconstruct 'truth' and 'reality' *per se*. Rather, he deconstructs specific texts in which foundational concepts such as 'truth' and 'reality' have been employed with insufficient rigour. For Gasché and Norris, Derrida does have something to say, some comment to make about philosophy and its uses. Furthermore, he is seen to offer *arguments* in support of his theories and observations.[7]

Christopher Norris also disputes Habermas's description of Derrida as a mystical non-cognitivist. Norris takes Derrida out of the Nietzschean heritage of anti-philosophy and situates him in the tradition which pursues the 'Kantian' problems of knowledge and reason. Norris takes issue with Habermas's assertion that Derrida so emphasizes the role of metaphor in philosophy that he effectively abolishes the difference between philosophy and literature. In response, Norris notes that Habermas (and Rorty) ignore

Derrida's early work, which is obviously philosophical, and focus too much on a few texts from the late 1970s which employ literary devices in the service of philosophical discussion. This is, furthermore, the essential point for Norris, because even when Derrida is at his apparently least serious and most poetic, his writing is still making philosophical headway.[8] Norris might have added that Derrida's 'literary' output is only a small part of his overall work to date and can hardly be used as the basis for a definition of his general point of view. Norris concludes that it is

> unfortunate that Habermas takes his bearings in *The Philosophical Discourse of Modernity* from a widespread but none the less fallacious idea of how deconstruction relates to other symptoms of the so-called post-modern condition. What Derrida gives us to read is *not* philosophy's undoing at the hands of literature, but a literature that meets the challenge of philosophy in every aspect of its argument, form and style.[9]

One of Rorty's comments on the debate is that Derrida 'makes noises of both sorts', giving encouragement both to himself and to Gasché.[10] This is an interesting remark. The Rorty–Habermas view of Derrida contains a strong element of truth. Derrida's texts do indeed lend themselves at moments more or less to one interpretation or the other. For a time at least in the late 1970s Derrida did experiment with stylistic devices and approaches that we normally associate with literature. In so far as he attempts to deconstruct a metaphysics (logocentrism) embedded within Western philosophy, the title 'post-philosophy' is not inappropriate. Derrida does try to place deconstruction beyond the reach of philosophical critique, and this does present a special challenge to the critic. Although he often claims to dislike the 'mystique' of deconstruction, and emphasizes the seriousness of his philosophical endeavours, his obscure style of writing has undoubtedly contributed to the mystification of his work.

Yet despite this, Rorty is able to write at length *about* Derrida's philosophy, the way it eludes criticism and its literary inventiveness. In all his statements about the impossibility of interpreting Derrida's writings, Rorty is at the same time *making* interpretations of them, and conceding that there is, after all, some interpretative conclusion or 'upshot' arising from reading Derrida. There is an inherent impossibility in the view that Derrida's philosophy is *sui generis*, since '*sui generis*' is itself a generic term. Rorty's conclusion – that Derrida's work is essentially play and that much of his writing is private and inscrutable – is already a totalizing interpretation. Someone who genuinely thought that Derrida's writings could not profitably undergo interpretation would be forced to pass over them in silence.

We have already seen that Derrida's philosophical project involves a convoluted engagement with language and the conditions of truth. Derrida seeks to exploit the excessive way in which language operates 'playfully' beyond logocentric control and organization. However, the playfulness of language is not – as Rorty implies – completely chaotic, unstructured and beyond description. From the work of Wittgenstein, we know that play clearly is a distinctively regulated activity, with a 'condition'; otherwise it would not be possible to distinguish it from non-play.[11] From the very outset, in his earliest descriptions of deconstruction, Derrida had said that 'one ought to be able to formulate its rules' (OG, p. 24). *'Différance* is not astructural', he asserts in a later text; 'it produces systematic and regulated transformations which are able, at a certain point, to leave room for a structural science' (Pos, p. 28) Thus it should be possible to ask about the patterns of play and the extent to which these patterns constitute an argument which is philosophically significant. Consequently, it should be possible to join some of the perceptions of Gasché and Norris with those of Rorty, and speak *at one and the same time* of Derrida's *rigour* and his *playfulness*.

Derrida considers this dynamic between play and structure on a number of occasions, but most notably in his essay 'Structure, Sign, and Play in the Discourse of the Human Sciences'. There are two senses, for Derrida, in which the play of a text does not constitute the absence of structure. First, play is that which unsettles the notion of 'a centre in the constitution of structure', deconstructing the notion that the centre is a *'fixed* locus' with a *'natural* site' (WD, p. 280, italics added).[12] This subversion of the 'centre' of a structure, therefore, does not rule out a 'non-centred' structure, 'the notion of a structure lacking any centre', although such a thing is, Derrida acknowledges, 'unthinkable' in a culture conditioned to see 'the centre' as the only possible means of structural organization.

The idea of non-centred structures may seem problematic. However, Derrida employs, for example, the serial form of narrative to attempt an escape from the apparently closed circle of presence-centred structures. Even when we consider some of Derrida's most 'literary' writing, we discover evidence of argument and sustained thematic organization. The 'Envois' section of *The Post Card*, for example, rests upon a shadowy but unmistakable narrative structure. Similarly, 'Cartouches', another apparently free-playing essay, contains a distinctive narration treating concepts as protagonists.

Elsewhere, considering the structure of music, Derrida supplies a metaphor for non-centred structure by appealing to the analogy of a 'constellation':

> This absence of both a border and any closure of propriety gives to this textual music what I will call ... its galaxic or ga-lactic structure. Galaxy is meant here, at least, as a multiplicity in a perpetually unfolding space, which has no external limit, no outside, no edge, a constellated autonomy which doesn't refer to anything but itself, feeding itself, inseminating itself or nurturing itself from its own breast. (Psy, p. 99) [13]

Derrida is not alone in using the metaphor of a constellation to describe the structure of philosophical thought. Walter Benjamin and Theodor Adorno have both employed this image in order to represent the organization of philosophical ideas beyond the controlling power of Enlightenment reason.

Gasché approaches the question of the disaggregated structure of Derrida's thought in relation to the Hegelian concepts of positive and negative infinity.[14] Derrida repeatedly asserts, most notably in *Dissemination*, that text in general is 'indeterminable' in any total sense, in such a way that interpretation is never final. Yet the indeterminability of what Derrida calls the 'general text' is not non-structural but takes its structure from the 'law of play'. Gasché argues that the general text's playful structure is not finally determinable and therefore constitutes what he calls a non-Hegelian 'structural infinity'. He distinguishes this 'structural infinity' both from Hegel's 'positive' infinity and from his 'negative' infinity, since these two forms of infinity are both effectively attempts at totalization. 'Structural infinity' stands staunchly between any form of infinity and any form of totalization.

Second, Derrida maintains that any discourse *against* the metaphysics of the 'centre', and this includes deconstruction itself, cannot escape collusion with the structures it seeks to undermine. 'In the repetition and return of play, how could the phantom of the centre not call to us?' asks Derrida (WD, p. 297). Therefore even Derrida's most elaborate anti-metaphysical texts cannot, by his own admission, escape metaphysically centred structures altogether. Indeed for Derrida

> there is no sense in doing without the concepts of metaphysics in order to shake metaphysics. We have no language ... which is foreign to this history; we can pronounce not a single destructive proposition which has not already had to slip into the form ... of precisely what it seeks to contest. (Ibid., pp. 280ff.)

Elsewhere Derrida comments that 'the designation of ... impossibility escapes the language of metaphysics only by a hairsbreadth ... [I]t must borrow its resources from the logic it deconstructs. And by doing so find its very foothold there' (OG, p. 314).

Thus two forms of structure – non-centred structures and residual metaphysical structures – ought to be discernible in Derrida's writing. As he states in his preface to *Dissemination*, even

> the adventurous excess of a writing that is no longer directed by any knowledge does not abandon itself to improvisation. The accident or throw of 'dice' that opens such a text does not contradict the rigorous necessity of its formal assemblage. The game here is the unity of chance and rule, of the programme and its leftovers and extras. (D, p. 54)

Derrida has clarified this perspective more recently when he denied ever having spoken or written about 'complete freeplay' of meaning (LI, p. 115).

Whatever hermeneutical problems face the reader of Derrida, these should not make an interpretation of Derrida either as impossible or convoluted as some critics suggest. Here we will contend, in agreement with Gasché, that there is inherent thematic coherence to Derrida's work, that his writing does belong to a philosophical tradition, that it does reflect particular philosophical attitudes, and that it is organized around a network of identifiable questions and motifs. Furthermore, it will be argued that patterns of thematic organization and argument are evident both in Derrida's so-called 'literary' work and in his 'philosophical' writing.[15] The texts which lend themselves most readily to Rorty's view of Derrida as a philosopher of play – the 'Genet column' in *Glas*, 'Envois' and 'Cartouches' – clearly present a special challenge to the philosophical reader. Arguments, philosophical or otherwise, seem scarce. However, themes *are* present, and there are arguments of a narrative sort which demonstrate Derrida's powers of philosophical innovation. This is not to ignore or deny the hermeneutical problems referred to above. Indeed, particular care will have to be taken in arguing for the coherence and identity of the thematic approach that will be used.

Deconstruction and the Theme of Death

The importance of the idea of 'death' in Derrida's philosophy has long been underscored, most recently in Catherine Pickstock's critique of Derrida in *After Writing*. Long before that, Geoffrey Hartman (in his highly influential work on Derrida, literature and philosophy, *Saving the Text*) identified what he called Derrida's thanatopsis or thanatopraxis.[16] Hartman also sets Derrida's interest in death in a religious context. Hartman sees the overcoming of death to find 'something positive' as 'the problem of religious thought'. This problem, however, also faces the philosopher since 'philosophy's attempt to have "nothing" as its presupposition merely veils the reality of death as the something that always precedes'. This, Hartman implies, is at the origin of Derrida's preoccupation with death. Geoffrey Bennington's 'Derridabase' raises the important question of Derrida's theology and of death in the context of the deconstruction of the metaphysics of the self.[17] Mark C. Taylor has often alluded to a theme of death in Derrida, as in his aphorism: 'The literature which preoccupies Derrida is the literature of death; the death that obsesses Derrida is the death of literature.'[18] David Wood has also spoken of Derrida's 'most intimate relation with death'.[19] Not least, Derrida himself has written: 'It's to death that already I owe everything I earn, I have succeeded in making of it, as I have with god, it's the same thing, my most difficult ally' (Cir, p. 172).

We will miss the significance of the theme of death in Derrida if we restrict our attention to texts where he discusses death in particular. It is not just 'death' – in what is called the 'proper' sense – that belongs to the theme to which we are giving 'death' as a title. The 'theme' of death also contains such other related concepts as absence, finitude, *sous rature* (or under erasure), the 'end', closure and non-presence. What therefore must be argued is that 'death' in Derrida's lexicon is not so much a fixed concept as the maternal metaphor in a familial field of related metaphors.[20] Derrida hints at the nature of this field in *Of Grammatology*, when he writes about 'the master-name of the supplementary series: death' (OG, p. 183). What does this mean?

This question is perhaps best approached negatively by saying what a field of related metaphors is *not*. The various words which relate within a field of metaphors are not merely a list of alternative signifiers which may be used to label the same object. This would amount to a field of metonyms rather than metaphors. As Paul Ricoeur puts it, 'metonymy rests on contiguity and metaphor on resemblance'.[21] The items in a field of metaphors belong together not because they may substitute for one another, but because they bear both *a family resemblance* and *a necessary dissemblance* to one another. Absence is not the same as death, yet the two can be said to share a relatedness. This is the basis of the coherence of the theme which we are to describe: a certain range of metaphors of negation and finitude used by Derrida are drawn together by the term death.

The notion of 'resemblance' enables us to define more precisely what has hitherto been described as a 'field'. The word *resemblance* derives from the French verb *ressembler*, which in turn stems from the Latin *similis*. *Ressembler* contains the notion of differentiated items which are in some sense drawn together. Wittgenstein also appeals to the notion of 'family resemblance' when he seeks to describe the patterns of similarity between games: 'the strength of the thread [of resemblance] does not reside in the fact that some one fibre runs through its whole length, but in the overlapping of many fibres'.[22] In 'The Double Session' Derrida acknowledges the requirement for a plural, differential or diacritical dimension to thematic criticism. A thematic critic must connect 'diverse nuances of meaning into one single complex' (D, p. 249). Derrida cites Ricoeur's 'law of intentional analogy' which attempts to 'reach all the themes linked by relations of affinity. This would involve, for example, moving from the azure to the window-pane, to the blank paper, to the glacier, to the snowy peak, to the swan, to the wing, to the ceiling' (ibid.). Derrida tries to show in this essay that any proposed field of simulation, in other words a 'theme', necessarily breaks down into dissimulation as the spread of its items multiplies and diversifies. Thus Derrida both recognizes the necessary *resemblement* of a theme and observes the tendency of all *resemblement* (simulation, mimesis, metaphor, and so on) to break down into dissimulation and difference. The quality of *resemblement* is therefore an indeterminable combination of similitude and dissimilitude, continuity and discontinuity, life and death. As Derrida puts it in another context, 'the issue ... is *to rebind* ... the question of *life death* to the question of the position ... of the theme or the thesis' (PC, p. 259).

Unlike a motif, a theme is not the identical repetition of the 'same', but the differentiated development of an idea through patterns of similarity and contrast. All this, therefore, may seem to be an unnecessarily complicated way of describing what is already commonly understood. However, there are two important reasons for undertaking this discussion. First, since there are those who strongly argue *against* the thematization of Derrida's writing, it is essential that the basis of these thematic claims is firmly secured at the outset. Second, the philosophical necessity to reflect upon the nature of 'theme' cannot be ignored. The extent to which a theme is held to be a function of identity or of difference is entirely apropos of the theme of death itself. In Derrida's analysis, identity (the same) is associated with the metaphysics of life (presence) and difference (the other) with the process of death (absence). Thus what is being argued here is that 'difference' is as crucial to the coherence of Derrida's theme of death as is 'identity'. This echoes the content of the theme itself, which implies that death cannot be excluded as life's 'other' but is crucial to both the possibility and the understanding of life. It is for this reason that Derrida's central theme must not be seen as a morbid necrophilia.[23] For the theme of death is the path that takes Derrida back to a philosophy of life as 'life/death': death in life and life in death.[24] 'Let us guard against saying that death is opposed to life. The living being is only a species of what is dead, and a very rare species' (C, p. 69).

Remembering his insistence on the non-totalizing character of text, it is important to note that, for Derrida, the theme of death takes the ultimately undecidable form of Gasché's 'structural infinity' or his own 'constellation'. The theme of death is an open field of *resemblement* rather than an exhaustive and closed categorization of Derrida's texts. Again, Paul Ricoeur makes an important point in this respect: 'A family resemblance first brings individuals together, before the role of a logical class dominates them.'[25] In this way, as an unbounded field of *resemblance*, the theme of death takes on a reflexive significance. As *resemblance* passes from item to item, and looping at points back upon itself, the theme slips into *dissemblance* and subverts itself. As Derrida puts it, 'metaphor always carries death within itself', sooner or later the carriage of metaphor snaps the chain of resemblance altogether. In view of this Derrida proposes, against Ricoeur's law of intentional analogy, an alternative definition of the limit of a theme:

> The angle and the intersection of a re-mark that folds the text back upon itself without any possibility of its fitting back over or into itself . . . one thinks one is seeing themes in the very spot where the nontheme, that which cannot become a theme, the very thing that has no meaning, is ceaselessly re-marking itself – that is, disappearing. (D, p. 251)

It is this 'very thing which has no meaning' (what Derrida calls the 'blank' or '*Khora*' or 'aporia' or 'chiasmus') that this study seeks to thematize under the title 'death'. Derrida's occasional contention that these 'blanks' cannot be thematized at all, however provisionally or tentatively, is constantly contradicted by his own identification of them. Whenever he tries to speak of the class of item that defies thematization, Derrida automatically creates a class of non-thematizable items, a paradox he names elsewhere as 'the species of the nonspecies' (WD, p. 293). So when he writes, for example, about 'the *constellation* of blanks' (italics added) which makes thematization impossible, his *refusal* of theme itself forces the *creation* of a theme (D, p. 257).[26] Consequently Derrida makes lists of the items which cannot be thematized: blank, veil, fold, re-mark, aporia, chiasmus, abyss, spacing, interval. On the basis of what, though, are such lists possible if not a theme? What Derrida is resisting is not so much the idea of theme as it is conceived here, but the possibility of a theme with a capital 'T' or a blank with a capital 'B' (ibid., p. 258). As that which cannot be totalized, 'the theme of death' as used in this study also necessarily contains 'the death of theme' as the play of metaphor gets spirited away into dissimilitude and contradiction. This is what in 'White Mythology' Derrida calls '*relève de metaphor*', the internal logic that means metaphor 'gets carried away with itself, cannot be what it is except in erasing itself, indefinitely constructing its deconstruction' (M, p. 268). (This is a process which is illustrated clearly in Derrida's set-piece example of *resemblement*, the essay 'Cartouches'.) Indeed 'death' is not only the title that will be given to the theme, but it also names the process of dissimilitude by which the theme develops. 'Death', as Derrida reminds us, is the name Hegel gives for change.

In his most recent writing Derrida has articulated the possibility of a theme of death. In *Aporias*, he explicitly says that he is 'choosing the theme of death' and speaks of 'the numerous instances where this theme has recurred: the aporetology or aporetography in which I have not ceased to struggle' (A, p. 15). In this text he also concedes that 'death' belongs to a semantic field: 'with the motif of the nonentity, or of nothingness, the motif of death is never far away' (ibid., p. 13).

Derrida uses the analysis of death and its related metaphors as a means of exploring the other of a metaphysics which is always grounded in the positive presence of 'life'. Whether it is Plato (who, Derrida notes in *Dissemination*, describes the *logos* as a *zoon*) (D, p. 79ff.) or Husserl (who is shown to ground phenomenality on a substratum of life) or Heidegger (whose humanism depends upon a particular determination of human life), Derrida associates *metaphysics* with *life*. Death or absence is the excluded alternative which although repressed by the structures of metaphysics is, none the less, essential to its life. Death is, to use a phrase of Derrida's, a 'crypt – one would have said, of the transcendental or the repressed, of the unthought or the excluded – that organizes the ground to which it does not belong' (G, p. 166). The meditation upon death, the contemplation of the repressed other, is what undoes metaphysics. It is also through the otherness of death, and on the far side of a deconstruction of metaphysics conceived as 'life', that we arrive at what may be called Derrida's theology: a theology which moves between life and death, between the old life-of-God theology of the metaphysics of presence and its repressed other: the theology of the death of God. This is not a new 'life-of-God' theology, in either 'negative' or 'positive' guises, or (as Mark C. Taylor argues) a thoroughgoing 'death-of-God' theology. Derrida's theology of difference 'means that God is or appears, *is named*, within the difference between All and Nothing, Life and Death. Within Difference, and at bottom as Difference itself. This difference is what is called *History*. God is *inscribed* in it' (WD, p. 116) .

This book will pursue the question of Derrida's theology through an analysis of his writings on Husserl and Heidegger. We will follow his deconstruction of Husserl and Heidegger, seeking to show how he uses the theme of death to uncover the grounds of both an impossible phenomenology and an impossible theology. This will enable us to determine more precisely the character of Derrida's 'impossible' God and assess its significance.

Notes

1   This faculty of faith is of obvious theological importance, and it will form a topic in a later chapter of this book.
2   Elsewhere Derrida refers to Eckhart's distinction between 'God' and 'Godness'.
3   The Western philosophical tradition is the theatre for Derrida's deconstruction of logocentrism. '*The history of ... metaphysics ...* has, in spite of all differences, not only from Plato to Hegel but also beyond these apparent limits, from the pre-Socratics to Heidegger, always assigned the origin of truth to the logos' (OG, p. 3). However, Derrida's philosophy is not merely a critical history of Western ideas. We will see in the following chapter how he launches a critique of Husserl's phonocentrism by venturing a general description of the condition of language in terms of delayed meaning. Derrida's reading of Husserl's text is the launch pad for a theory of language with universal significance. This illustrates the way in which Derrida uses the restricted stage of Western philosophy as the platform for philosophical reflection. It certainly is the case, Derrida argues, that 'we must begin *wherever we are*' (OG, p. 162), but deconstruction is also an attempt to think *against* and therefore *beyond* the concept of 'the West'. Derrida calls this endeavour an 'exorbitant' method (a thinking beyond the orbit of logocentrism). This is a most necessary move, since the very concept of 'the West' that Derrida uses so freely to *define* logocentrism *is itself* a logocentric concept. For a discussion of this issue, see R. Gasché, 'The Law of Tradition', in *Inventions of Difference* (Harvard University Press, Cambridge, 1994).
4   R. Rorty, *Contingency, Irony, Solidarity* (Cambridge University Press, Cambridge, 1989), p. 136.
5   J. Habermas, *The Philosophical Discourse of Modernity* (Polity Press, Cambridge, 1987).
6   R. Gasché, 'Infrastructures and Systematicity' in J. Sallis, ed., *Deconstruction and Philosophy: The Texts of Jacques Derrida* (University of Chicago Press, Chicago, 1987), p. 3.
7   Derrida has recently spoken unambiguously on this issue, describing the criticism that he does not offer arguments as a 'defamation' (C. Mouffe, ed., *Deconstruction and Pragmatism,* Routledge, London, 1996, p. 78). In this piece, Derrida also distances himself from Rorty's interpretation of his writing as 'private' and 'literary'.
8   Christopher Norris, importantly, makes the case for this in the 'Envois' section of *The Post Card,* arguing that the exchange of postcards shows 'how philosophy has excluded certain kinds of writing – letters, apocrypha, "unauthorized" genres of whatever sort – while allowing them a place on the margins of discourse from which they continue to exert a fascination and a power to complicate received ideas' ('Deconstruction, Postmodernism and Philosophy', in D. Wood, ed., *Derrida: A Critical Reader*, Blackwell, Oxford, 1992) p. 177.
9   Ibid., p. 191.
10 R. Rorty, 'Is Derrida a Transcendental Philosopher?', in D. Wood, ed., *Derrida: A Critical Reader.*

11   See L. Wittgenstein, *Philosophical Investigations*, tr. G. Anscombe (Blackwell, Oxford, 1974), §§68–71, pp. 32ff.

12   It is interesting to note that Derrida directly identifies the notion of 'non-centre' with both death and the absence of God. (See WD, pp. 294–300.)

13   See also D, pp. 257ff., where Derrida refers to 'a constellation of blanks' and 'a tropological structure that circulates infinitely around itself through the incessant supplement of an extra turn'.

14   Gasché, *Inventions of Difference*, pp. 129–49.

15   Derrida acknowledges the problems that arise when placing texts into 'philosophical' or 'literary' categories. However, he does not accept Rorty's view that in *Glas* and elsewhere he deliberately collapses philosophy into literature: 'I have never assimilated a so-called philosophical text to a so-called literary text' ('Is there a philosophical language?', in *Points ... Interviews, 1974–1994*, tr. Peggy Kamuf et al., Stanford University Press, Stanford, 1995, p. 217).

16   G. Hartman, *Saving The Text*, pp. xxv and xvii–xviii.

17   G. Bennington, 'Derridabase', in G. Bennington and J. Derrida, *Jacques Derrida* (University of Chicago Press, Chicago, 1993).

18   M.C. Taylor, *Altarity* (University of Chicago Press, Chicago, 1987), p. 298.

19   D. Wood, 'Following Derrida' in J. Sallis, ed., *Deconstruction and Philosophy: The Texts of Jacques Derrida*, p. 153.

20   In 'White Mythology' (*Margins of Philosophy*) Derrida famously argues *against* the philosophical evaluation of metaphor which only emphasizes the controlling aspect of metaphor and takes no account of the inherent attribute of metaphor as a 'carrier away' of meaning and thus as a dissembler.

21   P. Ricoeur, *The Rule of Metaphor: Multidisciplinary Studies in the Creation of Meaning in Language* (Routledge and Kegan Paul, London, 1986), p. 175.

22   L. Wittgenstein, *Philosophical Investigations*, §§67f.

23   As Catherine Pickstock argues in *After Writing* (Blackwell, Oxford, 1998).

24   Derrida uses this binarism as a neologism: *life death [la vie la mort]* in the title of an essay on Freud, 'To Speculate – On "Freud"' (PC, p. 259).

25   Ricoeur, *Rule of Metaphor*, p. 198.

26   The same can be said of Derrida's assertion later on that 'no possible theme of the fold would be able to constitute the system of its meaning or present the unity of its multiplicity' (D, p. 270). But Derrida *must* thematize the 'system of meaning' of 'the fold' precisely in order to refute the possibility of its thematization. There are other similar examples of such classification, for instance: 'the North, winter, death, imagination, representation, the irritation of desires – this entire series of supplementary significations' (OG, p. 309).

Chapter 2

The Living Present of God: Derrida's Deconstruction of Husserl's Theology

The question of the possibility of the transcendental reduction
cannot expect an answer. It is the question of the possibility of the
question, opening itself, the gap on whose basis the transcendental
I, *which Husserl was tempted to call 'eternal'... is called upon to ask*
itself about everything, and particularly about the possibility of the
unformed and naked factuality of the nonmeaning ... of its own
death.

(WD, pp. 167f.)

The Importance of Derrida's Writing on Husserl

Derrida's writing on Husserl has attracted surprisingly little attention.[1] Yet the reading of Husserl has both a distinctive and seminal position in Derrida's philosophy. Derrida's interest in Husserl can be traced back to his university studies when the problems of time, interpersonality and foundations in Husserl's philosophy were the subject of a thesis (written in 1953–54 but published over thirty years later as *Le problème de la genèse dans la philosophie de Husserl*, 1990). In the decade which followed, Husserl remained the dominant preoccupation of Derrida's lectures and publications: *Edmund Husserl's Origin of Geometry: An Introduction*; *Speech and Phenomena and other Essays on Husserl's Theory of Signs*; 'La phénoménologie et la clôture de la métaphysique'; and 'Genesis and Structure'. The critical standpoint that Derrida adopts in this period – the view that the Western 'metaphysics of presence' is subverted by the aporetic condition of the language in which it is promulgated – is the core perspective that guides his later work. What Derrida also develops through his reading of Husserl is the methodological technique known as 'deconstruction', although Derrida himself has been much less fond of this title than his commentators, particularly those in America.[2] These early works, although more philosophically conventional and much less fashionable than his more flamboyant, literary writing of the late 1970s and 1980s, contain a key to the enigmatic structure of Derrida's philosophical programme. In particular they disclose a theological preoccupation which never leaves his philosophizing.

Even in his thesis we can discern clearly many of the concerns of Derrida's mature writing. The thesis is what Derrida has called a 'panoramic' essay, surveying the treatment of 'genesis' or foundations in Husserl's writing. Derrida's argument – which is not so different from that effectively offered elsewhere in his writing – is that the quest for a foundation to philosophy is interminable and cannot be closed off (as Husserl claims) at a point of absolute origin: the philosopher searches back for a first beginning but finds her/himself travelling backwards in endless regress. Each apparently solid ground gives way to reveal a still deeper, or more entangled, set of assumptions. It is, significantly, in his thesis that Derrida first suggests that *lebendige Gegenwart* (living presence/living present) is the presupposed foundation of Husserl's phenomenology. This is a concept that Derrida will later call 'theological'. Although Husserl does use this concept in his published texts, the idea is most clearly explored in his unpublished writing (the *Nachlass*) in the Husserl Archive in Leuven where Derrida undertook research during the early 1950s.[3] In particular, he focused upon three groups of unpublished texts: Group B dating from 1921–23, which deals with the question of the so-called 'reduction'; Group C dating from 1930–34, which considers the problem of time and the possible constitution of 'original structures' (*Urstructuren*) of temporality, such as a continuous present; and Group D dating from 1926–32, where the issue of foundations or 'primordial constitution' (*Urkonstitution*) is discussed. Derrida's interest in the Husserl *Nachlass*, which is generally underestimated by critics (if it is mentioned at all), helped him to form a perspective on Husserl that we not only find in the early texts, but which echoes again and again through his later writing. Since, as will be argued, Derrida's perspective on Husserl is seminal for his philosophy as a whole, his reference to the *Nachlass* is of some importance.

Derrida argues in his thesis, as he does in later texts, that the main problems for Husserl are those of interpersonality and temporality. It will be seen below that this critical perspective is not original, but Derrida's discussion does contain many indications of the motifs of his later writing, in particular the idea of an irreducible alterity which makes 'impossible' Husserl's quest for a pure origin for phenomenological thought. In the thesis Derrida repeatedly describes this alterity as the 'dialectical' play of themes, 'a basic tension', in phenomenology:

> In the absolute identity of the subject with itself, the temporal dialectic, *a priori*, constitutes alterity. The subject appears to itself originally as a tension between the Same and the Other. The theme of a transcendental intersubjectivity establishing transcendence at the heart of the absolute immanence of the 'ego' is already announced. The ultimate foundation of the objectivity of intentional consciousness is not the intimacy of the 'I' with itself but Time or the Other, those two forms of existence which are irreducible to a single essence. (Pro, p. 126)

As Derrida observes in his 1990 preface or 'warning' to the reader, this dialectic or alterity prefigures the later notions of '*différance*', the 'supplement' of the origin and 'the trace', which problematize the purity of sense in language. Deconstruction is not mentioned by name, but the idea is clearly nascent in Derrida's identification of 'la contradiction dans l'acte de la réduction' (Pro, p. 31), and in his reference to the 'aporia' of phenomenology (Pro, p. 32 and pp. 129ff.). Husserl's essay 'The Origin of Geometry' is already of interest to him and although Derrida does not make an issue of language in this text, the question of Husserl's *Reaktivierung* ('recollection': the mechanism by which meanings are transposed from written text into thought) begins to raise the questions of signification which are addressed in the essay 'Speech and Phenomena' and *Edmund Husserl's Origin of Geometry: An Introduction*. The theme of death is not introduced by name, although its genesis is also clear enough. Elaborating his general argument for an originary dialectic, Derrida poses the question of the role of negation in the constitution of phenomenological foundations. He challenges Husserl's view of negation as a modification of the positivity of transcendental life, asking whether negativity must not be presupposed first as a condition of the possibility of intentional consciousness. The suggestion is that phenomenology rests upon a fundamental dichotomy of position and negation (Pro, p. 32 and pp.195–7). Here can be seen the structure of Derrida's argument in later texts, where he will state – following Heidegger – that death is more than just a modification of transcendental life, but that death is integral to the very possibility of the ego.

In his own estimation too, Derrida rates his work on Husserl as crucial and formative. He describes 'Speech and Phenomena' as 'the essay I like most', before even *Of Grammatology* and *Writing and Difference* (Pos, p. 14), two works that have attracted far greater attention. Derrida also gives a crucial place to *Edmund Husserl's Origin of Geometry: An Introduction*:

> Naturally, all the problems worked on in the Introduction to 'The Origin of Geometry' have continued to organize the work I have subsequently attempted in connection with philosophical, literary and even non-discursive corpora, most notably that of pictorial works. (TT, p. 39)

In 1984, talking to Richard Kearney, Derrida says

> Husserl taught me a certain methodological prudence and reserve, a rigorous technique of unravelling and formulating questions. But I never shared Husserl's pathos for, and commitment to, a phenomenology of presence. In fact, it was Husserl's method that helped me to suspect the very notion of presence and the fundamental role that it played in all philosophies.[4]

From other remarks it is clear that Heidegger can claim to have been Derrida's 'most constant influence', being more 'enigmatic and extensive' for him than Husserl.[5] Yet Derrida's encounter with Husserl was of very great and lasting significance. Derrida's discussion of Husserl's metaphysics is a test case for his general deconstruction of metaphysics, for it is, in his words, a confrontation with 'metaphysics in its most modern, critical and vigilant form: Husserl's transcendental phenomenology' (Pos, p. 5).

However, the significance of Derrida's early work should not be seen only in terms of his *critique* of Husserl or his *negative* reaction to Husserl's 'concealed metaphysics', because Derrida's encounter with Husserl also contributes *positively* to the development of Derrida's own philosophy. Husserl's *lebendige Gegenwart* is the foil against which Derrida can first position his own vocabulary: *différance*, the trace, arche-writing, and so on. Husserl's *epochē* and *Abbau* belong with Heidegger's *Destruktion* as the antecedents for 'deconstruction'. Finally, as will be argued below, Derrida does not properly escape Husserl's phenomenology, the 'philosophy of light' which strives to account for the way in which things come to be 'seen'. Gasché, among others, argues that Derrida belongs *within* the Husserlian tradition, absorbing from his reading of Husserl certain fundamental philosophical 'motifs', which resonate through Derrida's other writing. These motifs flow from the critical procedures Derrida employs to investigate *lebendige Gegenwart*, which is a notion he connects with Husserl's idea of God.

Derrida and the French Phenomenological Tradition

Studying Husserl in the early 1950s – twenty years after Sartre, Levinas and Merleau-Ponty – Derrida belongs to a second generation of French philosophers to have taken an interest in phenomenology. From the outset, Husserl's writing struck a chord with aspects of Bergson's philosophy of consciousness – a connection noted by early French phenomenologists such as Hering. Indeed Husserl is said to have claimed that his followers were 'the true Bergsonians'.[6] To the first generation of French 'phenomenologists', Husserl was a source of creative inspiration, directly influencing new philosophical developments. Levinas came to know Husserl in 1928–9 when he attended his lectures on intersubjectivity. Shortly afterwards he wrote a study of Husserl's theory of intuition and, with Gabrielle Peiffer, translated the *Cartesian Meditations* into French.[7] Levinas's absorption of Husserl's (and, more importantly, Heidegger's) phenomenology is too complex and subtle to describe in any detail here. However, it may be noted briefly that Levinas tends at once to transform and radicalize aspects of phenomenology in order to develop his own brand of ethical theology. Levinas takes a concept such as Husserl's *intentional* consciousness and suggests something anterior and 'other': a pre-reflective, non-intentional passive consciousness in which the phenomenality of the face of the 'other' wakens the self into a state of responsibility and an understanding of its own being.[8] Thus the ego, in complete contrast with Husserl, is a modification of the 'other'. Although this kind of 'phenomenological' approach is itself hardly Husserlian, the Husserlian influence is unmistakable.

By the time Sartre studied Husserl in the early 1930s, Levinas had already published a number of articles on phenomenology.[9] Sartre was rapidly enchanted by the notion of intentional consciousness, writing an essay on the concept and adapting it for use in his own theory of imagination.[10] Although Sartre became critical of phenomenology – in particular of the Husserlian ego which he believed to be 'shut up inside the cogito', reducing Husserl's philosophy to a version of Kantian 'phenomenalism'[11] – Husserl's influence was clearly formative and positive. And it was Sartre who, according to Spielberg, introduced Merleau-Ponty to Husserl's earlier writing in 1934. Merleau-Ponty was less inspired than Sartre by the early Husserl, but was particularly taken with the Husserl of *The Crisis of the European Sciences* and by 1939 he was studying Husserl's later unpublished writing in the Husserl Archive. His studies at the Archive were significant in two ways: first, Merleau-Ponty used these researches as the basis for his claim to be fulfilling Husserl's ultimate phenomenological intentions; second, material from Husserl's manuscripts contributed extensively to the formation of the *Phénoménologie de la perception* (1945), the first French major philosophical work to carry 'phenomenology' in its title.

Although there can be no doubt about the importance of phenomenology to Sartre, Levinas and Merleau-Ponty, there is nothing uniform or straightforward about the Husserlian influence upon these three thinkers. Sartre is moulded by the early Husserl and the emphasis upon intentional consciousness which permits transcendence of the Husserlian ego on the horizon of intentional acts and experience. Taking a different tack, Merleau-Ponty builds upon Husserl's late *Lebenswelt* writings to develop an ontology of 'ambiguity'. Levinas, in yet another way, uses phenomenology as a ladder to climb to a post-Husserlian, or even anti-Husserlian, philosophical theology. Yet for all this variation and criticism, Husserl's writing clearly provided an essentially positive impetus for a new range of French philosophies of the self and 'the other'. However adopted or even criticized, Husserl was nevertheless seen as a respected resource. By contrast, Derrida's approach to Husserl is altogether more hostile. Far from treating him as the initiator of a new direction in philosophy, Derrida sees Husserl as the final milestone in an old and failed metaphysical quest. As he puts it in 'Violence and Metaphysics', Husserl's phenomenology is the culmination of a 'Greek' metaphysics of light that stretches back to Plato. It is not surprising that of the three thinkers mentioned above the closest in approach to Derrida is Levinas, who poses the question of the 'other' of phenomenology. Derrida hardly makes reference to Sartre in his writing and he takes issue with Merleau-Ponty's interpretation of Husserl's view of history (EH, pp.111–13). Unlike Merleau-Ponty, whose researches in Leuven provided rich material for his exposition of phenomenology, Derrida uses the Husserl Archive to root out the evidence which will expose and condemn phenomenology as theology: an old-fashioned metaphysics of presence.

The Early Foundations of Derrida's Theological Ideas

The theme of death and theology, already outlined, has its genesis in Derrida's study of Husserl. Husserl's *lebendige Gegenwart* is, Derrida argues, the absolute substrate of transcendental consciousness: the condition of possibility of any phenomenological awareness. Derrida's critical technique – here as elsewhere in his writing – is to pose the question of the 'other' which is excluded by the formation of a concept of the absolute. Derrida asks what must be denied, repressed and excluded from the notion of *lebendige Gegenwart* in order to achieve the definition of the concept. *Lebendige Gegenwart* is clearly presence and therefore it resists absence; but it is, more significantly, 'living' and therefore not dead. 'Death' in the Husserlian scheme is, as Derrida puts it, 'a fact extrinsic to the movement of temporalization' (EH, p. 137). Thus, Derrida argues that *lebendige Gegenwart* is, with the slippage and plurality of space and time, always becoming a dying absence. Or to put it another way, *lebendige Gegenwart* is always deconstructed by an irreducible alterity that it can never banish.

Derrida's argument may not seem remarkable in itself. However, he attaches special significance to Husserl's conception of *lebendige Gegenwart*. *Lebendige Gegenwart* is, for Derrida, an essentially theological concept. Thus Derrida's deconstruction of it acquires additional importance. Derrida's writing on Husserl is certainly concerned with language, signification, time, alterity and the 'other', but it is also concerned with theology as an exemplary doctrine of 'presence'. For in all his writing on Husserl (with the arguable exception of his thesis) Derrida's purpose is to reveal phenomenology as a theological pursuit. Such an outright, generalized, and almost conventionally theoretical perspective is unexpected. Derrida is often described as a philosopher who does not advance a philosophy of his own and whose aim is merely to expose the flaws, contradictions and paradoxes in the philosophical writing of others. Certainly, Derrida does not set out to create a philosophical *system*. However, his work exhibits a very clear *philosophical attitude* and a definite, even grandiose, purpose.

This purpose is evident in all Derrida's writings on Husserl. The guiding question at the outset of 'Speech and Phenomena' is whether phenomenology, for all its methodological rigour, conceals 'a metaphysical presupposition' (SP, p. 4). In his essay 'Genesis and Structure', Derrida remarks that

> the constitution of the other and of time refers phenomenology to a zone in which its 'principles of principles' (as we see it, its metaphysical principle: the original self-evidence and presence of the thing itself in person) is radically put into question. (WD, p. 164)

Even in *Edmund Husserl's Origin of Geometry: An Introduction*, where Derrida claims that his '*sole ambition* will be to recognize and situate one stage of Husserl's thought, with its specific presuppositions and its particular unfinished state' (EH, p. 27, italics added), the discussion leads to a much more dramatic climax as Derrida concludes that the living-present foundation of phenomenology is effectively a version of 'God'. Derrida betrays his ulterior motive all too clearly in this conclusion since Husserl does not in fact refer directly to the living present anywhere in 'The Origin of Geometry'.[12] Here as elsewhere we see how Derrida uses the medium of his specific readings of texts to announce philosophical perspectives which he declares to be of general, even universal, importance. 'Speech and Phenomena' illustrates the same point. In the 'Introduction', Derrida explains that the examination of Husserl's theory of language is not a matter merely of technical interest but that the study of sign theory – in *The Investigations* in particular – will disclose 'the germinal structure of the whole of Husserl's thought' (SP, p. 3). This germinal structure is Husserl's hidden metaphysical theology. Moreover, the uncovering of metaphysics does not concern 'such and such metaphysical heritage' which 'here or there' has insinuated itself into phenomenology. Derrida wishes to expose the *entire* phenomenological method as 'controlled by metaphysics' (ibid., p. 5). Further on in 'Speech and Phenomena', Derrida makes it clear that his observations about Husserl's sign theory do not just concern specific texts or even the project of phenomenology. The condition of phenomenology also reveals what is constitutive of the whole 'history of metaphysics', 'the tradition that carries over the Greek metaphysics of presence into the "modern" metaphysics of presence understood as self-consciousness', and the very nature of philosophy 'which is always a philosophy of presence' (SP, pp. 16 and 63). Indeed we see how in later texts Derrida removes the concept of the living present from its Husserlian context and deploys it in the deconstruction of metaphysics in other writers, for example Rousseau in *Of Grammatology* and Marx in *Specters of Marx* (OG, p. 313; SM, p. xx).

What is revealed in the early texts on Husserl is the beginning of the colossal philosophical project which dominates Derrida's career: the deconstruction of Western metaphysics. What is of significance to Derrida in studying Husserl is the latter's ingenious use of philosophical structures which have sustained metaphysical thinking since Plato. For all the painstaking particularity of 'Speech and Phenomena' and *Edmund Husserl's Origin of Geometry: An Introduction*, it is the general and universal implications of these texts which gives them significance in Derrida's work as a whole.

This grates against some of the received wisdom about Derrida, even against some of Derrida's own protests. For it is above all the detailed reading of texts, and not the formation of grand theory, which is often taken to be the essential trait of Derrida's writing.[13] It is certainly true that Derrida pursues philosophy through the reading of specific texts. However, he turns close reading into something more than local study: in his hands it becomes the means of general disclosure and philosophical enlightenment. It is implicit in Derrida's writing that there is something special to be discovered through the careful, painstaking, critical reading of texts. Here is the paradox that Derrida so often observes in the writing of others. Even as his critique of Husserl cautions us about the spectre of metaphysical privilege that haunts the Western understanding of language, Derrida is making his own close-reading procedures into a means of privileged knowledge.

Derrida uses his critique of Husserl to develop the theme of 'the play of life and death' (SP, p. 100), which is so much in evidence in his later work. Although Derrida's professed interests are literary or semiotic, his treatment of Husserl is based on the view that 'phenomenology, the metaphysics of presence in the form of ideality, is also a philosophy of *life*' (ibid., p. 10). 'It is a philosophy of life ... because the source of sense in general is always determined as an act of *living*, as an act of a living being, as *Lebendigkeit*' (ibid.). Intentional consciousness, in other words, is always a living intentional act and not merely an abstract perspective. In itself, the characterization of phenomenology as a philosophy of life is nothing out of the ordinary. Misch argues this very case in his *Lebensphilosophie und Phänomenologie*. Heidegger also extends Husserl's thought in the direction of an *existential* phenomenology with the *Seinsfrage* or 'question of being' at its centre. By contrast Derrida's purpose is to expose a certain conception of 'life' as a structural feature of modern Western metaphysics – in particular the metaphysics which underlies the twentieth-century understanding of the life of the self – and implicitly to advance his own argument that life is characterized by that irreducible secondariness and contingency which has its archetype in writing and which is thematized in Derrida's work under the title of death.

Having established the general importance and meaning of Derrida's encounter with Husserl, four stages of investigation now lie ahead. First, an introductory sketch of Husserl's philosophy and its problems is needed in order to uncover the features of phenomenology which Derrida addresses in his critique. Second, a reading of Derrida's two key texts on Husserl: *Edmund Husserl's Origin of Geometry: An Introduction* and 'Speech and Phenomena'. This will show in what way and to what effect Derrida's reading of Husserl has a *theological* significance. Third, Derrida's main arguments about the theological character of 'the living present' will be evaluated in relation to Husserl's published and unpublished writings in this area. A concluding section will examine some of the theological implications of Derrida's treatment of Husserl.

A Summary Outline of Husserl's Philosophical Project

Husserl's philosophy arises out of a quest for a dimension of absolute certainty. Husserl was convinced that Western empiricism was too naïve and incomplete to be the basis of a truly certain science. Science, for instance, failed to offer an explanation of the consciousness of the empirical observer and her/his prejudices. Furthermore, Husserl saw little virtue in relativism, which ruled out the possibility of any absolute knowledge. Taking a quite different path, he attempted to uncover the trail of a 'positive science' which would steer between the hazards of empiricism and relativism. This science – which he called phenomenology – returned to Descartes's *cogito* as a point of certainty from which all other knowledge could be securely derived. Husserl renewed Descartes's quest for certainty with extraordinary rigour and tenacity.

It is difficult, perhaps, encountering the dense, technical language of Husserl's philosophy, to understand the attraction of phenomenology. Yet Husserl's philosophy is, at root, an ordinary, reasoned appeal to self-evidence. Husserl attempted to fulfil the age-old dream of philosophy and theology alike of finding the basis for certain knowledge, placing it upon a foundation that could not be shifted or undermined, and to produce a philosophy so 'obvious' that no one, of any time or culture, could ever dispute it. In this pursuit of 'first philosophy', Husserl followed Descartes in attempting to secure one absolutely indisputable pocket of knowledge and use this as the cornerstone of an apodictic knowledge of all things. To do this Husserl had to find a method of distilling the purest and most certain types of self-evident knowledge from what he called 'the Heraclitean flux' of human thoughts, perceptions, prejudices and presuppositions. In this way he aimed to discover 'those cognitions that are first in themselves and can support the whole storied edifice of universal knowledge' (CM, p. 14). In order to reach this most certain and indisputable basis of self-evident truth, Husserl devised a philosophical method, first advanced in 1907 and later set out fully in *Ideas* (1913), called the *epochē* or 'reduction'.[14] The *epochē* was Husserl's revision of Cartesian 'doubt', that is to say, a way of setting aside those things we cannot know with absolute certainty – the word *epochē* in Greek means 'holding back'. However, the *epochē* is not itself a process of doubt but a process of deliberate 'suspension' or 'bracketing'. The reality of what is 'reduced' in the *epochē* is not denied or doubted but put into abeyance. Husserl took the concept of the *epochē* from the ancient sceptics, understanding himself to be 'redeeming in a higher sense the truth of the radical subjectivism of the sceptical tradition'.[15] Where an issue cannot be decided one way or the other, the sceptics urged the suspension or *epochē* of judgement and Husserl uses this method to 'suspend' in its entirety what he calls 'the natural standpoint' – our common-sense view that there is an objective world and that experience of the objective world can be depended upon to furnish us with objective knowledge. Although the *epochē* is a continuous process, Husserl divides it into particular stages of reduction. The first stage, the so-called 'transcendental' or 'phenomenological' reduction, sets aside the entire empirical or 'natural' world and its presuppositions as an unreliable basis for knowledge. This involves 'suspending' all our judgements about the world of 'spatiotemporal' existence, to leave us in a neutral state, receptive to the cognitions of a consciousness purged of all empirical content and prejudice. This reduction is a shift of perspective from the natural standpoint (the everyday 'common-sense' attitude we adopt to the world) to the transcendental standpoint (the point of view of phenomenology). After the transcendental reduction, Husserl argued, we come to a new realization:

> If I keep purely what comes into view – for me, the one who is meditating – by virtue of my free *epochē* with respect to the being of the experienced world, the momentous fact is that I, with my life, remain untouched in my existential status, regardless of whether or not the world exists and regardless of what my eventual decision concerning its being or non-being might be. (CM, p. 25)

Thus, in the mental footsteps of Descartes, Husserl determined that the most self-evident of all self-evident things is the fact of human consciousness. Consciousness is self-evident because we cannot logically deny it. From this new transcendental standpoint Husserl maintained that the manifold stream of contingent world-objects could be perceived in a new way, giving 'a new kind of experience: transcendental experience' (ibid., p. 26). The transcendental ego becomes a 'disinterested onlooker' whose only motive is neutrally to describe 'what he sees, purely as seen, as what is seen and seen in such and such a manner' (ibid., p. 35).

The phenomenological reduction had the effect of distinguishing between two modes of, or sides to, life: the 'natural' life and the 'transcendental' life. The 'natural life'[16] is lived within an unquestioned and 'naïvely acquired world view' (PL, p. 15), taking experiences at face value and immersed within the flux of world events. The 'transcendental life', on the other hand, is detached from worldly concerns, a 'disinterested spectator' of natural life, treating the world as a mere phenomenon. The very use of the concept of separate 'lives' to designate the respective ambits of the natural and transcendental indicates the severity of Husserl's distinction. Each life has its own world order, with the self split into distinct 'natural' and 'transcendental' egos (ibid.). The natural self experiences the objective order of 'cosmic time' (that is, time which is calibrated or measured by clocks or calendars) whereas the transcendental self experiences 'phenomenological time' (IdI, pp. 234–7). Phenomenological time is the immediate pure interval of the 'now' in which transcendental life is sustained. Husserl further elaborates these distinctions in *The Crisis of the European Sciences* when he writes about 'the antagonism between "the life of the plane" and "the life of depth"' (CE, p. 118).

The two worlds of life are by no means equal in value. The natural life is uncertain, naïve and unquestioning, clouded with assumptions and prejudices. Purity of thought, language, experience and perception is only possible in the transcendental life. We do not have to look far, therefore, to see Husserl implicitly prioritizing the transcendental life as a higher state of life, more 'living' than the natural life. 'Natural being', Husserl remarks in the *Meditations*, 'is a realm whose existential status is secondary' (CM, p. 21). In *Ideas*, Husserl makes an interesting aside in parentheses; 'Every experience generally (every really living one, so to speak) is an experience "which is present"' (IdI, p. 310). Here Husserl implicitly distinguishes between *real* living which is possible in the transcendental life, and *mere* living, which occurs in natural life. Elsewhere Husserl implies that natural life is merely an observed phenomenon: if an object, say the human body, appears to manifest itself as an 'animate' phenomenon, then it has natural life.[17] Natural life, then, is not really 'life' at all, according to Husserl's account of all life as conscious. As with any dualistic account of the self, the question of the unity of the ego is raised as Husserl attempts at once to retain the continuity of life between the natural and transcendental, and yet to insist upon a discontinuity which separates transcendental life from mere natural living. It is also unclear, as Levinas observes, how exactly one shifts from natural into transcendental life.

> It seems that man *suddenly* accomplishes the phenomenological reduction by a purely theoretical act of reflection on life. Husserl offers no explanation for this change of attitude and does not even consider it a problem. Husserl does not raise the metaphysical problem of the situation of the *Homo Philosophus*.[18]

Although this first reduction achieved the major shift from the natural to the transcendental standpoint, 'a second stage of phenomenological research' was required to move from 'sensory' to 'categorical' intuition in order to reach a 'universe of absolute freedom from prejudice'. This second or 'eidetic' reduction involved the criticism of transcendental experience itself. The eidetic reduction aimed to focus intentional consciousness ever more deliberately upon that which is ideal (eidetic) in every contingent experience. Thus a die may be perceived in diverse actual and imaginable ways, writes Husserl, but this diversity must be reduced to *Wesenschau*, what is *essential* in the experience of the die. In this pursuit of universal *eidoi* phenomenology becomes what Husserl calls the 'Science of Essences'.

Husserl believed that the transcendental and eidetic reductions would achieve a standpoint from which all objects would be perceived not only with absolute *neutrality* and without prejudice, but also with regard for the *ideal* in every perception. However, one last reduction remained: the abstractive reduction. In an attempt to grasp absolutely his newly found dimension of certain knowledge, Husserl sought to reduce transcendental experience to its ultimate condition of possibility. This was the final 'abstraction' of phenomenology into its primordial foundation, what Husserl calls the 'reduction to my transcendental sphere of peculiar ownness or to my transcendental concrete I-myself, by abstraction from everything that transcendental constitution gives me as Other' (CM, p. 93). Husserl thus strips away everything that is alien to the essential consciousness of transcendental life. What remains is the pure substrate upon which all consciousness depends. This preconditional dimension of possibility for the transcendental ego is what Husserl at times calls 'the living present'.[19] The eidetic and abstractive reductions were, Husserl argued, only necessary for phenomenological *philosophy* as a means of securing the basis upon which phenomenology in general could be held to be apodictically true. As far as a new 'science' was concerned the transcendental reduction alone would permit humanity to enter a new plane of detached objectivity.[20]

Two Phenomenological Problems: Interpersonality and Time

Derrida's critique of phenomenology depends largely upon two well-known areas of weakness in Husserl's thinking: the problems of time and other persons. Indeed all idealistic philosophies are potentially vulnerable in the same way. Although there is little novel in Derrida's identification of these difficulties, he does develop his analysis of them in a very particular way, arguing that the problems arise from a long-standing Western metaphysics of identity which always suppresses temporal and spatial differences. Because Derrida's critique depends crucially upon Husserl's alleged failure to resolve the problems of interpersonality and time, it is worth briefly considering each of these problems in turn before looking at Derrida's own writing.

Husserl's first problem arises with other people. The *epochē* had so 'abstracted' the conscious subject (the transcendental ego), detaching it both from the empirical world of things and the community world of other persons, that giving an account of intersubjectivity presented Husserl with a major obstacle. Descartes's 'reduction' had left the mind of the subject isolated from the world of empirical objects, even from the human body. Husserl had 'corrected' this dualistic deficiency by ensuring that all talk of consciousness was of *intentional* consciousness, that is, consciousness *of* something. He then declared that consciousness was 'disinterested' in, but never disconnected from, the world of objects. Even intentional consciousness, however, could never be conscious of the conscious life of another person. Belief in the existence of other conscious persons failed phenomenology's litmus test of 'self-evidence' and was thus a presupposition of the very sort that was ruled out in the *epochē*. In the *Cartesian Meditations* Husserl is clearly troubled by this paradox – the Fifth Meditation which tackles the problem of intersubjectivity takes up nearly half the book. Husserl's solution is what David Bell calls 'a solipsistic escape from solipsism'.[21] Far from being a *problem*, Husserl declares solipsism to be the *guarantee* of intersubjectivity, effectively declaring absolute *subjectivity* to be the necessary precondition of any possible *inter*subjectivity.[22] Husserl, as Gadamer observes, stuck to this position throughout his writing on intersubjectivity:

> in the end he always relies on the same unambiguous solution to this difficulty (intersubjectivity): only on the basis of transcendental subjectivity, in the radical solitude of the transcendental ego – that is, only from the standpoint of a transcendental solipsism – can one legitimate the concept of 'we'.[23]

This ingenious argument ignores the fact that without direct *self-evidence*, all supposition of other consciousness must be seen as one of the prejudices of the natural standpoint and must be 'suspended' in the phenomenological reduction. There is, therefore, no *phenomenological* motive or argument for taking other consciousness seriously.[24] Husserl, as noted below, addressed this problem once more, again unsuccessfully, with his concept of a *Lebenswelt*: an ontological stratum anterior to consciousness.

Even within the short passage of the *Cartesian Meditations* Husserl's description of life runs into problems. We note that Husserl – anxious in the Fifth Meditation to dismiss the charge of solipsism and explain how phenomenology really does give a flawless account of intersubjectivity – wants to speak of life in other people. Yet other people do not present themselves to the transcendental consciousness as transcendentally conscious, but only as bodily and objective. Other people exist, just like any other object of phenomenal perception, but they do not 'live'. Whenever he writes about individual human beings, Husserl is careful in his use of terms: conscious subjects experience 'life'; other people are animate objects of whom existence is predicated by a conscious subject. However, towards the end of the Fifth Meditation, Husserl develops a concept mentioned only briefly in the First: that of the 'life-world': 'The transcendental sense of the world must also become disclosed to us ultimately in the *full concreteness* with which it is incessantly the *life-world* for us all' (CM, p. 136). Husserl's need to develop the concept of the life-world was heightened by the early Heidegger's revision of phenomenology. Unlike Husserl's subjective ego, Heidegger's *Dasein* had the basic condition of 'being-in-the-world' and was thus determined precisely within intersubjectivity. Gadamer describes *The Crisis of the European Sciences* as an attempt 'to give an implicit answer to *Being and Time*'.[25] Indeed we see how in Part III of *The Crisis of the European Sciences* Husserl turns directly to the unresolved problems of intersubjectivity, the existence of other persons and the common human life: 'How ... certain physical bodies in my perceptual field come to count as living bodies, living bodies of "alien" ego-subjects – these are now necessary questions' (CE, p. 107). In pursuit of answers, Husserl makes an interesting move away from his previously uncompromising idealism. He introduces the concept of 'we-subjectivity' (ibid., p. 109). 'We-subjectivity' is the community of consciousness of a common human life-world. Moreover, since this life-world is said to be *pre-given* in advance of any theory or science, Husserl attempts to give communal human life a place of pre-eminence in phenomenology. 'We, in living together, have the world pregiven in this "together", as the world valid as existing for us and to which we, together, belong, the world as world for all, pregiven with this ontic meaning' (ibid.). The argument of *The Crisis of the European Sciences* is that the so-called 'objective' sciences have entirely overlooked the life-world, focusing their investigations upon objects within the life-world without ever examining the 'we-subjectivity' which is prior to, and a precondition of, every particular science. For the scientist 'the full universal being of the life-world – especially in its function of making possible his theoretical world and what is given as belonging to it in particular – is completely unconsidered' (ibid., p. 383).

However, Husserl's 'life-world', as David Carr remarks, creates as many difficulties as it solves.[26] Not the least of these is that Husserl weakens the apodictic claims of phenomenology by extending them into communal subjectivity. In any case, as Derrida tartly observes, Husserl's 'life-world' is still really ego-centred: 'The transcendental *we* is not *something other* than the transcendental *Ego*. The latter's acts, even when they seem mandated by an ideal community, do not cease to be irreducibly those of a monadic "I Think"' (EH, p. 61). Husserl was caught in a paradox: in his earlier writing he gave an account of subjective, conscious life at the expense of community life. By the time of *The Crisis of the European Sciences*, he was attempting an account of community life at the expense of the transcendental standpoint.

The second dilemma facing Husserl was how to explain the process of time. When Husserl considered consciousness he clearly could not examine the consciousness of all things throughout all time. He needed to break the infinite 'Heraclitean' flux of time into manageable units for analysis. The time-unit Husserl needed was that which most nearly encased the episode of self-evident experience: the snapshot which captured the transcendental *Erlebnis*. For the purposes of argument Husserl had employed the everyday idea of the 'present moment' as a distinct unit of time. Thus his customary description of time inevitably appeared punctiliar: a series of moments of phenomenological experience. (Husserl, it should be noted, did not believe that time was *actually* broken up into 'points'; in *The Phenomenology of Internal Time-Consciousness* he recognizes time as essentially fluid, but he needed the punctiliar metaphor in order to narrate the process of phenomenological experience.) However, Husserl's use of the concept of the present moment created difficulties. First, he had to explain how universal time is possible when all time-experience is egological. Second, he had to overcome the logical difficulties of defining the constitution and duration of the moment of presence. Third, he had to explain how one could speak of presence when time is always 'on the move', slipping away and therefore, in a sense, always not-present.

'Long familiar problems' such as 'the "idea of time" ... present themselves,' writes Husserl, 'as transcendental and, naturally, as problem(s) of intentionality' (CM, p. 76). Husserl's understanding of time, set out in the Fourth Meditation, derives, as do all his arguments, from the self-evidence of intentional consciousness. Time is, therefore, neither a temporal environment for the transcendental ego nor an independent condition of existence, but a dynamic constituted by the active and passive operations of transcendental consciousness: for phenomenology all time is 'egological time' measured out by the consciousness of the ego. The present is the event-horizon of transcendental consciousness: everything that occurs must occur *for* the conscious ego and therefore *within* the present. Since there is no 'outside' to consciousness, there is also no 'outside' to the present. The past and future, and the 'egological present' of other persons, are not other than the present, but 'other presents'. All these 'presents' are held together, Husserl argues, in a unity within 'the law of compossibility'. This notion of 'compossibility' is difficult to grasp and, as Ricoeur observes, 'somewhat artificial'.[27] At this point even Husserl concedes that 'access to the ultimate universalities ... is very difficult' (ibid., p. 76). [28] Husserl's idea of compossibility is a way of attempting a general description of time beyond the exclusive experience of a particular ego. Certain conditions must exist, Husserl argues, in order that 'egological time' can be taken to occur for egos other than my own at any given moment. These conditions concern what Husserl calls 'the genetic structure of the ego in its universality' (ibid., p. 77). Kant, facing the same difficulty, declared space and time to be *a priori* conditions of phenomenological perception. Husserl, however, claims that 'one can see' the universal law of compossibility once it is laid 'open' by phenomenology and that its structure is 'accepted by us as obvious' (ibid., p. 77). Consequently, Husserl's concept of compossibility is philosophically dubious. Compossibility does not explain *how* egological time is intersubjectively connected, it merely asserts that compossibility is *obvious*. Thus Husserl might as well have attributed the connectedness of egological time to 'magic' or 'God'.

Husserl's concept of the continuous present, or as he occasionally calls it the 'living present', is also a philosophical problem. On the one hand he sees the present as a ubiquitous and infinite dynamic of consciousness with no specific duration. Yet when describing the phenomenological experience of the present, he has to freeze time into finite moments. Furthermore, Husserl's finite descriptions of presence are, perforce, always narrations of 'past presents'. This is because presence is always becoming a past even as it is being experienced as a present.

Paul Ricoeur sums up Husserl's twin dilemmas: 'All aspects of phenomenology converge upon the problem of the Other.'[29] Ricoeur conflates temporality and intersubjectivity into the category of Other, that is to say everything other than the solipsistic life of transcendental consciousness. In summary it may be said that Husserl used the phenomenological reductions to condense the world of persons and history down to the moment of subjective consciousness. From this vantage point the subject may hope for perception and communication without interpretational uncertainty or misunderstanding. However, Husserl failed to re-connect this privileged moment with the private worlds of other minds or the continuum of history. His Cartesian meditations leave the conscious subject stranded in solipsistic isolation. Thus it may be said that his philosophy brings the Cartesian project both to its climax and its closure. Never was 'first philosophy' so doggedly pursued; yet never did the pursuit, in the end, look so impossible.

Edmund Husserl's Origin of Geometry: An Introduction

It is appropriate to turn now to the detail of Derrida's writing on Husserl and see how the 'enigma of the concept of life' appears and reappears throughout; how Derrida argues that 'death' constantly contaminates Husserl's concepts of life and living; and how Derrida sees these issues as essentially theological. If Derrida is correct, then the whole of Husserl's philosophy and its quest for certitude rest upon the more or less explicit presupposition of 'the living present'. 'The entire Husserlian thematic of the living present is,' Derrida observes, 'the profound reassurance of the certainty of meaning' (WD, p. 60). It is this 'living present' which attracts Derrida's interest in his thesis (1953–4), in *Speech and Phenomena* (1967) and *Edmund Husserl's Origin of Geometry: An Introduction* (1962).

Although his short essay on origin and structure in phenomenology hints at the significance of the concept of death,[30] Derrida's first elaboration of this theme occurs in his long introduction to Husserl's essay, 'The Origin of Geometry as an intentional–historical Problem' (1939).[31] Here Derrida identifies what he calls 'the transcendental sense of death' as what unifies all history in relation to the living present. (EH, p. 88). In an attempt to explain how human knowledge can be passed from generation to generation, Husserl argues that written language is a secure container in which apodictic truths can be kept alive in order to be 'recollected' by the readers of the future. Derrida contests this view, arguing that the inherent instability of signs will not permit language to preserve meaning from slippage and distortion. Let us first examine Husserl's essay and then consider Derrida's critique of it.

In 'The Origin of Geometry' Husserl addresses the question of the pre-existing, ready-made, life-world which is described in *The Crisis of the European Sciences*. We stand, Husserl argues, within the ordinary world of history. The stability and certainty of this ordinary world are constantly corroded by the 'seduction of language' and 'the free-play of associative constructions' (CE, p. 362). However, this world has an 'essential structure that can be revealed through methodical inquiry' and which is composed of 'primary materials', 'primal premises', and possesses an '*a priori* structure' (ibid., p. 369). These ideal primary structures are those of geometry: propositions of such apodicity that they appear identically in every world-historical situation. However – and this is Husserl's crucial point – geometry is also a *tradition* which is disclosed to us through a history of datable discoveries. These discoveries occur as geometry makes itself obvious in the succession of 'cultural presents' which constitutes world history. Geometry is self-evidenced when we exploit our faculties of reflection and imagination – themselves self-evident – to suspend the facticity of the world-historical situation and contemplate the 'general set of elements going through all the variants' of possible experience. This is the origin of geometry: not the presence of a person who invented geometric thought, but the depth of a tradition of geometry's self-disclosure.

The significance of this argument lies in Husserl's attempt to historicize transcendental consciousness. His earlier emphasis upon the living present of the phenomenological life is now set in the context of a particular communal history. However, what Husserl means by 'history' is not the extrinsic, empirical history of world events, but an 'internal history' of phenomenological knowledge (EH, p. 34). This is the history of the sedimentation of geometric understanding – and of all forms of knowledge of which geometry is exemplary – within world culture, as layer by layer of apodictic truth deposits itself within civilization. At the origin of this sedimentation is an *a priori* foundation of primal self-evidence. This foundation is not only historically prior to all science and a precondition of the possibility of science, but also continually underlies the understanding of 'all historical facticities, all historical surrounding worlds, peoples, times, civilizations' (CE, p. 377).

This is a significant development in Husserl's thought. Since phenomenological knowledge is now the property not only of individuals but also of a community which stretches over time and space, there must be a certain communal conscious life within which knowledge is retained. Husserl call this 'a community of knowledge living in the unity of a common responsibility' (ibid., p. 362). Whereas the individual consciousness could make light of language because it could be said to exist in 'phenomenological silence' (its meaning always being immediately present to itself without indicative signification), a community has an absolute requirement for language if its members are to communicate. In order that the geometric achievements of one generation can be built on by the next, the ideal truths of geometry must be able to find a secure means of promulgation. Husserl is, therefore, obliged to attempt a description of the language which is to be used to communicate absolute truth.

Husserl describes a two-part process: first the self-evidence of geometry is deposited in language by an author; second it is 'cashed in' for self-evidence once again by a reader (ibid., p. 373). In characteristic fashion, Husserl makes a direct appeal to necessity and self-evidence as proof that the deposition and reactivation of self-evidence is possible in language.

> A continuity from one person to another, from one time to another, must have been capable of being carried out. It is clear that the method of producing original idealities out of what is pre-scientifically given in the cultural world must have been written down and fixed in firm sentences prior to the existence of geometry; furthermore, the capacity for translating these sentences from vague linguistic understanding into the clarity of the reactivation of their self-evident meaning must have been, in its own way, handed down and ever capable of being handed down. (Ibid., p. 366)

What Husserl declares to be both necessary and self-evident is *language*, 'written' language moreover, which is 'prior' to geometry. Thus writing assumes a sudden primordiality within phenomenology. For writing is now held by Husserl to be the pre-condition of the existence of an apodictic tradition that can pass between persons in time and space. Husserl is emphatic, moreover, that it is *writing* and not speech that can enable intersubjectivity. Speech is synchronic, but writing is diachronic, enduring even when its author is dead or asleep.

This is not at all to say, however, that Husserl sees language *per se* as part of pure ideality. Language belongs to a primary and secondary level of ideal objectivity. The tertiary level of pure ideal objectivity, the timeless origin of all truth, is beyond language and merely depends upon language for its appearance in world history, (EH, pp. 70–2).[32] As far as this aspect of Husserl's thought is concerned, there is no substantial difference between Husserl's position in *The Logical Investigations*, *Cartesian Meditations* and *The Formal and Transcendental Logic* and his position in 'The Origin of Geometry'. Language is still secondary to the independent primacy of pure ideality.

It is Husserl's interest in writing that provokes Derrida's extensive reflections on 'The Origin of Geometry' (they are far longer than Husserl's text). Husserl asserts that the possibility of inscription is an absolute requirement of ideal objectivity, for ideality could not be fully objective, fully constituted, if it were unable to present itself in language within the world-historical horizon. This requirement does not, however, sully the purity of ideal meanings: for meanings can endure even though languages can become 'dead', like ancient hieroglyphs, devoid of their originally intended meaning. Indeed it is precisely the fact that specific linguistic expressions do become obsolete or 'dead' that illustrates the freedom that ideal meanings have from any given linguistic formulation:

> The silence of prehistoric arcana and buried civilizations, the entombment of lost intentions and guarded secrets, and the illegibility of the lapidary inscription disclose the transcendental sense of death as what unites these things to the absolute privilege of intentionality in the very instance of its essential juridical failure. (EH, p. 88)

The failure of absolute truth to incarnate itself in everlasting laws results in linguistic expressions of truth which, as they become defunct, inevitably betray or degrade truth. Writing is, thus, what ought to guarantee ideal objectivity, yet belongs to the order of 'death'.

Husserl would no doubt have accepted that writing was essentially a realm of death, since it is the consciousness of the transcendental observer which 'recollects' the living meaning of the words. However, Derrida does not allow the life-giving powers of *Reaktivierung* to remain free from death. Derrida – reintroducing the problems of intersubjectivity and time – doubts whether such *Reaktivierung* is possible. In order that the original meaning of writing be properly grasped and the sedimentation of geometry not degenerate into a 'tradition emptied of sense', the reactivation must be a univocal and total reanimation of sense. When the sense of writing is 'recollected', however,

Husserl cannot guarantee that it is 'recollected' in a 'univocal' sense for different people at different times. Reactivation, Derrida argues, must always be equivocal since writing is 'a mobile system of relations and takes its source from an infinitely open project of acquisition' (EH, p. 104). Derrida continues, if *total* reactivation were possible and if every reactivation were a *total* reactivation of geometrical knowledge this 'would paralyze the internal history of geometry'(ibid., p. 105), leaving all progress of knowledge stuck at square one. Thus death returns to haunt the living structures of phenomenology: reactivated meanings are not finitely restricted and disintegrate into plurivocity. At this point, having considered the sense of death in writing, Derrida reaches the focus of his study: Husserl's living present. Derrida identifies the living present as the historical horizon, anterior limit and origin of phenomenological knowledge and a common life-world (ibid., p. 110).

In his deconstruction of living presence Derrida, in effect, asks how 'live' the living present really is. Although a radio transmission that goes out 'live' takes only a tiny period of time to reach the radio receiver, the transmission doesn't arrive exactly 'as it happens', but very shortly afterwards. In fact the transmission arrives 'dead' at the receiver. By the time the transmission arrives, the living present has already (to use Husserl's term) 'run off' (PI, pp. 27–30) and the received broadcast is already a recording of the past, a mere supplement to, a dead memory or trace of, the original presence of life itself. Thus, Derrida argues, the living present is experienced in retrospect and is characterized fundamentally by 'delay':

> Here delay is the philosophical absolute, because the beginning of methodic reflection can only exist in the consciousness of *another* previous, possible, and absolute origin in general. Since this alterity of the absolute origin structurally appears in *my Living Present* and since it can appear and be recognized only in the primordiality of something like *my Living Present*, this very fact signifies the authenticity of phenomenological delay and limitation. (EH, p. 152f.)

Husserl is aware of the possible temporal and spatial corruption of the living present when it undergoes transmission. His solution is to insist that the only adequate transmission is one of absolute repetition, in which there is no possibility of mutation. However, even the apparent security of absolute repetition (that is, self-reflection) does not guarantee the life of the living present since every reflection is also a distortion. In any case, as Derrida observes in a later text, even if the living present could be present to itself 'one's undifferentiated proximity to oneself is another name for death' (D, p. 331).

In an important section shortly before the end of his *Edmund Husserl's Origin of Geometry: An Introduction*, Derrida raises the question of Husserl's theology. He considers Husserl's unpublished remarks on God.[33] Husserl, as Derrida rightly notes, has 'bracketed the 'naïve metaphysics' of God in the 'factual' sense. However, Husserl leaves plenty of space for something divine in the transcendental sphere. Indeed, such a transcendental theology may be an inevitable conclusion of phenomenology. Derrida points out two senses in which Husserl invokes God. First, he argues that Husserl uses God as the label for the ground of the historical possibility of transcendental consciousness. In other words, God guarantees the continuity of the present through time and across persons. Second, Derrida notes that Husserl writes of God as a teleological destination towards which transcendental consciousness is travelling. Derrida suspects that Husserl understood God in both senses at once:

> God speaks and passes *through constituted* history, he is *beyond* in relation to constituted history and all the constituted moments of transcendental life. But he is only the Pole *for itself* of constituting historicity and *constituting* historical transcendental subjectivity. The dia-historicity of the divine Logos only traverses and goes beyond 'Fact' as the 'ready-made' of history, yet the Logos is *but* the pure movement of its own historicity.
> The situation of the Logos is profoundly analogous – and not by chance – to that of every ideality (such as our analysis of *language* has enabled us to specify this concept). Ideality is *at once* supratemporal and omnitemporal ... Are not supratemporality and omnitemporality also the characteristics of *Time itself*? Are they not the characteristics of the Living Present, which is the absolute concrete Form of phenomenological temporality and primordial Absolute of all transcendental life ? (EH, p. 148)

So Husserl sees God as *both* omnitemporal and supratemporal – *urzeitlich* and *überzeitlich*, in Husserl's terminology. At this juncture Derrida's argument makes its most significant turn with the rhetorical questions in the last two sentences of the extract. He thus reaches the climax of his argument: the description of phenomenology as theology and the identification of 'the Living Present' with 'God'. Furthermore, since the living present is contaminated by death, God by implication shares the same fate. Later sections in this chapter will consider how adequate Derrida's understanding is of God and the living present in Husserl.

Speech and Phenomena

'Speech and Phenomena' is listed among Derrida's 'essays on Husserl's Theory of Signs'. However, this text is not just an essay in the philosophy of language – at least not in so far as language is thought of as one among many interests of philosophy. As he investigates Husserl's theory of language, Derrida becomes preoccupied with Husserl's talk of 'life' – the 'transcendental' life of pure consciousness, the 'natural' life of existent creatures and the very concept of life, 'the common root that makes all these metaphors [of life] possible' (SP, p. 10). Some pages before Derrida concludes his first chapter, he openly declares the wider questions that structure 'Speech and Phenomena':

Ideality is the preservation or mastery of presence in repetition. In its pure form, this presence is the presence of nothing *existing* in the world; it is a correlation with the acts of repetition, themselves ideal.

Is this to say that what opens up the repetition to the infinite, or what is opened up when the movement of idealization is assured, is a certain relation of an 'existent' to his death? And that the 'transcendental life' is the scene of this relationship? It is too soon to tell. First we must deal with the problem of language. No one will be surprised if we say that language is properly the medium for this play of presence and absence. Is there not within language – is it not language itself that might seem to unify *life* and *ideality*? But we ought to consider, on the one hand, that the element of signification – or the substance of expression – which best seems to preserve ideality and living presence in all its forms is living speech, the spirituality of the breath as *phone*; and, on the other hand, that phenomenology, the metaphysics of presence in the form of ideality, is also a philosophy of *life*. (SP, pp. 9–10)

Thus the direction of 'Speech and Phenomena' becomes clearer: it is not just a delimited notion of language which is at stake in the text but the concepts of life and death, in all their forms and possibilities: presence and absence, being and nothingness, existence and non-existence, the something and the nothing. In short, the text raises the question of a metaphysics of 'life' in Husserl's philosophy. This is not to say that the philosophy of language is displaced by the concern with life, for Derrida concludes that the questions of language and the metaphysics of 'life' are aspects of the same issue. 'No one will be surprised if we say that language is properly the medium for this play of presence and absence.' However, it becomes apparent that Derrida cannot be labelled a 'philosopher of language' or a 'literary philosopher' without considerable qualification. The philosophy of language is not for Derrida a specialism within some more general philosophy of life – the philosophy of language is the philosophy of life itself.

Following the flow of Derrida's argument, we see how he widens the purview of Husserl's theory of language until it embraces the total of philosophy and life. Derrida begins 'Speech and Phenomena' with a bold thesis: that Husserl's differentiation, at the very outset of *The Logical Investigations*, of a 'twofold sense' of the sign – as 'expression' (*Ausdruck*) and 'indication' (*Anzeichen*) – reveals a 'metaphysical presupposition' which permeates the whole phenomenological method:

What is at issue, then, in the privileged example of the concept of the sign, is to see the phenomenological critique of metaphysics betray itself as a moment within the history of metaphysical assurance. Better still, our intention is to begin to confirm that the recourse to phenomenological critique is metaphysics itself, restored to its original purity in its historical achievement. (SP, p. 5)

The basis for the metaphysics of phenomenology – indeed of metaphysics itself – is a primordial foundation of pure ideality, infinitely repeatable through time. This form of absolute ideality has, Derrida asserts, a particular title both in Husserl's work and in the history of the metaphysics of presence:

> The ultimate form of ideality, the ideality of all ideality, that in which in the last instance one may anticipate or recall all repetition, is the *living present*, the self presence of transcendental life. Presence has always been and will always, forever, be in the form in which we can say apodictically, the infinite diversity of contents is produced. The opposition between form and matter – which inaugurates metaphysics – finds in the concrete ideality of the living present its ultimate and radical justification. (Ibid., p. 6)

The ideal, the foundation and guarantee of phenomenology, is given in the self-sameness of this spatiotemporal dimension of living presence: 'The living present ... is ... the conceptual foundation of phenomenology as metaphysics' (ibid., p. 99). Thus what Derrida calls 'the enigma of the concept of life' begins to assume the central position in this study of Husserl's sign theory.

Derrida argues that Husserl achieves the description of the ideality of living presence by separating language into two kinds: indicative language, which merely points to objects in the natural world; and expressive language, which emerges from the pristine realm of transcendental consciousness charged with the sentient power of intentional meaning.[34] Indicative language is devoid of the demonstrative faculty of expression. Indication, for instance, may *point to* the apparent conjunction of given existent objects/ states but cannot *demonstrate* any ideal necessity in their conjunction. Indication may allude but cannot demonstrate. Indication, then, being unable to offer 'a demonstration of apodictic necessities', can and must be bracketed with the rest of the contingent realm (SP, p. 29). Thus indication is set outside the ideal transcendental realm – beyond truth, reality and Being. This precautionary manoeuvre by Husserl guarantees, Derrida argues, the possibility of all subsequent reductions by establishing a non-actual, non-real, non-truthful, non-ideal, non-essential, non-evidential dimension in which anything contingent whatsoever will always successfully reduce down to zero. Furthermore, in the division of signs, Husserl discretely secures the territory of the living present, which Derrida argues is the cornerstone of phenomenology.

Within the transcendental sphere, Husserl treats language as an ideal entity: a purely 'logical', *a priori* grammar which is structured by rationality. Husserl sees the sense of commonplace discourse as governed by the conditions of a 'general grammar', but posits the existence of an inner *a priori* 'pure logical grammar' which better describes the conditions of 'mutual understanding among minded persons'. Logical grammar is eternal and ideal, merely repeating itself through time and between persons. This manoeuvre – setting a special region of 'logical *a priori* grammar' within language in general – gives away the substance of Husserl's metaphysics:

That this gesture, whereby the whole of phenomenology is already involved, repeats the original intention of metaphysics itself is what we wish to show here by pointing out in the first of the Investigations those roots which will remain undisturbed by Husserl's subsequent discourse. The factor of presence, the ultimate court of appeal for the whole of this discourse, is itself modified, without being lost, each time there is a question of the presence (in the two related senses of the proximity of what is set forth as an object of an intuition, and the proximity of the temporal present which gives the clear and present intuition of the object its form) of any object whatever to consciousness – where 'consciousness' means nothing other than the self-presence of the present in the living present. (SP, p. 9)

Although the foundational concept of living presence appears to provide a coherence and unity to all phenomenological talk of life, Derrida argues that there is a more embracing use of the word 'life' which, from a 'literary' perspective, underlies Husserl's use of the term 'living present'. 'The common root that makes all these metaphors (of presence and consciousness) possible still seems to us to be the concept of life' (ibid., p. 10). But the theme of this general 'life', which Derrida believes is so essential to phenomenology, remains unquestioned. The separation of two forms of sign, and the privilege of a logical *a priori* grammar, give rise to Husserl's double lives: natural and transcendental. Derrida argues, however, that Husserl never thematizes life as such, never asking what unity of life these separate lives might share. Thus Derrida argues that '"Living" is ... the name of that which precedes the reduction and finally escapes all the divisions which the latter gives rise to' (ibid., p. 15). Derrida, therefore appeals directly to the possibility of a unified economy of life, a more general economy than any used by Husserl, in order to undo the metaphysics of phenomenology. This more general economy of life is one that reaches into the absolute limit of the concept, that is to say 'death'. Here the metaphorical structure of Derrida's philosophy is being cast. The general economy of life which is not reducible to any individual life, as Husserl argues, is an economy of the alterity life/death.

J. Claude Evans questions the validity of Derrida's 'superstructural' ideas such as the 'life' which is presupposed by the dichotomy of the natural and transcendental lives and the 'showing' which is presupposed by the dichotomy of indication and expression. It is not enough, argues Evans, for Derrida merely to *use* superstructural 'conceptions' (such as '*différance*', arche-writing and so on); they must arise as the 'result of a demonstration that meets all the traditional requirements even as it shows that they cannot be maintained'.[35] Evans, though, rather misses Derrida's point. It is *Husserl's philosophy*, Derrida argues, which – despite the rigour of the reduction – requires the assumption of a 'superstructural' continuum across the divisions of the natural and transcendental and the expressive and indicative. Derrida offers a critique based upon the fact that these superstructural 'conceptions' must have logical and genetic priority in phenomenology. Consequently, the transcendental life cannot form a foundation since it must presuppose a superstructural, or 'general' economy of life. It is only at the last stage of his argument, having established the structural features of delay and difference at the source point of phenomenology, that Derrida advances the notion of '*différance*' as a superstructural tool in his critique.

Having thus drawn into question Husserl's 'restricted' economy of life, Derrida turns his critical gaze to the problem of intersubjectivity. During the *epochē*, both physical language and communicative speech must be bracketed. Physical signs – for example, writing and bodily expressions – have no inherent meaning-intention. For it is only *intentional* meaning (*Bedeutung*) that generates expression. Communicative speech from one person to another only has expressive meaning in the intentional consciousness of the individual subject. The communicative function of speech therefore does not occur, both speaker and listener remaining within the horizon of meaning permitted by their own intentional perspective. All communicative speech reduces to indicative discourse, which is in turn bracketed and set outside the domain of living presence. What remains of language after the reduction is soliloquy: transcendental consciousness speaking to itself. The consequence of this reduction is that the *presence* of the other effectively vanishes. The pure conscious intention of the other is not present to 'me' in the physical speech of the other, the intention of the other is merely mediate in speech but not immediate and self-present. 'The lived experience of another is made known to me only insofar as it is mediately indicated by signs involving a physical side' (SP, p. 39). Indication is what occurs when 'the living spirituality of the meaning-intention is not fully present' (ibid., p. 38). In all our relationships with the other, indication obscures expression and therefore pushes the presence of the other into non-presence. The other always appears as a non-presence, the empty indicative surface which has no intention and therefore no meaning. The life-world of the other's pure intentional consciousness is always absent in the living present. Consequently, Derrida argues, the appearance of the other is the appearance of death.

> We know now that indication, which thus far includes practically the whole surface of language, is the process of death at work in signs. As soon as the other appears, indicative language – another name for the relation with death – can no longer be effaced. (SP, p. 40)

In securing a realm of living presence for the transcendental ego, Husserl also brings into phenomenology a realm of deathly non-presence for everything beyond the transcendental frontier. It is language in general and writing ('physical signs') in particular which, Derrida argues, come to be the marks of death.

Derrida thus draws attention to the unavoidable obverse of life and the living present, that is, 'an irreducible nonpresence ... a nonlife, a nonpresence or nonself-belonging of the living present, an ineradicable nonprimordiality' which lies at the heart of Husserl's attempts to describe intersubjectivity. Husserl makes the absolute presence of non-presence a necessary condition of the presence of the living present. Ironically, therefore, Husserl is forced to give death, non-presence and absence a position of phenomenological certainty in order to sustain the life/death distinction which guarantees the apodicticity of the transcendental life. It is, for Derrida, this contradiction in the notion of living presence which undoes, or deconstructs not only phenomenology but the whole of Western metaphysics.

Sokolowski argues that some of Husserl's unpublished work, the C manuscripts, discloses a far more comprehensive description of living presence than is to be found in his best-known writings.[36] Sokolowski remarks that alterity and absence are positively included in Husserl's description of living presence. Evans argues a similar case, not from Husserl's unpublished work, but from the section on Wholes and Parts in The Third Investigation.[37] Derrida also notes the radical material in the C group of manuscripts, but takes Husserl's notion of *Ichfremde* as further evidence of Husserl's attempt to neutralize alterity (EH, pp. 80, 82, 87, 121 and 148–9). Husserl's objective is to describe a state of absolute prototemporal identity whose conditions already take account of the possibility of alterity. Derrida agrees that Husserl's living present must include all alterity, but in practice 'otherness' gets coerced into the sameness of a single identity: 'By its very dialecticalness, the absolute primordiality of the Living Present permits the reduction ... of all alterity' (EH, p. 86). But this only works if alterity can be reduced. The contention Derrida makes is that the 'other' never can be absorbed into the living present. So long as the present is determined as living, its excluded other must be 'death'.

It is not only the 'other' which intimates death, but the individual's relationship to himself as 'other', *Ichfremde*, or alter ego. The ideal realm of presence – which Derrida now explicitly calls 'platonic' – is prior (*pre*-sent) to the transcendental life of any individual self. It is only in the reduction or absence of the life of a self that the 'source-point' of transcendental life – that is, presence as such – is disclosed. At the level of highest phenomenological self-awareness, therefore, the self disappears:

> The relationship with *my death* (my disappearance in general) thus lurks in the determination of being as presence, ideality, the absolute possibility of repetition. The possibility of the sign is this relationship with death. The determination and elimination of the sign in metaphysics is the dissimulation of this relationship with death, which yet produced signification.
>
> If the possibility of my disappearance in general must somehow be experienced in order for a relationship with presence in general to be instituted, we can no longer say that the experience of the possibility of my absolute disappearance (my death) affects me, occurs to an I am, and modifies a subject. The *I am*, being experienced only as an *I am present*, itself presupposes the relationship with presence in general, with being as presence. The appearing of the I to itself in the *I am* is thus originally a relation with its own possible disappearance. Therefore *I*

am originally means *I am mortal. I am immortal* is an impossible proposition. We
can go even further: as a linguistic statement 'I am he who I am' is the admission of
a mortal. The move which leads from the *I am* to the determination of my being as
res cogitans (thus as an immortality) is a move by which the origin of presence and
ideality is concealed in the very presence and ideality it makes possible. (SP, p. 54)

In quite another context, Derrida speaks about this 'death' as an
'undifferentiated *proximity*' to self. Husserl's living present is the name of
this proximity: an absolute proximity within time, a punctiliar moment
without duration. Derrida, therefore, moves from the critique of
interpersonality to discuss Husserl's treatment of temporality.

Because Husserl has made the present moment – as a fixed point – so
crucial to the possibility of the transcendental standpoint and its pure
expression, Derrida says that any critique of the punctiliar present threatens to
undermine the entire phenomenological project. Derrida notes that Husserl is
strongly attached to the idea of the punctiliar present in *The Phenomenology
of Internal Time-Consciousness*. Although Husserl acknowledges that time is
not a series of full stops, but a flow – a 'running-off' of 'now-points' (EH,
pp. 29–30) – he still argues that time must have a 'source-point', a primordial
origin which is the beginning of time. Thus Derrida argues that Husserl's
'temporality has a non-displaceable centre, and eye or living core, the
punctuality of the real now' (SP, p. 62).

This privilege given to the present gives no offence to philosophy, Derrida
argues, because this certainty of presence *is* philosophy, whether the self-
presence of consciousness, or the self-presence of God. To remove presence
from philosophical thought is 'to remove every possible security and ground
from discourse' (ibid., p. 62). So when presence is challenged, a conflict is
created between philosophy and its Other, namely the thought of absence and
non-presence. For Derrida, this 'dominance of the now' not only underlies all
the metaphysical contrasts of form and matter, act and potency, but it also
links the old 'Greek' metaphysics and the modern metaphysics of
transcendental self-consciousness. Husserl is therefore, in this sense, a typical
metaphysician.

In a move, therefore, not only against Husserl but against the founding
principle of Western philosophy, Derrida begins a critique of Husserl's
'source-point' of the present 'now'. In describing the now of living presence,
Husserl faces a dilemma: on the one hand, the present now must belong in
continuity with not-nows (that is, previous and potential nows), otherwise
every present moment would come and go each time as if a new world were
appearing and disappearing. That is, memory and anticipation must be
permitted some continuity with the present. On the other hand, the certitude
of the now, its definite difference from the past and the future, must be
protected if phenomenology is to retain its living centre of presence and
thereby justify its apodictic claims. The now must exist in mutually exclusive
states: both continuous and discontinuous with the not-now.[38] Only pure

repetition can bridge these requirements. If every present now were, in some sense, an absolute reproduction of every past now, the purity of the present could be preserved. However, this points all nows backwards towards a point of origin, the first now or source-point of time. For every present is never as primordial as that which it repeats. Husserl's present is, Derrida argues, a mere trace of an earlier presence. 'Such a trace is,' Derrida concludes, 'more "primordial" than what is phenomenologically primordial' (SP, p. 67).

Husserl will not allow that memory, expectation and imagination are reducible to the immediacy of the present. Recalled and anticipated time are connected to the present but are not a part of it. Thus, Derrida argues, Husserl creates a radical discontinuity between 'perceptions' (made from the vantage point of the now) and non-perceptions (memories, expectations, imaginations and so on).[39] It is here, Derrida argues, that Husserl's explanation of temporality comes unstuck. Once non-presence becomes continuous with presence, the not-now with the now, the other with self-identity, then *alterity* becomes the condition for *presence*. Once the security of presence is thus shaken, phenomenology and the tradition of metaphysics to which it belongs are undermined.

Derrida finds in Husserl's living speech 'all the incidences of primordial nonpresence whose emergence we have already noted' (SP, p. 82). It is in speech, which is broadcast 'live' in absolute proximity to the *Bedeutung* of the speaker, that Husserl's living present appears in the world-historical sphere. 'My words are "alive" because they seem not to leave me: not to fall outside me, outside my breath' (ibid., p. 76). Speech belongs to the authentic 'ownness' of the transcendentally conscious self. Husserl's living speech is, for Derrida, in stark contrast to the deadness of writing, 'the signifier that is given over to the world':

> The living act, the life-giving act, the *Lebendigkeit*, which animates the body of the signifier and transforms it into a meaningful expression, the soul of language, seems not to separate itself from itself, from its own self-presence. It does not risk death in the body of the signifier that is given over to the world and the visibility of space. It can show the ideal object or ideal *Bedeutung* connected to it without venturing outside ideality, outside the interiority of self-present life. (Ibid., p. 78)

Speech is, for Husserl, the incarnation of ideality through the intentional creativity of *Bedeutung*. Speech is to ideality as the body is to the soul. The living present, however, ought not to require incarnation, argues Derrida, being present to itself in the silence of its own self-presentation. This incarnation, moreover, is yet a further extension away from the pure ideality of presence, introducing the possibility of something other than the Ideal, something bodily, something outward and dead. 'If speech must be "added" to the thought identity of the object, it is because the "presence" of sense and speech had already from the start fallen short of itself' (ibid., p. 87). Speech is thus the product of the difference created by these 'traditional distinctions' between the linguistic flesh and the ideal soul which it embodies. Thus

Derrida concludes that the living present is a supplement which will not reduce to anything other than primordial alterity, heterogeny and secondariness.

In his conclusion to 'Speech and Phenomena', Derrida re-emphasizes the general philosophical implications of his critique of Husserl:

> *The history of metaphysics therefore can be expressed as the unfolding of the structure or schema of an absolute will-to-hear-oneself-speak.* This history is closed when this infinite absolute appears to itself in its own death. *A voice without difference, a voice without writing, is at once absolutely alive and absolutely dead.* (SP, p. 102)

What Derrida means is that metaphysics, Husserlian or otherwise, is rooted in absolute conditions of impossibility. The search for self-presence is an attempt to close off world history, to 'squeeze the universe into a ball' of immediate consciousness. At this 'degree zero', presence is at once protected against the contamination of temporal and spatial flux and at the same time utterly obliterated. In the quest for an absolute life, presence ironically secures its own death. It is no accident that Derrida alights upon the contradiction of life by death as the dominant metaphor for the general condition of living presence. For what, among all possible human expressions of contradiction, could be more radical, more subversive, in a sense more *absolute*, than those concepts which embrace the circle of personal possibility: those of *my* life versus *my* death? In the attempt to designate the primordial alterity which undoes metaphysics, Derrida is inevitably drawn to 'the play of life and death' and to give this alteration a place of privilege in his own discourse.

The Question of the Living Present

Those familiar with Husserl's phenomenology may be surprised by the importance Derrida accords to a concept which is not always prominent in Husserl's published writing. So does the evidence of Husserl's writing support the interpretation of 'living presence' that Derrida offers?

Certainly there is overwhelming evidence in his published and unpublished writing that Husserl was concerned to determine the transcendental constitution of time, seeing the questions of 'time-consciousness' as the most basic of all questions of consciousness: 'These are extremely important matters, perhaps the most important in the whole of phenomenology' (PI, p. 346). Notwithstanding this, as Rudolf Bernet observes, Husserl often avoided treatment of this issue.[40] A concern with time can be traced like a thread through his career – from 1893 and the first of notes and lectures on time collected by Edith Stein in *Husserliana X* (1893–1917), including *The Phenomenology of Internal Time-Consciousness* (1905), to the later period of *The Crisis of the European Sciences* (1936) and his late and unpublished writings on time and primordial structures. However, the question of whether Husserl advanced anything approaching a coherent doctrine of 'the living present' is much less clear. Surveying his writing, it can be seen that Husserl makes a series of more or less different attempts to address the question of primordial temporality but that it is only in his unpublished work that he properly invokes the idea of a 'living present'. What Derrida does in asserting 'the living present' as the foundational concept in Husserl's thought is not so much to describe a fully worked-out Husserlian doctrine as to uncover what he believes to be the implicit presupposition of all phenomenological certainty.

To some extent Derrida recognizes the complexity of this issue: 'The unfinishedness of Husserl's reflections on primordial temporality – their richness, but also, as is said, the dissatisfaction they left their author – has long been underscored' (EH, p. 137). However, Derrida's enthusiasm for the idea of the living present carries him past the difficulties and objections that might restrain a more cautious critic. Derrida effectively amalgamates Husserl's various concepts and suggestions about primordial time into one essential concept. This amalgamation, while convenient, does not do justice to the subtlety of Husserl's analysis.

In his 1905 lectures on internal time-consciousness Husserl indicates the importance of primordial temporality, but declines to give the idea of a continuous present a technical name:

> A certain continuity of appearance – that is, a continuity that is a phase of the time-constituting flow – *belongs* to a now, namely to the now that it constitutes ... This flow ... is *absolute subjectivity* and has the absolute properties of something to be designated metaphorically as 'flow'; of something that originates in ... a primal source-point, the 'now' and so on. In the actuality-experience we have the primal source-point and a continuity of moments of reverberation. For all this we lack names. (PI, p. 79)

Husserl must have been pleased with this formulation because he repeats it more or less word for word in lectures given at Göttingen in 1909 (ibid., p. 382).[41] Crucially, in the 1909 version, Husserl emphasizes that absolute subjectivity is outside objectively constituted time, and thus effectively non-temporal. J.W. Brough in the introduction to his translation of *Husserliana X*, notes that these early remarks about the 'absolute flow' illuminate 'some of the key themes of phenomenology', not least the issue of the transcendental ego.[42] As he describes the way in which time appears to consist of a sequence of 'nows', Husserl does speak of the now as 'enduring' or 'flowing', but there is no hypostatization of the concept. Whether we should read these fleeting allusions as germs of a later theme of the 'living present' is difficult to say, but they do at least indicate that the question of the continuity of the 'now' in relation to transcendental subjectivity goes right back to the beginning of Husserl's project. Moreover, Husserl is, from the start, experimenting with the idea of a 'primal consciousness' (PI, p. 122) from within which time can be experienced as such.

In his later and influential text, the first volume of *Ideas* (1913), Husserl avoids a sustained discussion of the 'enigmas' of temporality, claiming only to be touching the 'fringe' of the problem (IdI, p. 236). However, the sketchy remarks he does make in the second chapter of the third section show that Husserl was continuing to assert the importance of what he now calls the 'infinite continuum of duration'. The precise phrase 'the living present' is not used, but Husserl comes close:

> *Perceptions* of things are primordial experiences ... in the sense which concrete experiences can be that at all. For closer inspection reveals in their concreteness only *one*, but that always a continuously flowing *absolutely primordial phase*, that of the living *now*. (Ibid., p. 221)

Despite such authoritative statements, the precise constitution of the temporal flow was to become an enduring problem for Husserl. In *Ideas I*, he says (without much explanation) that the flow should be thought of as a Kantian Idea. This is a patently unsatisfactory suggestion since the temporal flow of experience is not merely an idea within consciousness but the full content of consciousness itself. Nevertheless, Husserl insists that the temporal flow is 'absolutely and indubitably given' and says that the 'systematic study' of primordial time is 'a main task of general phenomenology' (ibid., p. 240).

Turning to Husserl's later writing we find the idea of the 'living present' as the character of a 'primordial world' or substrate to transcendental experience indicated clearly enough (although not explained in any detail at all) in the *Cartesian Meditations*. In the Fifth Meditation, as we have seen, Husserl completes the so-called 'abstractive *epochē*' to the ego's sphere of 'ownness'. What concerns Husserl here, among other things, is *'an essential structure which is part of the all-embracing constitution* in which the transcendental ego ... lives his life'. On a separate sheet, included in Strasser's edition, Husserl makes a note on this point, referring to this all-embracing constitution as 'the flowing present'.[43] Later Husserl clarifies the status of this structure as the *'all-embracing apodictic Apriori'* which is 'fully determined' and 'firmly identifiable again and again' (CM, p. 103). Having a universal and *a priori* character the living present becomes the basis for that which guarantees the unity of cultural 'worlds' and the 'worlds' of other persons. Husserl argues that the constitution of separate worlds presupposes 'something "primordially" and something "secondarily" constituted'. Thus our worlds may apparently be separate at the secondary level, but share in a common dimension at the primordial level:

> At each of the levels in question, the primordial enters, with a new stratum of sense, into the secondarily constituted world; and this occurs in such a fashion that the primordial becomes the central member, in accordance with orientational modes of givenness. The secondarily constituted, as a 'world', is necessarily given as a horizon of being that is accessible from the primordial and is discoverable in a

particular order. It is already thus, in the case of the first, the 'immanent' world which we call the stream of subjective processes. As a stream of mutual externalities, this stream is given in an orientation around the primordially given living present, from which everything else outside it (but belonging to immanent temporality) is accessible. (Ibid., p. 134)

These references are all made very much in passing however, and *Cartesian Meditations* does not contain any sustained consideration of 'the living present' and its constitution.

In the year or two that followed the writing of *Cartesian Meditations* Husserl did make a concerted attempt to set out the basis of the living present and the C group of manuscripts, dating mostly from 1930–32, are largely devoted to this task. In these texts Husserl relaunches a radicalized form of the *epochē* involving a 'reduction to the sphere of ur-temporality, in which the first and original sense of the being of time as a steady flux comes to light – time precisely as the living-flowing present'.[44] The significance of this *epochē* is that it seeks to push the reduction beyond transcendental subjectivity itself, beyond the mere flow of experience or consciousness, back to the purity of Time itself.[45] This dimension necessarily precedes all others, as Husserl explains:

> In the end the origin of epochs, objects, and worlds in every sense, lies in the ur-flow of the living present or put better, in the transcendental ur-ego, which lives its ur-life as ur-flowing present moments and as the present in general, and thus in its way Being exists in an ur-temporality, which constitutes, in the form of a stream, an ur-time and an ur-world.[46]

Despite the greater attention given to the topic in the C Group, Husserl's difficulties remain, and this passage illustrates well the problem that he faces. The more forcefully he attempts to assert the foundation of the living present, the more proliferative becomes his vocabulary of concepts of foundation: *Urwelt, Urzeit, Urleben, Urstrom, Ur-Ego*. But far from shoring up the foundations, this new echelon of concepts merely begs the question of the possibility of a deeper foundation with its own vocabulary of ultra-primordial concepts. The living present, far from creating a solid base, opens up age-old problems of regression. The effect is philosophical vertigo.

It is perhaps owing to such problems that Husserl's confidence in a definitive concept of the 'living present' does not extend even to *The Crisis of the European Sciences* (written between 1934 and 1937), where he is altogether more cautious about naming the ground of primordial temporality. The use of the definite article, and the talk of a 'substrate', implies something concrete, and raises impossible difficulties about both the empirical and logical status of '*the* living present'. Consequently, Husserl's tone is more hesitant than in the C group or the *Cartesian Meditations*: 'To be sure, words taken from the sphere of the natural world, such as "component" and "stratum" are dangerous and the necessary transformation of their sense must be noticed' (CM, p. 174). Husserl describes the spatiotemporal *character* of the life-world and what he is now calling the 'flowingly-statically present' nature of the transcendental life, but he does not assert the 'living present' as a foundation for the ego's experience. Indeed Husserl closes off the possibility of thinking of there being a 'foundation' for the ego: 'Having arrived at the ego, one becomes aware of standing within a sphere of self-evidence of such a nature that any attempt to enquire behind it would be absurd' (ibid., p. 188). Even the transcendental ego is not a reified thing (that, argues Husserl, would also be absurd) but merely a dynamic: the 'ego-pole of transcendental acts' (ibid., p. 186).

At times in *The Crisis of the European Sciences* Husserl's approach to the primordial constitution of the transcendental sphere is almost apophatic.

> Not even the single philosopher by himself, within the *epochē*, can hold fast to anything in this elusively flowing life, repeat it with always the same content, and so become certain of its this-ness and its being-such that he could describe it, document it, so to speak (even for his own person alone), in definitive statements. (CE, p. 178)

Furthermore, Husserl openly recognizes the difficulties of infinite regress that dog foundationalism: 'Every "ground" that is reached points to further grounds, every horizon opened up awakens new horizons' (CE, p. 170). Later he asserts that 'the point' of phenomenological research 'is not to secure objectivity but to understand it' (ibid., p. 189).

In *Experience and Judgement*, Husserl takes yet another approach to the issue. Instead of conceiving of primordial temporality as an ongoing living present, Husserl characterizes basic time as 'a linear continuum of the flow of firsthand presents', each succeeding the next in an infinite process of 'becoming' (EJ, p. 385). Thus time-consciousness appears like a row of light bulbs switching on in succession: 'Every new original present which lights up is a new immediate "positing" with a "content"' (ibid., p. 383). This continuum is a reality not only for each individual ego, but is part of 'a continuum of continua, a continuous series of continuous coexistences' (ibid., p. 383) which constitutes objective time for everyone and is a characteristic of the world of nature which is itself 'the absolute substrate in a pre-eminent sense' (ibid., p. 139). This is all very different from the view in the C texts where the new *epochē* uncovers a living-present stratum *distinct from* the succession of conscious experiences: 'This flowing-living present is not that which we otherwise hitherto described transcendentally-phenomenologically as a stream-of-consciousness or a stream-of-experience.'[47] Husserl's conception of natural objectivity in *Experience and Judgement* is different from the idea of the 'life-world' in *The Crisis of the European Sciences* and his insistence on the objectivity of punctiliar time is different again from the subjective 'now-points' of the early writings.

In review, Husserl's treatment of primordial temporality clearly does not amount to anything like a coherent doctrine. Rather, we experience Husserl struggling with a fundamental problem: how to perceive and describe that which is ultimately presupposed in every perception or description. In 1905 Husserl speaks of this as an area where 'names' are 'lacking'. Thirty years later those names are as elusive as ever. Yet in repeatedly attempting to speak about the precondition of transcendental subjectivity, Husserl was powerfully asserting the actuality of that precondition. Whatever the shortcomings of Derrida's analysis, he does at least draw our attention to the fundamental issue of primordial time in phenomenology, exploiting remarks in the *Nachlass* to lend a title to what remains for Husserl a dimension without a definitive description and without an official name.[48]

The Question of Husserl's Theology

The other half of Derrida's argument about the living present is that it should be seen as a theological concept. As Derrida puts it succinctly in an essay on Artaud, the 'being-present-to-itself' of speech intimates 'the absolute Logos, the living present of God' (WD, p. 237). In general terms, the observation that phenomenology implies a theology is not new. Husserl himself says as much, and many students and successors developed phenomenology in more explicitly theological directions. Derrida's observations make a particular argument about the character of Husserlian theology, seeing Husserl's apodictic claims for transcendental phenomenology as typical of a Western metaphysics built on a hierarchical distinction between speech and writing. But how justified is Derrida's claim about Husserl's theology?

Had Husserl and his successors not explicitly linked phenomenology with theology, we might still reasonably have made the connection. Certainly there are many aspects of phenomenology that seem to disclose a theological ambition. In itself the goal of Husserl's quest gives an implicit indication of its theological possibilities. The aim of phenomenology is, Husserl asserts, to be a 'science of Essential Being', an attempt 'to realize the idea of Absolute Knowledge', a 'Knowledge of Essence' and to disclose 'the essential nature of the Real'. The goal of being the science of Essence is coupled with the motivating conviction that such Essence exists and may be discovered. Nor is phenomenology to be a merely regional science, but a universal science, a queen of sciences, spanning what Husserl saw as the flawed disciplines of empirical science and speculative philosophy: 'All the sciences will now be ... living branches on the tree of the one universal science.'[49] Kolokowski remarks that to have attained Husserl's phenomenological standpoint 'amounts to gaining the position of the Gods'.[50] Indeed, once purged of error, the transcendental standpoint of the conscious ego aims at complete certainty. The only point of view that might exceed this would be the integrated perspective of every individual standpoint, what Husserl cautiously calls 'the community of transcendental egos'. At the very least, such a meta-science (or literally *omni*science) may be said to have adopted the ambitions of theology for authoritative truth. We might also say that the goals of phenomenology hint at a usurpation of the domain of theology and the replacement of its vocabulary with that of a transcendental philosophy. Phenomenological investigation would thus replace the religious consciousness. Perhaps Husserl was hinting as much when he concluded the *Cartesian Meditations* with a reference to the Augustinian cogito: 'Turn into yourself: Truth dwells in the inner man'.

During the phenomenological reductions the transcendental ego clearly emerges as having theological potential. For phenomenological consciousness is the location of absolute knowledge and essential reality. The transcendental ego is not a thing, an object like all others, which merely exists *for* transcendental consciousness. 'The transcendental ego ... is', as Husserl puts it, 'not a subject, but *sui generis, "the"* subject.' [51] In *Ideas II*, Husserl calls the intentional ego 'spiritual'. He also on occasion refers to the ethical goal of human life as *Seligkeit* or 'blessedness', in which all transcendental egos combine harmoniously. Furthermore, Husserl speaks in Heideggerian terms of each transcendental ego having a special calling (*Beruf*).[52]

Husserl's followers were not slow to see the theological potential of phenomenology. Spielberg notes that Landgrebe and Fink both headed off in this direction: 'Husserl's two most qualified interpreters have both moved beyond and away from the master's conception toward a more or less theological metaphysics.'[53] Landgrebe's vision, for example, was of a metaphysical world order to which the human is bonded and which is necessarily opened up by the phenomenological viewpoint.[54] Edward Farley shows how phenomenological influences flow, either directly or through an intermediary (for example Scheler's *Lebensphilosophie* or Heidegger's existentialism), into the writings of a number of theologians, among others Paul Tillich, Paul Ricoeur, Dietrich von Hildebrand, Henri Duméry and Auguste Brunner.[55] Although an exploration of the pattern of this influence is not within the scope of this study, it needs to be noted that Husserl's philosophy did, either directly or indirectly, provide a stimulus to twentieth-century theology. This stimulus continues today in the writings of Steven Laycock who has constructed a theology around the provocative suggestion that we are the eyes of the divine mind.[56]

Among Husserl's protégés it is notably Heidegger, in the period before the development of his particular existential phenomenology in *Being and Time*, who raises the question of phenomenology and Christianity. Theodore Kisiel has surveyed in detail Heidegger's lectures from 1915 to the writing of *Being and Time* in the mid-1920s.[57] Kisiel describes this decade as that of the 'Ur-Heidegger', when Heidegger published nothing and about which until recently little has been generally known. However, Heidegger's lectures from that period show how interested he was in combining his Catholic and seminarian education with Husserl's method of phenomenological description. It was in this period, at the time of his Lectures on Religion from 1920 to 1921, that Heidegger famously declared 'I am a Christian theologian!'[58] Taken by itself, this can be a misleading remark, but it does at least indicate a powerful Christian-religious influence on the early Heidegger. Kisiel documents how in the years 1917–19 Heidegger experiments with the idea of religio-mystical consciousness (particularly that of Eckhart) as a paradigm for phenomenological awareness.[59] Mysticism seemed to offer a model of a 'formless' consciousness denuded of prejudice, detached from the worldly and everyday standpoint, open entirely to the objectivity of things in themselves, and oriented towards that objectivity with a motivation towards the absolute in all its purity. From such a perspective the alignment of religion with phenomenology could easily be made. A decade later, in his lecture 'Phenomenology and Theology',[60] Heidegger takes a different view (the one we normally associate with him), crisply separating theology from phenomenology. Theology is a 'positive science' with a thematized area of inquiry. As such, 'theology' shares a footing with the natural sciences. Theology is the study of God, but since God can only be known through faith, God is thus not a *positum* of the kind found in the natural sciences. However, as a positive science, theology remains one of 'ontic' investigation. Phenomenology (understood by now in the Heideggerian rather than the Husserlian sense) is 'the name for the procedure of ontology, which essentially distinguishes itself from all other, positive sciences'.[61] Since 'every ontic interpretation operates within the basic context of an ontology', the *science* of theology is regional to that of phenomenology. Heidegger insists that this does not mean that 'theology is being led on the leash by philosophy', arguing that philosophy/phenomenology merely acts as an *ontological corrective* to theology (and the other positive, ontic sciences), clarifying theology's grasp of its subject matter. Heidegger's essay does not explore the possibility that the subject matter of theology might coincide precisely with the ontological (or transcendental in Husserl's case) constitution of phenomenology.

More significantly, it is Husserl himself who ultimately recognizes the theological implications of phenomenology.[62] In an apocryphal story, when asked by Roman Ingarden to name the most fundamental philosophical problem, Husserl is reported to have replied 'the problem of God, of course'.[63] Although very few commentators on phenomenology or philosophical theology refer either to Husserl's implicit or his explicit theological remarks, both support Derrida's general contention that phenomenology is essentially theological. The lack of attention to this area of Husserl's thought may arise from the dual way, from a phenomenological point of view, in which theology may be considered. One may (and this is what Derrida does) consider theological traits in the *method* of phenomenology itself, seeking to identify theological presuppositions in the *a priori* structures of transcendental consciousness. Alternatively, one may *subject theology to* the *a priori* structures of phenomenology such that God and theology appear as phenomena within the ego's conscious purview. In much of Husserl's published work, but notably the first volume of *Ideas*, he

argues that any empirical concept of God must be secondary to the conditions
of the pure *a priori* structures of transcendental consciousness. God cannot,
as Husserl puts it, alter the fact that $1 + 2 = 3$ (IdI, p. 138). God must therefore
be regarded as an object within the phenomenal perception of the ego,
existing *for* the ego and not prior to or in spite of it. Some commentators
erroneously take this to be Husserl's final word on God and theology.[64] This
empirical concept of God is the product of what Husserl calls at the end of
Cartesian Meditations 'naïve metaphysics', which operates 'with absurd
things in themselves'. However, Husserl is emphatic that the absurdity of
'naïve metaphysics' does not rule out 'metaphysics as such', which concerns
the 'supreme and ultimate questions' of the purpose and possibility of
consciousness itself. In his later years, Husserl acknowledged the possibility
that the consideration of God might properly belong to the first-order
questions of phenomenology: primordial temporality, teleology, the basic
constitution of the ego, the constitution of the life-world and of interpersonality.

There are traces of these later reflections in Husserl's earlier writing. In his
earliest writing on time, Husserl had observed that 'the divine consciousness
is the ideal correlate of objective time and of the objective world and world-
evolution' (PI, p. 180). In other words God lives in an infinite 'now', eternally
present, a perspective which in its complete experience of time has in fact
become non-temporal. Since in these texts Husserl was establishing the 'now'
as a term of convenience for the moment of transcendental experience, it is
unlikely that he was oblivious to possible analogies between the divine
experience of time, and the time-dimension of the transcendental ego. This
analogy is drawn more explicitly in *Ideas II*, where Husserl compares God's
perspective with the human point of view. Since the 'spiritual' human view
requires sensuous bodily perception, Husserl argues that God, the 'absolute
spirit', would himself require a body in order to be capable of a perception
analogous to ours.[65] Although the purpose of *Ideas II* was not theological but
was to establish the philosophical basis for the priority of the 'human' over
the 'natural' sciences, Husserl's emphasis on a 'spiritual' world upon which
the 'natural' world depends is pregnant with theological possibility. Nature is
what Husserl calls the 'intersubjective' material substrate for the spiritual
lives of transcendental egos:

> Nature is an intersubjective reality and a reality not just for me and my
> companions of the moment but for us and for everyone who can have dealings
> with us and come to a mutual understanding with us about things and about
> other people. There is always the possibility that new spirits enter into this nexus.
> (IdII, p. 90)

But the intersubjective nexus of the natural world is contingent upon the
absolute nexus of 'spirit':

Spirits are precisely not unities of appearances but are instead unities of absolute
nexuses of consciousness; more exactly, they are Ego-unities. And appearances
are correlates of nexuses of consciousness which themselves have absolute being.
And if appearances are constituted intersubjectively, then we are led back
precisely to the plurality of persons who can comprehend one another. A correlate
as such has its support in persons and in their lived experiences, and their absolute
being precedes the relative being of the appearances ... All natural existence
depends upon the existence of absolute spirits. (Ibid, pp. 315–6)

This area of Husserl's writing is notoriously difficult to interpret, not only
because of its intrinsic ambiguity, but because Husserl does not pursue the
concepts in subsequent publications. In his later writing – such as the *Cartesian
Meditations* – Husserl turns away from the spiritual experiment of *Ideas II*,
ceasing to talk about 'spirits' at all and simply speaking of a 'transcendental'
sphere which is distinguished from the spheres of 'psychology' and 'nature'.
Chronically uncertain about these problems of so-called 'basic constitution'
and the difficulty of finding a solution, Husserl postponed publication of *Ideas
II* and it was published posthumously in 1952.[66]

In the better-known first volume of *Ideas*, published in 1913, there are
further clues to Husserl's hidden theological perspective. His famous
'reduction' of God in section §58 is noteworthy not so much for its
'suspension' of an other-worldly view of God as for the scope that it allows
for a theology located in the realm of the 'transcendental' rather than the
'transcendent'. Even as he denies God as an exterior reality, Husserl
reinforces the importance both of an 'Absolute of Consciousness', which he
has earlier called 'the principle of principles', and of the fact that
'transcendental purification cannot mean the disconnecting of *all*
transcendents' (IdI, p. 174).

These intimations of a hidden theological disposition are confirmed by
Husserl's private conversations and unpublished writings. Dorian Cairns
records Husserl's table-talk on the subject:

The term God is used occasionally by Husserl in private conversation to mean the
community of transcendental egos which 'creates' a world, but this is for Husserl a
'private opinion'. [67]

This 'private opinion' is, as Klaus Held observes, also expressed in Husserl's
later unpublished writing when he speaks of a religious inner direction or
introjection (*Innenrichtung*) which discloses God as the ground of an internal
intersubjectivity (*Innern Intersubjektivität*), a community of 'persons'
(*Gemeinschaft*) illuminated by the self-reflection of the transcendental ego:[68]

This inner direction is parallel with the phenomenological inner direction, by
which the way passes through my inwardness into the realm of all others (as inner-
Others, not as exterior people, as spatio-temporal realities) thus through first to the
World and to one's own and other *Dasein*.[69]

The journey along this inward path, which leads back to the world of other persons is also stretched out in time and has a teleological direction which Husserl also sees as theological 'the being-process of transcendental intersubjectivity'[70] motivated by a 'universal absolute will' which Husserl calls 'godly'.

> The universal absolute will, which lives in all transcendental subjects, and which makes possible the individual-concrete being of transcendental all-subjectivity, is the divine will.[71]

This theme had been developed a few years earlier by Husserl in an unpublished discussion of 'cultural life, theology and knowledge'. Here the theology is more explicit and more religious. Not only does Husserl describe the teleology of consciousness as 'divine', but he emphasizes the importance of a belief in this divinity. Once one has accepted the reality of the teleological process, Husserl argues that theological language, and indeed theological belief, both become inevitable:

> But how else are we to understand this other than by the idea of God? How else but in terms of an absolute teleology prevailing through 'I' and 'I-life', through all consciousness and this is itself similar to a personal being in its personal challenges [*Forderungen*], expressed in the absolute challenges within the Soul – I can only be blessed [*selig*], I can only exist in all suffering, misfortune, in all the irrationality of my world, if I believe that God exists and that the world is God's world, and intend with the whole strength of my soul to hold fast to the absolute obligation [*Sollen*], and this is in itself an absolute will, for I must believe absolutely that He exists. Belief is the absolute and highest challenge. [72]

There are some clear Hegelian resonances here (as R.A. Mall has observed[73]), but there are also echoes of a Kierkegaardian 'dialectic of inwardness': Husserl reaches awareness of divinity down the internal channel of phenomenological exploration. The transcendental journey inwards leads to the transcendent intersubjective field and eventually to the teleological ground of the divine.

For Husserl, God is the final step in phenomenological discovery, only when we have fully grasped the nature of transcendental life can we grasp the understanding of the transcendence of God: 'the ethical–religious questions are the last questions of phenomenological constitution'.[74] Husserl appears to be using God as a working title for the precondition of the transcendental life. This leads Pivcevic to conclude that Husserl is employing God like Berkeley (whom he admired) to explain intersubjectivity and public time.[75] So God enters the Husserlian scheme at the point of its greatest ambiguity and incoherence. God is invoked as that which must necessarily be presupposed as the condition of possibility of a purposeful and trans-subjective transcendental consciousness.

This theology is not exactly the one that Derrida identifies in Husserl.

Derrida argues that Husserl's theology consists primarily of an assertion of the self-presence of consciousness. Furthermore, Husserl does not talk about the living present in theological terms (and this is an obstacle that Derrida does not tackle). For Husserl, theology does not start with the self-presence of consciousness, but begins as consciousness seeks to *transcend* its self-presence in order to realize its ethical obligation to others, to the 'world', and towards a future society. Derrida acknowledges this briefly, citing from one of the E manuscripts (Ms. E III 4, 'Teleology') which locates the absolute logos 'beyond transcendental subjectivity' (EH, p. 146). However, Derrida dismisses the reality of any such transcendence, arguing that the transcendental subject is trapped within the horizon of its living presence. The transcendental subject must move towards the other or the future *within* its living present or else forfeit its transcendental life. This argument may have some merit but it cannot disguise the fact that Derrida does not deconstruct Husserl's teleological conception of God as such, but only the implicit metaphysics Derrida detects in the temporal constitution of the ego. This leaves the question of Husserl's professed ethical and teleological theology hanging unanswered in mid air. Husserl's theology emerges from a concern to establish the basis for ethics: responsibility to the other and the aspiration of a more just future. Derrida's reluctance to engage with these questions at this stage – his alleged ethical procrastination – rebounds upon him in the form of the criticism that deconstruction fails to take ethics seriously. The irony is that when Derrida does take up ethical themes more directly, he strongly asserts the necessity of the otherness of the other, a Husserlian conclusion following directly from the transcendental constitution of the ego.

Concluding Remarks: Theology and Impossibility

As Derrida's writing progresses through its various encounters, his reading of Husserl retains its importance. Derrida continues to use 'the living present' as an exemplary instance not only of the metaphysics of subjectivity, but also of the metaphysics of presence in general. As 'the most radical and most critical restoration of the metaphysics of presence' (OG, p. 49), Husserl's living present provides a test case for the deconstruction of metaphysics in general – whether it is 'living speech' in *Of Grammatology*, the *Lebendigkeit* of Hegelian *Geist* in *Glas*, or the 'living presence' of the ethical subject in *Specters of Marx*.

However, Husserl's role in Derrida's philosophy is more than that of an exemplary and defeated adversary. At the end of his short essay 'Form and Meaning', Derrida speaks about 'two lines of thought' which may be seen to flow from Husserl's philosophy. One concerns the formal conditions of knowledge, the Cartesian-Kantian project, which arguably reaches its climax in Husserl and continues in various kinds of 'structuralism'. The other concerns the 'sense of being', the ontological security of presence which underpins Husserl's entire scheme of knowing. It could be argued that out of

Derrida's studies of Husserl there is a bifurcation in the theme of death which proceeds along the tracks of these two 'lines of thought'.[76] On the one hand Derrida pursues the question of death in the 'scene of writing' and how 'writing' (in both its general and vulgar senses) is the deathly other of living speech. This draws him into readings of Saussure, Rousseau, Lévi-Strauss, Freud and Plato. On the other hand Derrida may be seen to pursue the question of 'being' and death through readings of Bataille, Levinas, Hegel and Heidegger. This bifurcation could be read as a division of Derrida's philosophy into separate epistemological (linguistic) and ontological dimensions. But such a division would not be faithful to his intention. It is central to Derrida's purpose to assert that writing is always a 'written being' and being is always a 'being written', that the binarism of ontology and epistemology cannot be sustained: 'the unity of the sense of being ... is, in the last instance, a unity of the word' (OG, p. 22). In 'Form and Meaning' Derrida concludes that there is 'probably no choice between the two lines of thought' and that his task is 'to reflect on the circularity which makes one pass into the other indefinitely'. Derrida hints that this will take him beyond philosophy, that it will shift his thinking to a new site where the questions of 'negativity, nonbeing, lack, silence' can be considered not as a deficiency or problem but as an opportunity.

Of course this is only partly a criticism of Husserl. At the end of *Edmund Husserl's Origin of Geometry: An Introduction*, Derrida only argues that Husserl is *unsuccessful* in taking thinking beyond the division of epistemology and ontology. The *identification of the need* to unsettle the separation of the two fields is a *positive* feature of the 'living present' which Derrida absorbs into his own project. It is one of the ironies of Derrida's philosophy that although he rejects the phenomenological quest for certain foundations, his own work can be read – perhaps *should* be read – as an attempt to establish a super-phenomenology, with such concepts as arche-writing, the trace and aporia providing an uncertain non-ground from which non-phenomenality deconstructs phenomenality conceived as life. The question of the possibility or impossibility of this non-phenomenal non-ground lies at the heart of Derrida's philosophical writing.

Later chapters will argue that Derrida and Heidegger – in the quest for ever-more radical foundations – are entirely complicit with phenomenology. Can deconstruction not be read as an interminable *epochē* which, as a matter of principle, never reaches a ground of certainty? Could not such a principle of uncertainty, which would be an anti-principle, be read as an alternative to the 'living present', different from a *constitutive* point of view, but with a *performative* affinity? Is there a sense in which, for all his *resistance* to phenomenology, Derrida *reinforces* the phenomenological gesture? And if this gesture is in Husserl essentially *theological*, what should be deduced about the 'theology' of deconstruction?

Once seen in a fraternal light, the similarities, congruences and alliances between Derrida and Husserl become more prominent and more significant.

Both seek to 'overcome' metaphysics; both adopt a technique that involves the meticulous dismantling of inherited concepts and patterns of thought; both claim to have inaugurated a new age in philosophy; both (in the end) tend towards a theological mysticism: for Husserl the mysticism of egological time, for Derrida the mysticism of linguistic difference. It is telling that the philosophies of Derrida and Husserl both slide into mystical apophasis the minute they are pressed to describe foundational concepts. As we have seen, Husserl speaks vaguely of 'a dimension where names are lacking'. Derrida too, in 'Différance', says that *différance* is 'not a name' and that the 'play' of language 'cannot be named' (SP, p. 159).[77] For all their differences and despite the 'deconstruction' of phenomenology, there is still a theological alliance between Husserl and Derrida.

The deconstruction of the Husserlian ego and its 'theology' provides Derrida with many resources for his later consideration of the question of ethics and human responsibility. Derrida's demonstration of the impossibility of the Husserlian ego and of living presence brings him back to a staunchly Husserlian affirmation of the undecidability, and therefore the essential *secrecy* of the ego. Derrida's ethical themes of hospitality, democracy, forgiveness, friendship and responsibility all presuppose the discretion of the ego, that other persons cannot be known but must be approached with openness to their otherness. Husserl's insight that the otherness of the other is not a philosophical problem but the basis of any meaningful ethics of responsibility is carried on in Derrida, who sees humanity as individuated and singular in a way that calls for a respectful social and interpersonal order. The demonstration of the impossibility of the living present of consciousness is *positive* in that it *establishes* the impossible self as a starting point for ethical thinking. Exactly the same may be said for Derrida's deconstruction of Husserl's theology: this is an *inaugural* act, a positive thinking of the impossible God.

At this stage in his career at least, Derrida is not explicitly calling deconstruction theological. Indeed, taking a superficial look at some of his early essays – say, 'Différance' and *Of Grammatology* – we could easily conclude that the Derrida of the 1960s has no interest in exploring the theological implications of deconstruction. After all, he does say categorically in 'Différance' that *différance* 'is not theological, not even in the most negative order of negative theology' (SP, p. 134); and Derrida rants joyfully in *Of Grammatology* about the closure of the 'theological' 'age of the sign'. But this is only half, or less than half, of the story. With Derrida nothing remains one-sided, not even – not least – his own pronouncements. In an attempt to wrest the concept of language from the grip of metaphysics, Derrida acknowledges that deconstruction must engage metaphysically. Thus, despite his attempt to overcome metaphysics, he also says that 'différance remains a metaphysical name' (ibid., p. 159). It is for this reason that he speaks about the 'closure' (*clôture*) of metaphysics, rather than the end.[78] So there is a metaphysics and theology *of* deconstruction and *after* deconstruction.

Derrida deconstructs Husserl's theology, in part, by installing his own in its place. He challenges the 'metaphysical assurance' and theological self-presence of Husserlian consciousness by counterposing the necessity of the undecidability of an absolute theological presence (or absence). To be sure, this is a different kind of theology, a theology that tries to be self-erasing or self-emptying, a theology that is trying all the time not to be 'theological'. However, it remains a theology and Derrida returns to it again and again in his later writing. He credits Husserl with 'an admirable modern revolution of metaphysics, going beyond the whole history of metaphysics to re-instate it at the purity of its origin' (PCM, p. 15). Derrida perhaps deserves a similar accolade, in so far as deconstruction purifies metaphysics in *différance* rather than abolishing it.

Derrida's 'purification of metaphysics' rests in the determination of theology as 'impossible'. Derrida's critique of Husserl concludes that 'the living present', a 'pure' phenomenality and God are impossible ideas. The 'irreducible ... nonlife' of the living present means that it can never occur *as such*. It can only appear in the form of an impossible idea. This goes for the entire range of fundamental distinctions in Husserl – including the thinking of God: 'Their possibility is their impossibility' (SP, p. 101).

A Husserlian Rejoinder

From Heidegger's work, Husserl was aware of the possibility of a form of *epochē* which would end up, like deconstruction, in a tangle of paradoxes. In *The Crisis of The European Sciences*, Husserl describes what can go wrong with a radical phenomenology when it tries to sidestep the question of the transcendental ego and move directly to an exploration of pre-egological grounds. Since, for Husserl, all forms of philosophical investigation necessarily depend upon the ego's intentional activity, any philosophical attempt to out-manoeuvre the ego will also have to presuppose the ego. In Husserl's estimation a (Heideggerian/Derridean) radical phenomenology never makes any progress, but simply chases after itself in an endless, and pointless, circle of subject–object paradoxes. In the end, says Husserl, this sort of phenomenology will justify itself by holding up these paradoxes as achievements:

> What is peculiarly proper to this phenomenological-transcendental radicalism is that ... rather than having a ground of things taken for granted and ready in advance, as does objective philosophy, it excludes in principle a ground of this or any other sort. Thus it must begin without any underlying ground. But immediately it achieves the possibility of creating a ground for itself through its own powers, namely, in mastering, through original self-reflection, the naive world as transformed into a phenomenon or rather a universe of phenomena. Its beginning course ... is necessarily one of thinking in naive self-evidence. It possesses no formed logic and methodology in advance and it can achieve its method and even the genuine sense of its accomplishments only through ever

renewed self-reflections. Its fate (understood subsequently, to be sure, as an essentially necessary one) is to become involved again and again in paradoxes, which, arising out of uninvestigated and even unnoticed horizons, remain functional and announce themselves as incomprehensibilities. (CE, p. 181)

For Husserl, such paradoxes are resolved when the 'uninvestigated and unnoticed' horizon of the transcendental ego is clarified, and the subjective, living present activity of the ego is acknowledged as a ground. Perhaps, if Husserl had lived to issue a rejoinder to Derrida, he would have asked about the 'uninvestigated horizon' of deconstruction, challenging Derrida to be more explicit about the 'theological' ground from which deconstruction launches itself. In fact, as his career continues, Derrida does become more explicit about his impossible God, indeed about his *faith* in the impossible God. But at this juncture in his thinking the idea of 'the impossible' – its value, its necessity, its paradoxes – is still at a protean stage. Derrida's engagement with Heidegger enables a more profound thinking of impossibility in relation to subjectivity and the way in which the thought of one's own death, the thinking of Being and the concept of the 'other' can clarify the impossible conditions of any phenomenology or of any revelation.

Notes

1 Given the importance of Derrida's writing on Husserl, it is strange that critics have tended to pay scant attention to it. W. McKenna and J. Claude Evans, eds, *Derrida and Phenomenology* (Kluwer, Dordrecht, 1995) contains a selection of critical essays. P. Völkner, *Derrida und Husserl: zur Dekonstruktion einer Philosophie der Präsenz,* (Passagen Verlag, Vienna, 1993) is the earliest treatment of the topic. Volume 32 of *The Southern Journal of Philosophy* (1993) is a collection of papers on Husserl and Derrida written in response to the publication of *Le problème de la genèse dans la philosophie de Husserl*. Recently Dermot Moran's *Introduction to Phenomenology* (Routledge, London, 2000), has included a chapter on Derrida and Husserl as has Christina Howell's *Introducing Derrida* (Polity, Oxford, 1999).
2 Derrida speaks disparagingly of 'that nebula named "deconstruction in America"' (Mem, p. 108).
3 Derrida was not alone in his interest in the Husserl Archive. Vincent Descombes reports 'the fascination exercised over a whole generation by the then unpublished manuscripts of Husserl' (V. Descombes, *Modern French Philosophy,* Cambridge University Press, Cambridge, 1980, p. 64).
4 R. Kearney, ed., *Dialogues with Contemporary Continental Thinkers* (Manchester University Press, Manchester, 1984), p. 109.
5 Ibid.
6 Cited in H. Spielberg, *The Phenomenological Movement: An Historical Introduction* (Martinus Nijhoff, The Hague, 1971), p. 399. Spielberg conducts an invaluable survey of the progress of the reception of Husserl in France.
7 E. Levinas, *La théorie de l'intuition dans la phénoménologie de Husserl* (Alcan, Paris, 1963); tr. A. Orianne as *The Theory of Intuition in Husserl's Phenomenology* (Northwestern University Press, Evanston, 1973).
8 For Levinas's own description of this treament of intentionality see 'Ethics as First Philosophy' in S. Hand, ed., *The Levinas Reader* (Blackwell, Oxford, 1989).

9   See for instance 'Sur les "Ideen" de M.E. Husserl', *Revue Philosophique de la France et de l'Etranger*, CVII, 3–4 (1929): 230–65; or 'Freibourg, Husserl et la phénoménologie', *Revue d'Allemagne et des pays de langue allemande*, V, 43 (1931), pp. 402–14.

10 See J.P. Sartre, 'Intentionality: An Idea in Husserl's Phenomenology', tr. J.P. Fell, *Journal of the British Society for Phenomenology*, vol. 1, no. 2 (May 1970) and J.P. Sartre, *Imagination*, tr. F. Williams (Cresset Press, London, 1962).

11 J.P Sartre, *Being and Nothingness*, tr. H. Barnes (Routledge, London,1989), pp. 73 and 84f.

12 In fact Husserl had given up using this term by 1936. However, to be fair to Derrida, Husserl does address the question of primordial time, calling it 'flowing-static vitality … the vital movement of the co-existence and the interweaving of original formations and sedimentations of meaning'. *The Origin of Geometry* as it appears in Derrida's translation in *Edmund Husserl's Origin of Geometry: An Introduction*, pp. 173f.

13 See for instance C. Norris, *Derrida* (Fontana, London, 1987), pp. 15ff; R. Bernet, 'On Derrida's "Introduction" to Husserl's *Origin of Geometry*', in H. Silverman, ed., *Continental Philosophy 2: Derrida and Deconstruction* (Routledge, London, 1989), pp. 139–53.

14 The description which follows outlines the *epochē* of the *Cartesian Meditations*. Husserl's theory of the *epochē*, like so much of his philosophy, was reworked. In *The Crisis of the European Sciences* Husserl sees the successive *epochē* as 'corrections' of each other: 'As against the first application of the *epochē*, a second is required, or rather a conscious reshaping of the *epochē*' (CE, p. 186). Husserl also argues that the *epochē* should be more than an individual activity; it should involve the entire culture in 'a total transformation of attitude' (ibid., p. 148). This so-called 'universal *epochē*' has the ambitious goal of 'radically changing all human existence' (ibid., p. 151). The emphasis here is rather different from that of the *Cartesian Meditations* where the *epochē* takes place 'each for himself and in himself'. In *Experience and Judgement* – published in 1939 but comprising material from 1910 onwards and fully drafted by the mid-1930s – for example, the *epochē* is recast as *Abbau* (dismantling) in a twofold retrogression, employing the terminology of 'life-world' that is characteristic of Husserl in *The Crisis of the European Sciences*. The first retrogression reduces from the pre-given natural world to the transcendental life-world, the second retrogression from the life-world to the 'subjective operations' which give rise to the life-world (EJ, §11). Such revisions of the *epochē* are technical and do not fundamentally alter the nature of Husserl's phenomenology. However, the notion of *Abbau* has attracted the interest of writers on deconstruction, notably Gasché in *The Tain of the Mirror*. Gasché sees *Abbau*, like Heidegger's *Destruktion*, as prefiguring 'deconstruction'. It will be argued here, in general agreement with Gasché, that the *epochē* itself, whether conceived as *Abbau* or 'bracketing', is the genealogical ancestor of deconstruction.

15 *Lectures on First Philosophy*, cited in Dermot Moran, *An Introduction to Phenomenology* (Routledge, London, 2000) p. 148.

16 Between *Ideas* and *The Crisis of the European Sciences* Husserl uses the term 'natural' in quite contradictory ways. In *Ideas* the natural life is the life governed by prejudice and presupposition. However, in *The Crisis* Husserl speaks about the pre-theoretical life world as 'original natural life' (see Carr's introductory comments to *The Crisis of the European Sciences*, tr. D. Carr, Northwestern University Press, Evanston, 1970, p. xxxix). Here 'natural life' is that described in *Ideas*.

17 'I become the disinterested spectator of my natural and worldy ego and its life' (PL, p. 15).

18 Levinas, *The Theory of Intuition in Husserl's Phenomenology*.

19 Since we have been citing the *Cartesian Meditations* we note Husserl's reference to 'living presence' in §46 as he concludes the abstractive reduction (CM, p. 102).

20 See for example Husserl's remarks about the transcendental *epochē* in §40 of *The Crisis of the European Sciences*. (CE, pp. 148ff.).

21 David Bell, *Husserl* (Routledge, London, 1990), p. 215. Bell argues that the difficulty

described here is 'neither a theoretical problem, nor a practical obstacle in the way of intersubjective understanding' (p. 220). Bell accepts Husserl's argument that the consciousness of the other must necessarily be 'other' and therefore inaccessible. However, this ignores Husserl's insistence upon the 'abstractive reduction', where the reduction of the 'other' itself is a phenomenological imperative. Indeed, Husserl must take phenomenological research back to its absolute logical foundation, since it is upon just such a foundation that phenomenology stakes its claims. Bell dismisses the third reduction too easily as an aberration when it is really at the core of the problem. Sartre, seeing solipsism as the inevitable consequence of any philosophy that depends upon the subject–object relation, argues that 'Husserl cannot escape solipsism any more than Kant could' (*Being and Nothingness*, p. 235). Ryle also notes 'a progressive trend visible in the philosophy of Husserl and his followers towards a rarefied Subjective Idealism or even Solipsism' (M. Murray, ed., *Heidegger and Modern Philosophy*, Yale University Press, New Haven, 1978, p. 55).

22 'If what belongs to the other's own essence were directly accessible, it would be merely a moment of my own essence, and ultimately he himself and I myself would be the same' (CM, p. 109). The later Husserl maintains the same stance (CE, pp. 184–6).

23 H. Gadamer, 'The Science of the Life World', in *Philosophical Hermeneutics* (University of California Press, 1977), p. 187.

24 Derrida also addresses this issue in a discussion of Levinas and Husserl in 'Violence and Metaphysics' (WD, pp. 123f.). Derrida agrees that there can be no transcendental basis for assuming the transcendental experience of the other. However, he supports the argument that the transcendental ego guarantees the otherness of the other in two respects: first, the other as another body; second, the other as an unknown subject/ego with unique experiences. However, Derrida skips over the problem of how the other can be apodictically identified as an ego, and not merely imagined or presupposed by analogy. Derrida implies that it is through language, speech and communication that the other is disclosed as an alter ego: 'The egoicity of the other permits him to say "ego" as I do; and this is why he is Other, and not a stone ... This is why, if you will, he is face, can speak to me, understand me and eventually command me' (WD, p. 126). Derrida says that the necessity of recognizing the other as alter ego is an ethical, in other words a necessary Kantian, imperative. But this sets the presupposition of the alter ego into a different logical category from the apodictic knowledge of the other as another body. Derrida returns to this point in his discussion of ethical responsibility in *The Gift of Death*, this time giving the otherness of the other a Levinasian theological interpretation: 'Since each one of us, everyone else, each other is infinitely other in its absolute singularity, inaccessible, solitary, transcendent, nonmanifest, originally non-present as my ego (as Husserl would say of the *alter ego* that can never be originally present to my consciousness and that I can apprehend only through what he calls appresentation and analogy), then what can be said about Abraham's relation to God can be said about my relation to *every other (one) as every (bit) other*, in particular my relation to my neighbour or my loved ones who are inaccessible to me, as secret and transcendent as Jahweh' (GD, p. 78).

25 H. Gadamer, 'The Phenomenological Movement', in *Philosophical Hermeneutics*, p. 161. Although Gadamer is correct in that Husserl develops the concept of *Lebenswelt* to address the question of the communal consitution of egos, it should be noted that Husserl's use of the concept of *Lebenswelt* predates the publication of *Being and Time*. Spielberg records that Husserl uses the idea as early as 1924 in 'Kant und die Idee der Transzendentalphilosophie', *Husserliana* VII, 232, 2.6. See Spielberg, *The Phenomenological Movement*, p. 741.

26 E. Husserl, *The Crisis of the European Sciences*, translator's introduction, pp. xxxviii–xlii.

27 P. Ricoeur, *Husserl: An Analysis of his Phenomenology* (Northwestern University Press, Evanston, 1967), p. 110.

28   Husserl makes other attempts at offering an account of intersubjectivity, such as in *Ideas II*, where the 'spiritual' world of lived experiences is seen as the absolute basis for the natural world. See pp. 56–57 above.

29   Ricoeur, *Husserl*, p. 195.

30   In 'Genesis and Structure' (WD, pp. 154–68), Derrida suggests that we ask the question of what precedes the transcendental reduction and the transcendental 'I'. In particular, this question must ask about the possibility of the death of the transcendental ego (ibid., p. 168).

31   Published in English as an appendix to *The Crisis of the European Sciences and Transcendental Phenomenology*, tr. David Carr (Northwestern University Press, Evanston, 1970).

32   Primary ideal objectivity is the existence of words as empirical objects that can appear again and again in quite different situations. Secondary ideal objectivity is the sense or intention-content of words which passes beyond their empirical appearance. Both primary and secondary idealities are 'bound' by temporal restrictions. Tertiary ideal objectivity, however, goes beyond all contingency and finds its paradigm in the omnitemporal structures of geometry.

33   However, Derrida does not treat them directly, but via A. Diemer, tr. A. Lowit and H. Colombié, 'La Phénomenologie de Husserl comme métaphysique', *Les Etudes Philosophiques*, 9, (1954).

34   The 'expressive' signs have a sense which Husserl names '*Bedeutung*' – they express the ideal and logical form of transcendental consciousness. The 'indicative' signs have a sense which Husserl calls '*Sinn*' – they indicate sensible objects in the world-historical sphere.

35   J. Claude Evans, *Derrida and the Myth of the Voice* (University of Minnesota Press, Minneapolis, 1991), p. 54.

36   R. Sokolowski, *Husserlian Meditations* (Northwestern University Press, Evanston, 1974), pp. 158–62.

37   Claude Evans, *Derrida and the Myth of the Voice*, p. 128.

38   Derrida has already made this point in *Le problème de la genèse dans la philosophie de Husserl* (Pro, pp. 167f.).

39   Husserl, however, is not consistent on this point: at §17 he denies that perception and nonperception are continuous (PI, p. 42); at §16 however, he says 'perception and nonperception continually pass over one another ... Moreover, it is true that even this ideal now is not something *toto caelo* different from the not-now but continually accommodates itself thereto' (ibid., p. 40; cf: SP, p. 65).

40   R. Bernet, I. Kern and E. Marbach, *An Introduction to Husserlian Phenomenology*, (Northwestern University Press, Evanston, 1993), p. 101. Bernet et al. cite the first volume of *Ideas*, where time-consciousness is described as a 'sphere of problems of exceeding difficulty'.

41   Bernet et al. note complementary remarks in manuscripts dated *c*.1908 about the 'absolute, primordially constituting conciousness' (*Introduction to Husserlian Phenomenology*, p. 109).

42   E. Husserl, *On the Phenomenology of the Consciousness of Internal Time*, p. LV. However, Brough brushes off far too easily what he calls the 'mystical' and 'metaphysical' implications of the 'absolute flow', arguing that Husserl offers no hint of this in these early texts. This is simply not true, because Husserl does use the idea of God's omniscience to describe the condition of an absolute temporality which becomes non-temporal by virtue of its total experience of time. (See Husserl, *On the Phenomenology of the Consciousness of Internal Time*, p. 180 and the discussion of Husserl and theology on pp. 53–59 above.)

43   The note is cited in Dorian Cairn's edition of E. Husserl, *Cartesian Meditations* (CM. pp. 93ff.).

44   Husserl, Ms. C. 3. I. 4a.

45 See Husserl, Mss. C. 3. I. 4a; C. 6; C. 12. 2a.
46 Husserl, Ms. C. 2. I. 5a.
47 Husserl, Ms. C. 3. I. 4a.
48 It should be mentioned that Derrida is guided to this interpretation by others, notably the Vietnamese phenomenologist Tran Duc Thao. See Tran Duc Thao, *Phenomenology and Dialectical Materialism* (Kluwer, Dordrecht, 1986); and his essay 'Dialectical Logic as the General Logic of Temporalization', in *The Logic of the Living Present, Analecta Husserliana*, vol. 46, ed. A.T. Tynieniecka (Kluwer, Dordrecht, 1995).
49 Husserl, Ms. F. I. 32. 41a. Cited by Bernet et al., *An Introduction to Husserlian Phenomenology*, p. 219.
50 L. Kolokowski, *Husserl and the Search for Certitude* (University of Chicago Press, Chicago, 1975), p. 81.
51 D. Cairns, ed., *Conversations with Husserl and Fink* (Martinus Nijhoff, The Hague, 1976), p. 59.
52 Cairns, *Conversations*, p. 35.
53 Spielberg, *The Phenomenological Movement*, p. 601.
54 See L. Landgrebe, 'Phenomenology and Metaphysics', *Philosophy and Phenomenological Research*, vol. 10, no. 2 (1949–50), p. 197.
55 E. Farley, *Ecclesial Man: A Social Phenomenology of Faith and Reality* (Fortress Press, Philadelphia, 1975). Farley separates phenomenology's influence on theology into three broad categories: first, there is the phenomenology *of* theology, which subjects theology to phenomenological analysis, seeking to establish the eidetic structure of theological discourses and religious consciousness. In this category, Farley cites, among others, Rudolf Otto's *Die Heilige* (1917). Second, there is transcendental–phenomenological theology, which (aligning theology with the Kantian transcendental project) seeks to establish the conditions required for religious knowledge and belief. In this category Farley cites, among others, Brunner's *Glaube und Erkenntnis* (1957). Third, there is existentialist–phenomenological theology, drawing either on the later Husserl or Scheler/Heidegger, which seeks to describe the ontological conditions of religious possibility. Here Farley cites in particular the 'fundamental theology' of Tillich and Bultmann.
56 S. Laycock, *Foundations for a Phenomenological Theology* (The Edwin Mellen Press, Lewiston, 1988).
57 T. Kisiel, *The Genesis of Heidegger's Being and Time* (University of California Press, Berkeley, 1993).
58 Letter to Karl Löwith, 19 August 1921, published in D. Papenfuss and O. Pöggeler, eds, *Zur philosophischen Aktualität Heideggers: Vol. 2 Im Gespräch der Zeit,* (Klostermann, Frankfurt, 1990).
59 Kisiel, *Genesis of Heidegger's Being and Time*, pp. 80–108. Kisiel cites texts from Heidegger, *Frühe Shriften* (Klostermann, Frankfurt, 1972).
60 Translated in J.G. Hart and J.C. Maraldo, eds, *The Piety of Thinking* (Indiana University Press, Bloomington, 1976).
61 Ibid., p. 21.
62 The most comprehensive study of Husserl and theology is by A. Bello, *Husserl Sul problema di Dio* (Edizions Studium, Rome, 1985). Other important writing on the subject includes the following: G. Bucher, 'The Metaphor of the Sacred, or the Allegory of Origin', in *From the Sacred to the Divine: Analecta Husserliana*, vol. 43 (Kluwer, Dordrecht, 1993). Louis Dupré, 'Husserl's Thought on God and Faith', *Philosophy and Phenomenological Research*, vol. 29, no. 2, 1968–69 and *A Dubious Heritage: Studies in the Philosophy of Religion after Kant* (Paulist Press, New York, 1977). J. Hart, 'The Study of Religion in Husserl's Writings', in M. Daniel and L. Embree, eds, *Phenomenology of the Cultural Disciplines* (Kluwer, Dordrecht, 1994). D. Guerrière, ed., *Phenomenology of the Truth Proper to Religion* (State University of New York Press, New York, 1990). J. Hart and S. Laycock, eds, *Essays in Phenomenological Theology* (State University of

New York Press, New York, 1986). M Henry et al., eds, *Phénoménologie et Théologie* (Criterion, Paris, 1992). E. Housset, 'Husserl et le Dieu d'Aristote', *Les Etudes Philosophiques*, 4 (1995). L. Landgrebe, 'Phenomenology and Metaphysics', *Philosophy and Phenomenological Research*, vol. 10, no. 2 (1949–50). S. Laycock, *Foundations for a Phenomenological Theology* (The Edwin Meller Press, Lewiston, 1988). R. Mall, 'Theology and Phenomenology', *Husserl Studies*, vol. 8 (1991). J. Mohanty et al. *Phenomenological Inquiry*, vol. 14: 'Phenomemological Approaches to the Divine', (1990). S. Strasser, 'Das Gottesproblem in der Spätphilosophie Edmund Husserl's, *Philosophisches Jahrbuch*, 67 (1958). S. Strasser, 'History, Teleology and God in the Philosophy of Husserl', in *Analecta Husserliana*, vol. 9 (Kluwer, Dordrecht, 1976).

63   See L. Dupré, 'Husserl's thought on God and Faith', *Philosophy and Phenomenological Research*, vol. 29, no. 2 (1968–69), p. 201.

64   See for example J. Edie, *Edmund Husserl's Phenomenology: A Critical Commentary*, (Indiana University Press, Bloomington, 1987), pp. 72 and 74.

65   'Obviously, the absolute spirit would also have to have a Body for there to be mutual understanding, and thus the dependency on sense organs would have to be there as well' (IdII, p. 90).

66   *Ideas II* was written in 1912, revised by Edith Stein in 1916 and 1918, but despite further work by Landgrebe in the 1920s was not published in Husserl's lifetime. The other major text on this topic is the manuscript 'Natur und Geist', prepared in 1913.

67   D. Cairns, ed., *Conversations with Husserl and Fink* (Martinus Nijhoff, The Hague, 1976).

68   K. Held, *Lebendige Gegenwart* (Martinus Nijhoff, The Hague, 1966), pp. 173–84. Held refers to Ms. E. III. 9. 'Instinkt, Welt, Gut, Teleologie, Normstruktur der Personlichkeit' (1931–33).

69   Husserl, Ms. E. III. 9. 22b.

70   Husserl, Ms. E. III. 4. 42a.

71   Husserl, Ms. E. III. 4. 44b.

72   E. Husserl, Ms. A.V. 21. 15b. See also Husserl, Mss. A. V. 24a, 24b and 25a.

73   R. Mall, 'Theology and Phenomenology', *Husserl Studies*, vol. 8 (1991).

74   Cairns, *Conversations*, p. 47. Husserl himself elaborates on these in Husserl, Mss. E. III. 4. 19a and 19b.

75   E. Pivcevic, *Husserl and Phenomenology* (Hutchinson, London, 1970), pp. 15f.

76   Christopher Norris tends towards this broad distinction by separating Derrida's 'epistemological' (Husserlian) and 'ethical' (Levinasian) interests in the conclusion to C. Norris, *Derrida* (Fontana, London, 1987).

77   Derrida has commented directly on the fact that both he and Husserl try to speak of what cannot be named (TS, p. 68).

78   See Derrida's comment on the 'problem of closure' as that of the relations between belonging and the opening [*la percée*] (WD, p. 110).

Chapter 3

Death, Self and World:
Heidegger's Reversal from Husserl

*Life's being is also death. Everything that enters into life also
begins to die, to go towards its death, and death is at the same time
life.*

(IM, p. 131)

*A mere shift of attitude is powerless to bring about the advent of
the thing as thing.*

(PT, p. 182)

Introduction

Having opened up the theme of death in Derrida's reading of Husserl, the next
task is to prepare the ground for an analysis of Derrida's deconstruction of
Heidegger, by examining Heidegger's engagement with Husserl. This will
illuminate the structure of the essentially *phenomenological* tradition in
which Derrida stands. In particular we will see the evolution of another kind
of phenomenology – Heidegger's phenomenology as 'privation' – which
Derrida develops into his own impossible phenomenology of 'disappearance'.

Derrida 'turns' or 'reverses' from Heidegger's philosophy much as
Heidegger 'reverses' from Husserl's. Heidegger attempts to pass through
Husserl's consciousness to secure his thinking on the ground of Being.
Derrida, in turn, attempts to pass through Being and appeal to the un-
grounded ground of arche-writing and *différance*. All three appeal to a
deepening of revelation, a more self-evident *phainesthai*. Each attempts to
make an ever-more primitive disclosure. Thus each is a 'phenomenologist' in
the sense that each clears a space – by *epochē*, *Destruktion* or deconstruction
– for a 'showing'. In Husserl's case the *epochē* uncovers the basis of apodictic
knowledge. In his turn Heidegger argues that knowledge is unrooted until the
question of the being of the knower has been resolved. In a further reduction,
Derrida appeals to a difference 'older than Being itself': *différance* (M, p. 67).
What separates Derrida from the other two is his more self-conscious – and
reluctant – participation in the quest for grounds. Derrida, aware of the
tradition which threatens to engulf him, attempts to gesture at something
'other' than a ground. Yet even as he resists the tradition, he deepens his
complicity. The appeal to *différance* is an act of sabotage which goes wrong

(ibid., p. 67). For *différance* becomes the ground *par excellence*: a ground so profound in its uncertainty that it cannot even say whether or not it is a ground. Yet Derrida is himself conscious, and makes the reader conscious, of this paradox, noting that '*différance* is itself *enmeshed*, carried off, reinscribed, just as a false entry or false exit is still part of the game, a function of the system' (M, p. 27).

Within this triangle, 'Husserl–Heidegger–Derrida', Heidegger and Derrida share a congruent reaction to Husserl. Heidegger and Derrida both attempt to gesture at a dimension behind Husserlian consciousness: Heidegger at Being, Derrida at 'writing'. Furthermore, both thinkers achieve this by using a phenomenology 'without reserve'. As Ricoeur puts it, 'Heideggerian and post-Heideggerian hermeneutics, though they are indeed heirs to Husserlian phenomenology, constitute in the end the reversal of this phenomenology to the very extent indeed that they also constitute its realization.'[1] Derrida, surpassing the other two, uses the same tactics on Heidegger. In the history of these reversals, from the publication of *Being and Time* in 1927 to Derrida's first discussions of Heidegger,[2] the question of death plays a crucial role. Derrida, as we have seen, identifies death as the other, excluded by Husserl's living presence. Heidegger, much more than Derrida, explicitly thematizes death and gives it a distinctive role not only in his early existential analysis of *Dasein*, but also in his later philosophy of language, allowing him to develop a concept of existential selfhood which transcends the solipsism of Husserl's ego. Finally, it will be argued that it is essentially through the question of death that Derrida is able to pursue his charges of a metaphysics of Being and metaphysical humanism against Heidegger, leading Derrida to a still greater anteriority in the uncertain difference between death and life. The task of this present chapter is to determine the character of the Heideggerian reversal from Husserl in preparation for an analysis of the Derridean reversal from Heidegger.

Knowledge versus Being

Edmund Husserl hoped that his former pupil and successor as Rector of Freiburg University, Martin Heidegger, would continue to promote and explore 'phenomenological research'. Indeed Heidegger himself, at least up to the writing of *Being and Time*, saw his own writing as 'phenomenological' and built directly upon the work of Husserl. However, Heidegger's development of phenomenology was at once an expansion and a subversion of its Husserlian origins. In his 1925 lecture course (which developed concepts later to appear in *Being and Time*) Heidegger's growing ambivalence is evident. At the same time as making 'trenchant' criticisms of Husserl, Heidegger declares apologetically that 'it goes almost without saying that even today I still regard myself as a learner in relation to Husserl' (HC, p. 121). John Van Buren has offered an assessment of the importance of

Heidegger's early writings, arguing that both the disenchantment with Husserlian phenomenology, and Husserl's disapproval of Heidegger's innovations begin from as early as 1919.[3] Certainly, within *Being and Time*, it became clear to Husserl that Heidegger wished to develop phenomenology in a radical new anthropological and existential direction. Husserl's marginal notes to *Being and Time* indicate his displeasure. He felt that the translation of phenomenological terms into Heidegger's existential jargon – transcendental ego into *Dasein*, for instance – was unnecessary and confusing. Furthermore, Husserl felt that his ideas were being exploited and corrupted by Heidegger. Scribbled in the margins of Husserl's copy of *Being and Time* is the irritated comment: 'What is said there is my own teaching deprived of its deep grounding.'[4] In the introduction to *Being and Time*, Heidegger goes to some lengths to stress the continuity between his own thought and Husserl's. Heidegger describes phenomenology as 'the science of the Being of entities – ontology' and describes his approach as that of a 'universal phenomenological ontology' (BT, pp. 161ff.). In texts written after 1927 however, Heidegger ceases to align himself with phenomenology in such a direct fashion. Even within *Being and Time* Heidegger delivers an unremitting attack on Descartes which must have made uncomfortable reading for Husserl.[5] In correspondence with Husserl after *Being and Time*, Heidegger identifies the problem of the being of 'the world' as the key issue both of *Being and Time* and of his contention with Husserl. Heidegger sees fundamental distinctions opening up, within this notion of 'world', between 'epistemological' phenomenology and 'fundamental ontology'. What, however, does Heidegger mean by 'the world' and how is this central to Heidegger's reversal from Husserl?

In *Being and Time* Heidegger lists four possible meanings for the term 'world'. The first indicates the gamut of things considered merely ontically and in an abstract sense and without any particular perspective. The second indicates the same realm of things, but considered ontologically from the point of view of their being. The third refers to the same ontic universe as the first, but viewed this time from the perspective of *Dasein*. This is *Dasein*'s world and has, consequently, 'a pre-ontological existentiell signification'.[6] The fourth, which Heidegger calls 'worldhood', is an ontological–existential concept embracing the entire *a priori* possibility of world as such. Later Heidegger explains that worldhood is constitutionally 'a system of relations' (BT, p. 122). It is the third and fourth senses of world which are of interest here.

To set his own sense of world in relief, Heidegger contrasts it with a mere 'ontology' of the world which sees the world as the environment of a conscious observer, a tendency which is 'most extreme' in Descartes (and, by implication, in Husserl). A 'pre-phenomenological' attitude is required to see beyond the Cartesian/Husserlian ontology of world, and to uncover the primary concept of the world's worldhood as such. Yet this pre-phenomenological viewpoint cannot be attained in the abstract, but can only be accessed through the existential condition of *Dasein*'s being-in-the-world.

It is thus what Heidegger terms *Dasein*'s 'involvement' (*Bewandtnis*) in the world which is epistemologically determinative not only of *its* world, but of worldhood *in general*:

> *That wherein* [*Worin*] *Dasein* understands itself beforehand in the mode of assigning itself is *that for which* [*das Woraufin*] it has let entities be encountered beforehand. *The 'wherein' of an act of understanding which assigns or refers itself, is that for which one lets entities be encountered in the kind of Being that belongs to involvements*; and this 'wherein' is the phenomenon of the world. And the structure of that to which [*woraufhin*] *Dasein* assigns itself is what makes up the worldhood of the world. (BT, p. 119)

The totality of these involvements as a 'system of relations' constitutes the world's worldhood. *Dasein*'s constitutive being, its 'basic state', is thus 'being-in-the-world'. This means that there is no condition of *Dasein* prior to its 'being-in-the-world', since to remove *Dasein* from the world (which would be an impossibility) would require it to surrender its basic state and thus be the dissolution of its being. So *Dasein* is woven into the world's system of relations.

Importantly, the world's worldhood is not a static, but a dynamic (*ecstatic*) structure determined in a particular way by every particular *Dasein*'s involvement. Moreover, since the world is also temporal, its structures not only have a synchronic but also a diachronic dimension. *Dasein* is always within-the-world, here or there, at this or that time. It can always be both *mapped* and *dated*. The world's diachronic structure also means that *Dasein*'s involvements concern not only the objects which appear in the immediate temporal horizon, but also those situations which lie in the future. It is in this way that Heidegger can introduce death as a feature of *Dasein*'s world.

Although this sounds anti-Husserlian, there is still considerable room for confusion in the talk of '*Dasein*' and 'world', which implies a Husserlian subject–object structure. Heidegger's description of *Dasein*'s fall or 'downward plunge' (*Absturz*) into the world strongly implies the separate egoicity of *Dasein*, as if it were a thing in its own right. Although the language is potentially misleading, this is not at all what Heidegger intends. If we *already* conceive of *Dasein* as an ego, then Heidegger concedes that falling would suggest 'an isolated "I" or subject, as a self point from which it moves away' (BT, p. 223). Conceived existentially, on the other hand, *Dasein*'s fall is not from beyond the world into the world, but from one mode of being-in-the-world to another. '*Dasein can* fall only *because* Being-in-the-world understandingly with a state-of-mind is an issue for it' (BT, p. 224). In other words, the falling of *Dasein* is only a spatial *metaphor* for an existential condition. Thus *Dasein* falls not so much into something else as 'out of itself into itself'. In his 1925 summer lecture course, Heidegger puts this more explicitly:

From what has been said about the being of *Dasein* as in-being, namely that this in-being does not refer to anything like a spatial in-one-another, we can at least formally gather that world is the wherein of *Dasein*'s being. Accordingly, the 'wherein' does not refer to a spatial container. (HC, pp. 167–8)

If the world is not *Dasein*'s container, what sense should be given to the 'in' of 'in-being'? So long as we insist on thinking of *Dasein* as an 'entity', says Heidegger, in-being will remain a puzzle. It is only when the totality of *Dasein* and world is conceived as the pre-given unity of 'being-in-the-world' that the sense of the 'in' becomes apparent (ibid., pp. 165). Effectively, then, 'being-in-the-world' is a non-negotiable axiom for Heidegger's ontology: 'In-being ... before all else has to be seen as an inherent kind of being and accepted as such' (ibid.). There is no way to explain 'in-being' – it just *is* an existential truth: human *Dasein* is always and everywhere 'in-the-world'. How could it be otherwise?

So the issue at stake is the precise 'ontology' of the world itself, and whereas Heidegger's ontology begins with the world in general and the question of Being, Husserl's begins with 'consciousness' and the world which exists for it. In *La théorie de l'intuition dans la phénoménologie de Husserl* written shortly after *Being and Time*, Levinas puts Husserl's position succinctly: 'the origin of all being, including that of nature, is determined by the intrinsic meaning of conscious life and not the other way round'. [7] Thus for Husserl the world exists as an environment of intentional objects:

The Objective world, the world that exists for me, that always has and always will exist for me, the only world that ever can exist for me – this world with all its objects ... derives its whole sense and its existential status, which it has for me, from me myself, *from me as the transcendental Ego*. (CM. p. 26)

In other words, philosophy not only must begin, but does actually begin, from the conscious life of each particular person. For obvious reasons, we cannot expect Heidegger to make a sustained and open critique of Husserl in *Being and Time*. However, he offers a disguised critique of Husserl by discussing the shortcomings of Descartes's construction of the world as an extension of transcendental concepts such as space. Husserl's 'intentional consciousness' is a development of what Descartes means by 'extension'. For Descartes, objects can appear at all only in so far as they are appropriated by structures of mind: 'so something which I thought I was seeing with my eyes is in fact grasped solely by the faculty of judgement which is in my mind'.[8] Although Husserl replaces Descartes's 'mind' with 'consciousness' as the structure of the subject, his understanding of the subject's relationship with the world is substantially the same: the world can only appear *to* intentional consciousness. Ryle describes Husserl's position accurately when he says that Husserl 'reached the point of saying that *Sein* is nothing else than the correlate of *Bewusstsein*, i.e., Being is just what Consciousness has as its "accusative"'.[9] Thus a Cartesian/Husserlian ontology of objects will always understand 'the being of a thing' as a function of judgement/intentionality. This view subordinates the question of being to that of knowing in a way which is unacceptable to Heidegger. For Heidegger the question of the being of the knower is existentially prior to the question of what can be known, judged or intended. Being-in-the-world logically precedes any knowledge of the world: 'Knowing is a mode of *Dasein* founded upon Being-in-the-world. Thus Being-in-the-world, as a basic state, must be Interpreted beforehand' (BT, p. 90).

In his 1925 lecture course at Marburg, Heidegger makes a more sustained and particular critique of Husserl than we find in *Being and Time*. Against what he saw as Husserl's increasingly psychological phenomenology, Heidegger argues for a 'phenomenology that is grounded in the question of Being'. He describes this as a development of the phenomenological theme which proceeds

> in a counter phenomenological direction. This ... does not serve to drive phenomenology outside of itself but really brings phenomenology right back to itself, to its ownmost and purest possibility ... Phenomenological questioning in its innermost tendency itself leads to the question of the being of the intentional and before anything else to the question of the sense of being itself. (HC, pp. 135–6)

It is in the name, then, of a more perfect phenomenology that Heidegger criticizes Husserl. Heidegger's existential phenomenology radicalizes Husserl's abstractive reduction, finding a deeper dimension than consciousness. Consciousness is found to have a being which is not in any sense abstracted from its worldly environment. This being is *Dasein*, which is not 'within-the-world' merely as a spectator, but as an entity which has its *being* 'in the world'.

So the relationship of *Dasein*/ego to the 'world' contains the difference between Husserl and his pupil. (And as will be seen in the next chapter, Derrida will argue that it is precisely these concepts that in Heidegger contain 'the profoundest metaphysical humanism: and I do mean the profoundest', and which he will deconstruct to disclose a condition of alterity which he calls 'origin-heterogeneous'.[10]) Husserl's ego stands opposite the world of things as subject to object whereas Heidegger's *Dasein* is 'within-the-world'. For Husserl the 'other' is, as we have seen, structurally separate from the ego, such separation being a logical precondition of the otherness of the other. But for Heidegger the 'other' is also a *Dasein* within-the-world like every other *Dasein*. Heidegger is quite emphatic that *Dasein* is not a subject: 'Subject and object,' writes Heidegger, 'do not coincide with *Dasein* and the world' (BT, p.87). Whereas for Husserl knowledge is possible precisely within the bi-polarity of ego and world, for Heidegger 'knowing is a mode of Being of *Dasein* as Being-in-the-world' (ibid., p. 88). In asserting itself, therefore, *Dasein* is not in any sense separating itself from the world: '*In saying "I", Dasein expresses itself as Being-in-the-world*' (ibid, p. 368). 'Furthermore,' writes Heidegger, 'the perceiving of what is known is not a process of returning with one's booty to the "cabinet" of consciousness after one has gone out and grasped it' (ibid., p. 89). Phenomenology, then, gave itself to two interpretations: for Husserl phenomenology is primarily epistemological, for Heidegger phenomenology is a question of ontological interpretation.[11]

Death and the Authentic Self

Although Heidegger rejects Husserl's conscious ego, he recognizes the validity of the question of *Dasein*'s self-identity or what he calls the 'who' of *Dasein*. Heidegger's assertion that the 'world is always one that I share with Others', that *Dasein* is a *with-world* (Mitwelt) (BT, p. 155), and that the world is essentially a shared system of relatedness, does not preclude an understanding of selfhood in two senses. First, Heidegger speaks of the 'I' 'in the sense of a non-committal *formal indicator*' (ibid., p. 152), in other words as regulative rather than constitutive: the 'I here' is merely 'a locative personal designation' (ibid., p. 155) which 'maintains itself' through manifold experience. This Kantian self is essentially a 'they-self' which has not yet reached authentic 'Being-one's-self'.[12] Second, Heidegger identifies an 'authentic selfhood' which is achieved when the selfhood of *Dasein* appropriates its own 'way of existing'. Thus the 'who' of *Dasein* is the Self, but understood in Heidegger's very particular sense of the word.

It is in the transition from the merely Kantian 'they-self' to the authentic, existential self that the question of death is brought to the fore. Whereas for Husserl it is the *life* of intentional consciousness which enables a determination of the transcendental ego, for Heidegger it is the *death* of self, or at least the anticipation of death, which makes his existential conception of the self possible.

Death accomplishes the move from the 'they-self' to the 'authentic self' by asserting death as the personal property of a given *Dasein*. Since it is not possible to die the death of another, death is *Dasein*'s 'ownmost, non-relational' possibility, which belongs, in its totality, to *Dasein*. Of course it is possible to *witness* the death of another as an event in the world, but this is not an *existential* experience of 'being-towards-death'. Death, therefore, belongs to the other only as an observable phenomenon, whereas 'being-towards-death' is not an intersubjective experience at all, but belongs entirely to the particular *Dasein* concerned. This is absolutely crucial in the determination of the self of *Dasein* as a self, since 'being-towards-death' alone is what can be grasped as the state of 'being-one's-self':

> Death does not just 'belong' to one's own *Dasein* in an undifferentiated way; death lays claim to it as an individual *Dasein*. The non-relational character of death, as understood in anticipation, individualizes *Dasein* down to itself. (BT, p. 308)

Heidegger connects death and selfhood in the concept of 'care'. *Dasein*'s engagement in the world consists in its 'involvement' with the possibilities of the world situations into which it is 'thrown'. *Dasein* exists continually in relation to these possibilities, always 'projected' forward 'ahead-of-itself' into one possibility or another (ibid., pp. 330f.). This condition of projection into possibility, or 'potentiality-for-being', is what Heidegger means by 'care'. Although the Kantian 'they-self' serves the mundane function of uniting the everyday field of *Dasein*'s possibilities, as the 'I' which accompanies all my representations, it is ontologically unsatisfactory since it takes for granted the being both of the world and of the self as structural preconditions of consciousness. Furthermore, the 'they-self' is always dependent upon the world, understanding itself through things within the world. By contrast, *Dasein* must grasp itself in its own being; in other words it must grasp itself as 'care', as the 'potentiality-for-being-one's-self'. Among all the possibilities which stand before *Dasein*, one possibility in particular is crucial for the determination of *Dasein*: death. Death is not only *Dasein*'s *unique* possibility, 'which cannot be outstripped', since no other possibility requires *Dasein*'s eradication, but death is also each and every *Dasein*'s *personal* possibility, its own 'potentiality-for-Being'. 'Care', which describes *Dasein*'s orientation towards possibility, finds its ontological ground in death, in fact 'Care *is* Being-towards-death' (BT, p. 378, italics added). Death, therefore, defines and clarifies each *Dasein*'s sense of being itself.

Thus Heidegger's self is a non-thing. Authentic selfhood is not selfhood in the ordinary sense of 'having' a self. Indeed the authentic self does not exist as such since the self is effectively nothing more than *Dasein*'s reflexive relation of identity. It is only those who are caught up in the 'they' who must go on about *having* a self, authentic *Dasein* merely has to *be* its self (BT, pp. 369–70). 'Being-one's-Self', when understood ontologically, is 'being-towards-death', since 'my' death is what enables me to think of being a self at all. Looking forward as it does to its own demise, *Dasein*'s selfhood is inextricably tied up with an orientation towards its own finitude: 'I can be authentically only in anticipation' (ibid., p. 310). Heidegger's self, therefore, has no present existence, but only a future possibility. However, this possibility is the impossibility of its existence, since the self only appears at its vanishing point. There is a sense, therefore, that the authentic self is a no-thing, always deferred, which can be grasped only as it slips through the fingers into nothingness. Yet a continuing and 'resolute' orientation towards this impossible possibility of self can enable *Dasein* to maintain its own sense of self. *Dasein* will only be concerned about its continuing identity if it has become 'lost' in the 'they'. So any lack of self-constancy in *Dasein* is not a philosophical problem, but an existential symptom of *Dasein*'s distracted falling-away from its own 'being-one's-Self' (BT, p. 442).

Heidegger's analysis of the self at times verges on mysticism. It seems that his 'self' is nothing more than *Dasein*'s relation to its own identity. Yet this self-relation is effectively an orientation towards a no-self. So it is not clear exactly what *Dasein is*, in order that it *can* relate to itself. This is a problem which will be discussed shortly. What is significant here is that Heidegger does not posit the self as existing before 'care', but uncovers the self within experience, as the self-constancy of *Dasein*.

Privation as Phenomenality

Although the importance of 'death' in Heidegger's philosophy cannot be overstated, what he means by 'death' is not altogether clear. What do the 'life' and the 'death' of *Dasein* mean, when *Dasein* is not a simple biological entity, but an existential condition? Is *Dasein*'s 'death' a merely metaphorical sense of ending? Indeed, does *Dasein* have a 'life' at all in the normal sense of the word?

It is well known that at the outset of *Being and Time*, Heidegger resolves to avoid discussing *Dasein* in terms of 'life', preferring instead to use the language of 'existence' (BT, p. 72). In summary, Heidegger is anxious to resist any talk which suggests that the question of being can be investigated by studying being as a phenomenon 'out there'. To think of human being in terms of 'life' implies that human being can be conceived as an empirical 'object'. Since we are always already inside human being, indeed always actually *being* human, it is not possible to stand aside from our lives in order to examine them. Human being must be considered as an existential condition rather than an observed or even a lived 'experience'.

There are three particular ways in which the word 'life' confuses the investigation of *Dasein*. First, Heidegger associates the concept of 'life' with ideas of subjectivity and reified consciousness. This is understandable enough: to be 'alive' is easily taken both colloquially and philosophically to mean the same as being 'conscious'. To equate *Dasein* with 'life' might therefore lead to the (wrong) conclusion that *Dasein* is the same as consciousness. Second, Heidegger dismisses the study of *Dasein* as 'life' in the anthropological, biological, social, or psychological senses. These are 'sciences of life', which again seek to 'know' 'life', and which have indefinite 'ontological foundations'. Thirdly, Heidegger distances his own philosophy from so-called 'philosophies of life' which focus in a personalized way upon individual 'living experiences' (*Erlebnisse*), but in which '"life" itself as a kind of Being does not become ontologically a problem' (BT, pp. 71–5). *Lebensphilosophie* thus focuses upon the content of experience and not upon its fundamental possibility.

These qualifications notwithstanding, Heidegger does permit life to be understood and investigated in a very particular way:

> Life, in its own right, is a kind of Being; but essentially it is accessible only in *Dasein*. The ontology of life is accomplished by way of a privative Interpretation; it determines what must be the case if there can be anything like mere-aliveness

(*Nur-noch-Leben*). Life is not a mere Being-present-at-hand, nor is it *Dasein*. In turn *Dasein* is never to be defined ontologically by defining it as life (in an ontologically indefinite manner) plus something else. (BT, p. 75)

This is a curious and ambiguous statement. Robinson and Macquarrie take it to mean that 'in order to understand life merely *as such*, we must make abstraction from the fuller life of *Dasein*' (ibid., p. 85 n.1). Life, therefore, would be understood by considering what *Dasein* would be like if deprived to the extent that it was merely alive. But the theme of privation has a much wider significance. Heidegger uses privative interpretations on a number of occasions in *Being and Time* to indicate a kind of phenomenality which can occur in a negative fashion. For example, he uses a privative interpretation to explain the difference between perceiving something 'as' itself and merely 'seeing' it:

> When we merely stare at something, our just-having-it-before-us lies before us *as a failure to understand it any more*. This grasping which is free of the 'as' is a privation of the kind of seeing in which one *merely* understands. (BT, p. 190)

Similarly, mere listening to something 'all around' is defined as a privation of 'hearing which understands', the process of coming near is described privatively as *Entfernung* (or de-distancing), and the phenomenon of 'falling' as a privation of a certain self-awareness of *Dasein*. Elsewhere Heidegger speaks of a negative method (*prohibitiv*) of approaching *Dasein*'s authentic being-towards-death. Thus, Heidegger explains, privation is a structural feature of phenomenality itself. For showing takes place as 'not being concealed', as un-covering or dis-closure (*Entdeckung*):

> The factical uncoveredness of anything is always, as it were, a kind of *robbery*. Is it accidental that when the Greeks express themselves as to the essence of truth, they use a privative expression – *a-letheia*? (BT, p. 265)

Under such conditions, *Dasein* itself is inevitably defined privatively: 'to *Dasein*'s state of Being, *disclosedness in general* essentially belongs' (ibid, p. 264). *Dasein*'s disclosure is possible in a privative way of being towards *Dasein*'s closure, in other words 'being-towards-death'. *Dasein* comes into focus as it disappears. It will come as no surprise that Heidegger's privative interpretation of the life of *Dasein* is of intense interest to Derrida.[13] Indeed, Derrida will employ just such a procedure in his own reversal from Heidegger.

So for Heidegger, life cannot be disengaged from death for separate analysis. *Dasein*'s 'life' is meaningless, indeed inconceivable, without the deathly shadow of its ownmost possibility. This contrasts powerfully with Husserl's ontology, in which the pure life of consciousness is determinative of everything. But having given death such a crucial position in the life of *Dasein*, and all that is disclosed within that life, Heidegger's account of death requires particularly detailed interpretation.

Heidegger is painstaking in his paradoxical definition of the 'ontological' character of 'death': 'Death is the possibility of the absolute impossibility of *Dasein*' (BT, p. 294). Thus *Dasein* discloses itself to itself through what Heidegger terms 'no-longer-*Dasein*'. Furthermore, Heidegger is emphatic that the true death of *Dasein* is to be understood as a possibility and not as an actual or certain event. Thus the death of *Dasein* has nothing to do with the biological death of a living organism, or the event of *Dasein*'s ending at such-and-such a moment. *Dasein*'s death is the possibility of *Dasein*'s impossibility: 'it must be understood as a *possibility*, it must be cultivated as a *possibility*, and we must *put up with* it *as a possibility*' (ibid., p. 306). So 'being-towards-death' is not an awareness of a temporal event, but an orientation towards non-being as a possible alternative condition to being. The sensation of 'being-towards-death' is therefore not the natural fear of dying, but the ontological angst of non-existence.[14] This orientation to non-being, though, is accessible only through one's own *Dasein*. This non-being (death) is always only understood authentically as the non-being of a given *Dasein* and not as non-being (death) in general. It is for this reason, we must conclude, that Heidegger insists upon using the term 'death' – with all its personal, anthropological connotations – rather than a concept such as 'non-being' or 'absence'.

To clarify the exact nature of the death towards which *Dasein* must orient itself, Heidegger distinguishes between three forms of death: *sterben*, *verenden* and *ableben*. Animals die (*verenden*) as a result of the loss of life in the biological sense. Humans also die (*sterben*), but *Dasein* dies (*ablebt*) through the 'demise' of its existential condition. Derrida has focused upon these distinctions in texts from the late 1990s. The point he makes, rightly, is that Heidegger uses this hierarchy of death to separate the death of *Dasein* from the common or garden biological death of an organism (whether human or animal). Thus death can become more than an objective physical state, and more the proper existential death (*Ableben*) which can form the basis of a Heideggerian ontology of selfhood.

After *Being and Time* much changes in Heidegger's philosophy, and although the concept of death does not disappear, Heidegger scales down its role considerably. At the time of the *Beiträge zur Philosophie (vom Ereignis)* in the mid- to late 1930s, Heidegger rejects outright any reading of *Being and Time* as a philosophy of death:

> How miserable and cheap ... it is to single out that phrase 'being towards death', to attribute a great *Weltanschauung* to it – and then to impose this view on *Being and Time*. Apparently this analysis works out especially well, when *Being and Time* is read moreover as a 'book' about 'nothingness'. And so we reach the glib conclusion: Being towards death equals being towards nothingness and this equals the being of *Dasein*! (BP, p. 284)

This is not to say that being-towards-death has no role to play, but Heidegger emphasizes its methodological importance in clarifying the ontological basis of *Dasein*:

Death comes here into the area of ground-laying consciousness not in order to teach a *Weltanschauung* or philosophy of death, but first of all to lay bare the reason for the question of being and to open up *Da-sein* as the un-grounded ground. (Ibid., p. 286)

In *An Introduction to Metaphysics*, written in the mid-1930s, Heidegger recasts the idea of death in a dramatic Nietzschean narrative of human existence as a violent and daring beating out of paths into an alien environment of things.[15] *Dasein* is understood (far less passively than in *Being and Time*) as *deinotation,* meaning both 'strangeness' and 'power'. Standing alone and homeless in the vast and terrible arena of Being, human beings exploit the power of language to 'break out' into Being, violently 'breaking it up' to create an orderly and submissive world. Man is 'the violent one' who sets forth into the un-said, who breaks into the un-thought, compels the un-happened to happen, risking 'dispersion, instability, disorder and mischief' (IM, p. 161). But this 'violent one' is constrained:

All violence shatters against *one* thing. That is death. It is an end beyond all consummation (*Vollendung*), a limit beyond all limits. Here there is no breaking-out or breaking-up, no capture or subjugation. But this strange and alien (*unheimlich*) thing that banishes us once and for all from everything in which we are at home is no particular event that must be named among others because it too ultimately happens. It is not only when he comes to die, but always and essentially that man is without issue in the face of death. In so far as man *is*, he stands in the issuelessness of death. Thus his being-there is the happening of strangeness. (Ibid., p. 158)

Death shows humanity that its apparent technological mastery over Being is an illusion. We throw ourselves violently against Being only to be shattered by it, and by our mortality. But in this shattering, Being is disclosed.

Although the tone of *An Introduction to Metaphysics* is markedly different from both *Being and Time* and the later texts on language, there are two features of this text which are important to the progression and continuity of Heidegger's thinking on death. First, as in *Being and Time*, death holds the position of that which enables *Dasein*'s self-realization. Second, we see the relationship between Being, death and language, which is stressed here more emphatically than in *Being and Time*.[16] It is this question of language, above all, which dominates the later writings. Thus the issue of language and death is raised:

Mortals are they who can experience death as death. Animals cannot do so. But animals cannot speak either. The essential relation between death and language flashes up before us, but still remains unthought. It can, however, beckon us toward the way in which the nature of language draws us into its concern and so relates us to itself, in case death belongs together with what reaches out for us, touches us. Assuming that the mover which holds the world's four regions in the single nearness of their face-to-face encounter rests in Saying, then only Saying confers what we call by the tiny word 'is' and thus say after Saying. Saying releases the 'is' into lighted freedom and therewith into the security of its thinkability.

Saying, as the way-making movement of the world's fourfold, gathers all things up into the nearness of face-to-face encounter, and does so soundlessly, as quietly as time times, space spaces, as quietly as the play of time-space is enacted.

The Soundless gathering call, by which Saying moves the world-relation on its way, we call the ringing of stillness. It is: the language of being. (OL, pp. 107–8)

Mortals stand to death as language stands to the silence of its speaking. As with mortals, so with the words of language: they appear authentically only as they are 'broken up' by death or stillness. Thus death, the silence of life, is the stillness of language in its human modality. This stillness of Saying is the basis for phenomenality: 'Saying is showing', writes Heidegger (OL, p. 126 / PT, pp. 201 and 205). In 'The Thing' we read that death, too, has the same privative phenomenality:

Death is the shrine of the Nothing, that is, of that which in every respect is never something that merely exists, but which nevertheless presences, even as the mystery of Being itself. As the shrine of Nothing, death harbours within itself the presencing of Being. As the death of Nothing, death is the shelter of Being ... Mortals are who they are, as mortals, present in the shelter of Being. (PT, p. 179)

Remembering Heidegger's famous formula about language as the 'house of Being', his description of death as the 'shelter of Being' indicates a phenomenological equivalence between death and language. Just as death discloses by taking away the reality of human being (and thus Being in general), so language speaks by not speaking of the being of beings.

Problems of Selfhood

The carefully conceived notion of a self that is a no-thing avoids what Heidegger calls the 'reification' of consciousness. 'It is constantly suggested that what we have in advance is a Self-Thing ... the ontological question of the Being of the Self must turn away from any such suggestion' (BT, p. 370). Yet this presents Heidegger with some difficulties, as he acknowledges in the final passage of *Being and Time*: 'What *positive* structure does the Being of "consciousness" have, if reification remains inappropriate to it?' (ibid., p. 478). Heidegger – rather less confident here than in the opening pages – refers to this as 'the conflict as to the Interpretation of Being'. He excludes what he calls 'curiosity' as a possible means of asking the question of Being, but he does not properly resolve the issues of consciousness and of the way in which the question of being gets asked. Heidegger tells the reader that 'one must seek a *way* of casting light on the fundamental question of ontology' and that *Being and Time* is merely 'on the way' (ibid., p. 487).

Although it is clear enough what Heidegger is trying to achieve with this conception of the self, it is still not clear whether his existentially conceived self can ask the question of Being. Thus in Heidegger's text the notion of what he calls 'particular *Dasein*' is often apparently interchangeable with a range of pronouns that he uses to address both himself and the reader. Moreover, Heidegger must say that *Dasein* 'knows' or 'hears' or 'understands' or is 'anxious', although it is not entirely clear how *Dasein* can accomplish these actions. Despite his best attempts to transcend Husserl, consciousness keeps reasserting itself in Heidegger's description of *Dasein*. In fact Heidegger implicitly assumes the presence of a knowing self of the Kantian type in order to write about the questioning activity of *Dasein*. For although he maintains that the question of being is part of the being of *Dasein*, it is not at all clear how *Dasein* performs the analytical and linguistic task of framing, asking and investigating questions. Heidegger writes in a non-specific way about a 'we' that formulates the question, but does not clarify the sort of 'we' that he has in mind (BT, pp. 24–5). Ryle suspects that Heidegger has 'surreptitiously imported' a 'conscious being' which 'is not explicitly recognized'.[17] This suspicion is shared by Jean-Luc Marion, who writes of 'the recuperation of a Cartesian horizon' in *Being and Time*.[18] Marion contends that the question of the subjectivity of *Dasein* does not get resolved, leaving a space in which the Cartesian ego must be assumed.

Although Heidegger tries to side-step consciousness, it remains problematic in his description of *Dasein* and the question of Being, and his critique of Husserl faces some difficulties of its own. He establishes a clear order of philosophical inquiry, effectively 'bracketing' consciousness by arguing that the question of the Being of knowing must be asked before the question of the knowing of Being. But how exactly is the question of Being *asked* and who asks it? Does not the question of Being presuppose the being of a conscious speaker capable of asking it? Has Heidegger, therefore, not presupposed Being (or at least 'a being') before asking the question? And is this presupposition not a product of a conscious mind? If this is the case, is not Husserl correct to insist that the priority of consciousness simply cannot be avoided? Is not Heidegger admitting as much when he concedes that 'only as phenomenology is ontology possible' (BT, p. 60)? These questions uncover a fundamental problem – the tension between ontology and epistemology – which Heidegger, by his own admission, is not able to solve in *Being and Time*.

At the beginning of *Being and Time* Heidegger is, defensively, aware of this difficulty. The inquirer after Being is, he argues, a being which possesses the question of Being as part of its structure: that is to say, *Dasein*. But Heidegger insists that the being of *Dasein* is not a conceptual presupposition of the conventional sort – in the sense of an 'axiom' from which other propositions can be deduced. The process is not one of 'presupposing' something but of 'laying bare the grounds for it and exhibiting them' (BT, p. 28). The priority of *Dasein*, as a being containing the structure of the question of Being, is thus established because 'it has announced itself' (ibid., p. 28). This process of 'laying bare the grounds' is later termed '*Destruktion*' and involves the removal of historical accretions and sediments which have obscured both the question of Being and the structure of *Dasein*. *Destruktion* functions like the *epochē* to clear the way for something to 'appear' phenomenologically – in this case the question of Being itself. Thus, as the question of Being is uncovered, so also is the inquiring structure of *Dasein*. Yet *Dasein*, as Heidegger insists, is not supposed to be a personal concept or just another word for 'the human being'. *Dasein* is the condition of human being. As such, in what sense can a 'condition' be said to ask questions? Is it not, in the end, still a *person*, a conscious inquirer, who must ask the question of Being, even if that person is informed by the inquiring, existential condition in which he finds himself?

It is not possible to find detailed answers to these questions in *Being and Time*. Although Heidegger intended to 'work out the question of Being' in a third division to part 1, he withdrew this section while it was with the publishers and the completed version never appeared. As a result there are only faint clues in *Being and Time* as to his intentions. In particular, *Being and Time* hints at two possible modes of articulating the question of Being which are developed in Heidegger's later writing: silence and poetry. In his discussion of the concept of 'care', Heidegger describes the 'call' (*Ruf*) which draws the authentic self away from the they-self:

> The call dispenses with any kind of utterance. It does not put itself into words at all ... Conscience discourses solely and constantly in the mode of keeping silent ... The fact that what is called in the call has not been formulated in words, does not give this phenomenon the indefiniteness of a mysterious voice, but merely indicates that our understanding of what is 'called' is not to be tied up with an expectation of anything like a communication. (BT, p. 318)

This silent, wordless call is made from the depths of *Dasein*'s forgotten Being. The call is the uncovering of *Dasein*'s 'uncanny' (*unheimlich*) position in the world which is obscured by the idle talk of the they-self. The proper listening to language does not take place automatically. Heidegger is contemptuous of what he calls *hinhören* ('listening-away') which is what happens when one listens to the talk of the 'they'. The way that the 'they', with all its voices on the subject, covers up the existential fact of death is contrasted with the pure voice of conscience which speaks to *Dasein*: 'Losing itself in the publicness and the idle talk of the "they", it fails to hear its own Self in listening to the they-self' (BT, p. 314; see also pp. 299–300). So (as Derrida points out) Heidegger distinguishes a special sort of hearing, *horchen* (translated by Robinson and Macquarrie as 'hearkening' or, as Derrida puts it, listening with a 'pricked-up ear'), which has the super-sensitive phenomenological capacity of listening to the noises which are given only in *Dasein*'s world. In his discussion of the nature of proper hearing, Heidegger also mentions the existential possibilities of silence and poetry.

This is the solution to the question of Being which is elaborated and developed by the later Heidegger, particularly in his essay 'Language'. He suggests that a faulty understanding of language has dominated the whole Western tradition and has 'remained the same for two and a half millennia'. This tradition sees 'language as audible utterance of inner emotions, as human activity, as a representation by image and concept' (PT, p. 193). But Heidegger argues that there is an older, forgotten understanding of language as something which speaks itself. Humans speak by *not* speaking, by listening to the speaking of language and responding. In such a context, the question of Being cannot properly be asked by a conscious subject. The question is asked by language itself: humanity merely listens and responds.[19] Although this mystical solution describes how the question of Being is spoken, the phenomenological problem of consciousness stubbornly remains. The notion of listening, which also features significantly in *Being and Time*, and *What is Philosophy?* begs the question of the listener who hears and can report the speaking of language.

The problem Heidegger faces goes very deep. The very language in which thought must take place conspires against his evasion of consciousness. The structure of subject and predicate consistently reinforces the Husserlian scheme of consciousness and object. Whenever Heidegger says that *Dasein* has *done* something, such as asking or listening, he begs the question of Husserl's intentional ego. In his later writing Heidegger reaches the conclusion that thought cannot take place naïvely, but must subvert itself: 'the evil and thus keenest danger is thinking itself. It must think against itself, which it can only seldom do' (PT, p. 8).

This question of the 'who' stands between Husserl and Heidegger as their common reproach to each other. Marion describes Husserl's ego as 'the intimate adversary of *Dasein*'.[20] Heidegger reproaches Husserl for overlooking the existential 'who' of *Dasein*. Husserl's reply is a reproach to Heidegger for presupposing the transcendental 'who' of the conscious ego. The issue at stake is the meaning of human life: whether our life is ultimately defined by the intentional immediacy of a lived present, or by the future orientation towards finitude and death.

Conclusion

For all this difference, Heidegger and Husserl share not only the common methodology of phenomenology, but also its dream. Heidegger's strategy is to pose the question of something more primordial than the foundation of Husserl's living presence. This question is the question of Being, a question which is structurally built into the condition of *Dasein*. Heidegger undertakes what is, effectively, an *epochē* to what is essential, ownmost, individual, non-relational and certain in human being. This, in the end, is death.

The similarity between Heidegger's privative interpretation (which arrives negatively at an understanding of *Dasein* by grasping it as the absence of no-*Dasein*) and Husserl's programme of reduction (which arrives negatively at the basis of consciousness by the reductions) is striking. Through these reductions both Heidegger and Husserl are attempting to uncover an absolute and certain phenomenality. Husserl's aim is to establish the *certain basis* for knowledge whereas Heidegger aims to establish the absolute *possibility* of human existence (*Dasein*). For Heidegger only possibility is certain. There is no super-certainty which can 'outstrip' the certain possibility of death (BT, pp. 308–9). Whereas for Husserl the determinate condition of human being is self-present, 'living' conscious experience, for Heidegger the determinate condition of *Dasein* is the presence-through-absence of 'being-towards-death'.

Being-towards-death is the final and most telling 'reduction' in Heidegger's radicalization of phenomenology. For *Dasein* to show itself phenomenologically, 'in its wholeness', it must 'bracket' itself in an absolute reduction to nothingness. 'Upon reaching its wholeness and precisely in it, it becomes no-longer-*Dasein*. Its wholeness makes it vanish' (HC, p. 308). In a reverse image of Husserl's abstractive reduction to a dimension of certainty founded upon the experience of living consciousness, Heidegger reduces *Dasein* to its 'phenomenological basis' in its experience of the possibility of its own death. The phenomenological gesture in Husserl and Heidegger is structurally the same: both attempt to secure a foundation which is apodictically certain in the sense that it cannot be 'outstripped'. This gesture yields what Heidegger calls the 'phenomenological ground' of *Dasein*. Thus Heidegger, like Husserl, is concerned to open up a 'ground' for philosophy. Husserl's ground has been described by Derrida as the 'living present'. Heidegger's ground is Being oriented towards its own oblivion.

Heidegger's attempt to uncover a phenomenality more phenomenal than that of transcendental phenomenology is, as we have seen, both a fulfilment and rejection of Husserl's thought. 'In such an inquiry', Heidegger warns us, 'one is constantly compelled to face the possibility of disclosing an even more primordial and more universal horizon' (BT, p. 49). Heidegger tries to take phenomenology further back into primordiality, yet transgresses phenomenology in the process. Heidegger's 'privative interpretation' results in an approach to 'life' and 'presence' which quite opposes Husserl's unity of conscious experience. The Being of *Dasein* is understood to lie outside of itself both in its being-towards its own death and in its temporal structure as 'not-yet'. The presence of *Dasein* thus arises from its absence in a revelatory paradox which Heidegger describes as the 'concealment in which unconcealedness (*Aletheia*) is based' (QB, p. 91).

Notes

1   P. Ricoeur, 'On Interpretation', in A. Montefiore, ed., *Philosophy in France Today* (Cambridge University Press, Cambridge, 1983), p. 191.

2　'*Ousia* and *Grammē*', first published in *L'endurance de la pensée: Pour saluer Jean Beaufret* (Plon, Paris, 1968); 'The Ends of Man', first given as a lecture at Cornell University in 1968.

3　J. Van Buren, *The Young Heidegger: Rumour of the Hidden King* (Indiana University Press, Bloomington, 1994).

4　Cited in Terrence Malick's introduction to his translation of Heidegger's *The Essence of Reasons* (Northwestern University Press, Evanston, 1969), p. xii.

5　Heidegger's marginal notes to *Being and Time* show that this disguised attack on Husserl was calculated and deliberate. He describes the treatment of Descartes as 'a critique against Husserl's stratified construction of "ontologies"'. In a letter to Jaspers of 1926, Heidegger comments that if *Being and Time* 'is written "against" someone, then against Husserl' (both quotations cited in Van Buren, *The Young Heidegger*, p. 211).

6　Heidegger defines '*existenziell*' in the opening pages of *Being and Time*: 'The question of existence never gets straightened out except through existing itself. The understanding of oneself which leads along this way we call "existentiell" (*existenziell*)' (BT, p. 33).

7　E. Levinas, 'The phenomenological theory of being', in S. Hand, ed., *The Levinas Reader* (Blackwell, Oxford, 1989), pp. 12f.

8　R. Descartes, *Meditations on First Philosophy*, tr. J. Cottingham (Cambridge University Press, Cambridge, 1986), p. 21.

9　G. Ryle, 'Heidegger's *Sein und Zeit*', in M. Murray, ed., *Heidegger and Modern Philosophy* (Yale University Press, New Haven, 1978), p. 56.

10　OS, pp. 12 and 107–8.

11　This is what in his 'Dialogue on Language' (written 1953/4) Heidegger speaks of as *hermeneutical* phenomenology. Here Heidegger sees 'hermeneutics' as an 'adjunct word' to 'phenomenology' (OL, p. 28).

12　Heidegger does not use this adjective, but it is clear from his discussion in *Being and Time* (BT, pp. 364–70) that this is what he has in mind. He praises Kant for not conceiving of the self as a substance, but resists any hint in Kant of the self as a formal subject.

13　OS, ch. 6; Psy, p. 411.

14　Heidegger characterizes 'fear' as 'being afraid in the face of something' (BT, p. 181). He contrasts fear with anxiety (BT, pp. 230ff.), which is a response to *Dasein*'s general condition of 'being-in-the-world', the 'basic-state' of which is 'being-towards-death'.

15　Published in 1953, but given as lectures in summer 1935.

16　The connection between the 'call of conscience' and death is an implicit part of *Being and Time*. We are 'called' to the authentic thinking of death. For a consideration of the relationship in Heidegger between 'death' and the 'voice' see G. Agamben, *Language and Death: the place of negativity*, tr. K. Pinkus and M. Hardt (University of Minnesota Press, Minneapolis, 1991).

17　Ryle, 'Heidegger's *Sein und Zeit*', p. 63.

18　J.L. Marion, 'Heidegger and Descartes', in C. Macann, ed., *Critical Heidegger* (Routledge, London, 1996).

19　There are hints of Heidegger's later philosophy of language in *Being and Time*, in particular the emphasis on 'listening' (BT, pp. 203–10).

20　Marion, 'Heidegger and Descartes', p. 94.

Chapter 4

From Prophecy to Mysticism: Derrida's Reading of Heidegger

Two texts, two hands, two visions, two ways of listening.
Together simultaneously and separately.
(M, p. 65)

Introduction

Derrida has a curious relationship with Heidegger. Although Heidegger is clearly a major influence, Derrida has not undertaken a systematic study of his philosophy. What we find is a number of articles and essay-length volumes spread over thirty years. Through these various engagements, there is occasionally a sense of withholding, even avoidance, and the voice of a relationship which is only partly determined. This implicit ambivalence is probably a reflection of Heidegger's complicated influence on Derrida. Derrida self-consciously inherits from Heidegger the mission of exposing and undermining the ontotheological errors of the Western tradition. But even as he draws upon Heidegger's writing, Derrida distances himself, accusing Heidegger of a hidden complicity with the very metaphysics that he is seeking to overcome:

> What I have attempted to do would not have been possible without the opening of Heidegger's questions. And first ... would not have been possible without the attention to what Heidegger calls the difference between Being and beings, the ontico-ontological difference such as ... it remains unthought by philosophy. But despite this debt to Heidegger's thought, or rather because of it, I attempt to locate in Heidegger's text – which, no more than any other, is not homogeneous, continuous, everywhere equal to the greatest force and to all the consequences of all its questions – the signs of a belonging to metaphysics, or to what he calls onto-theology. Moreover, Heidegger recognised that he had to borrow ... the syntactic and lexical resources of the language of metaphysics, as one must always do at the very moment one deconstructs this language. (Pos, p. 10)

This equivocal relationship is further complicated by the question of Heidegger's war record. Hugo Ott records the intense level of hostility to thinkers not taking a staunch anti-Heideggerian line in the mid-1980s.[1] It was impossible for Derrida to continue as a 'Heideggerian' without offering both some explanation for his own affiliation and some mitigation for Heidegger. *Of Spirit: Heidegger and the Question* (1987) appeared in the thick of a debate sparked by the republication in 1983 of the 'Rectorship Address' alongside Heidegger's apologia, *The Rectorship 1933–34: Facts and Thoughts*. Derrida's contribution to the debate is typically obscure, not dealing with the history of Heidegger's politics, but attempting to tease out the acceptable and unacceptable presuppositions of the philosophy. This involves opening up the ambiguity of Heidegger's thought, or as Derrida prefers it in the plural, 'the thoughts and unthoughts of Heidegger' (OS, p. 6). For Derrida the issue is tied up with Heidegger's celebration in the Rectorship Address of 'spirit', which in turn derives from Heidegger's metaphysical humanism. Derrida does not say as much, but the implication is that his own philosophical critique of Heidegger's metaphysics has always also been a political critique of Heidegger's ethics. So Derrida reproaches Heidegger for 'spiritualising' Nazism (OS, p. 39), which is also the ontotheologization[2] of Nazism because '*Geist*' is 'the most fatal figure' of the return of metaphysics. But there are ambiguities and ambivalences in Derrida's deconstruction of Heidegger's metaphysics, which consequently complicate his assessment of Heidegger's politics, with the result that the so-called 'Heidegger question' remains for Derrida an 'open' one.[3]

So the influence of Heidegger is clearly significant, yet full of uncertainty. On the one hand, Derrida is inspired by Heidegger's attempt to overcome Western metaphysics, and takes a lead from Heidegger in developing deconstruction (from Heidegger's *Destruktion*) and *différance* (from his ontico-ontological difference and the later term 'Dif-ference'). On the other hand, Derrida discovers in much of Heidegger's writing remnants of an enduring metaphysics: Heidegger's 'speaking of being' is an example of what Derrida calls the metaphysics of the voice; Heidegger's search for the 'proper name' of Being is for Derrida a nostalgic and impossible metaphysical quest; and Derrida criticizes the 'metaphysical humanism' of Heidegger's *Dasein*, which he sees illustrated in (among other places) Heidegger's talk of 'spirit'. This ambivalence plays itself out through all Derrida's readings of Heidegger.

The critical analysis which follows will attempt two things: first, to uncover the shape, purpose and tone of Derrida's relationship to Heidegger; and second, to show in the process how in the course of his Heideggerian studies, Derrida clarifies an idea of 'impossibility' which becomes essential to the development of his theological thinking. Of particular interest will be Derrida's interpretation of Heidegger's being-towards-death, not just how Derrida discusses it, but how in his early writing he avoids the issue, even withholding mention of the term. Having brought the concept of death to the very centre of his critique of Husserl, having identified the interrelationship of death and the other in 'Violence and Metaphysics', having asserted 'the principle of death and of difference in the becoming of being' in *Of Grammatology*, having raised the question of *Dasein*'s temporality in '*Ousia* and *Gramme*', and having discussed precisely the question of human finitude in 'The Ends of Man', it is strange that in his publications before 1980 Derrida barely touches upon Heidegger's being-towards-death. This silence is all the more uncanny because in his most recent writing, Derrida turns again and again to this concept, finding it a fecund source for his own formulation of 'aporia'.

Although the approach taken below will remain broadly consistent with the earlier discussion of Husserl by carefully analysing Derrida's most important writing on Heidegger,[4] the task in this case is much more complicated. Derrida's deconstruction of Husserl is neatly set out in texts from a specific period and is focused on a more or less specific issue. Yet, as has been noted, Derrida's encounter with Heidegger ranges not only across texts, but over time and between topics. These difficulties are compounded by the fact that some of Derrida's commentary on Heidegger appears in texts that have a wider purpose and field of reference. In order to disclose an underlying coherence of Derrida's writing in this area, it is helpful to bring texts together into loose periodic categories. The structure for this classification is taken from 'Violence and Metaphysics' which, as Derrida's first engagement with Heidegger, forms a 'natural' (or at least convenient) point of access.

'Toward this unthinkable–impossible–unutterable...'

We see the structure of Derrida's relationship to Heidegger first sketched out in the 1964 essay 'Violence and Metaphysics'. Derrida's admiration for Heidegger is grounded upon the perception that Heidegger had thought 'difference' in a more profound way than Levinas,[5] even though Derrida acknowledges that Levinas makes alterity a more dominant theme. Throughout the essay, Derrida also appeals to Hegel's infinity as better conceived than Levinas's. In Derrida's opinion Levinas attempts to assert a total, infinite alterity, without realizing that the true infinity must also include its own opposite: in this case, the figure of the same. Levinas's attempt at totalization is, says Derrida, essentially *empirical* because of the priority it gives to the *exterior* as an infinite. In this sense Derrida sees Levinas as non-philosophical, preferring the mystical infinity of alterity to the rational sameness of the Greek logos. By contrast, Heidegger's thought of Being strives to include its opposite: its own dissimulation, veiling, hiddenness and oblivion. 'Since Being is history for [Heidegger], it *is not* outside difference, and thus, it originally occurs as (nonethical violence), as dissimulation of itself in its own unveiling' (WD, p. 184). What Derrida sees in Heidegger's thought – and what moulds the development of his own thinking – is this dissimulation of unveiling, the 'phenomenality as disappearance'. This is the privative strategy Heidegger uses to effect his super-phenomenological reduction to the pre-egological reality of *Dasein*, the same strategy that appears later in a less anthropological form in Being.

'Violence and Metaphysics' is primarily written as a critique of Levinas's analysis of Husserl and Heidegger. Levinas sees Husserl and Heidegger – for all their differences – as two of a kind, 'two Greeks' who can only be understood within the Western tradition of philosophy from Plato. This is a tradition ruled by the 'domination of the Same': in Husserl the self-same presence of the phenomenological perspective, in Heidegger the self-same thought of Being. In Derrida's portrayal, Levinas sets himself at a common distance from both Husserl and Heidegger, the differences between the two mattering less than the similarities. The fact that Husserl admired Plato for prioritizing reason and Heidegger blamed him for obscuring Being is a difference which is 'fraternal in its posterity' since both thinkers are essentially 'Greek' in their search for a self-same unity as the ground of philosophy.

Derrida follows Levinas's journey from Husserlian phenomenology via Heideggerian ontology to a post-Heideggerian philosophy. Beginning with Levinas' argument for a metaphor of 'light' which dominates phenomenology and is implicit in the entire Platonic tradition, Derrida follows Levinas's Heideggerian turn towards ontology and away from the conception of 'the real world as a world of knowledge'. Finally, Derrida plots Levinas's more vociferous reaction to Heidegger. In Levinas's view, Heidegger himself does not escape from the Platonic metaphors of light and the philosophy of consciousness. Heidegger's perspective is always 'inside' being, looking out on to the world. In the search for something 'other' than Greek philosophy, Levinas tries to move beyond the interiority of Heidegger's *Dasein* towards the abstract givenness, and absolute alterity, of the 'il y a'. For Levinas – taking up an idea that has been noted in Husserl's conception of interpersonality – the otherness of the other is both irreducible and prior to the unity and self-sameness of the Greek logos. This otherness has its primary expression in the face-to-face encounter. As an absolute Other, the face of another person is also infinite and therefore in a sense divine: the human face is the image of God's face so that 'the Other resembles God'.[6] At this point in the essay, Derrida introduces a concept of his own that will be significant in his later writing. Since the face of the other is not God himself but a *resemblance*, Derrida finds an opportunity to take up the Levinasian concept which he will make his own, asserting that 'we are in the *Trace* of God'. The face or trace of God, the face or trace of the other, is the ground of Levinas's ethical philosophy, a ground which is prior to Husserl's and Heidegger's.

The main part of the essay is a discussion of Levinas's relationship to Husserl and phenomenology in which, broadly speaking, Derrida argues that Levinas fails to develop concepts significantly different from those already present or implicit in Husserl. As a consequence, Levinas's metaphysics 'presupposes ... the transcendental phenomenology that it seeks to put in question' (WD, p. 133). Furthermore, where Levinas does depart from Husserl, he sets up difficulties which undermine his own arguments. The discussion culminates in a critique of Levinas's conception of the other as absolute exteriority.[7] Derrida contends that exteriority can only be understood as a complement to interiority, and that it must be presupposed that the other has an 'interior' ego, the same as my ego, if the subject is to have any ethical responsibility towards the other as fellow human being. The point Derrida makes is that for the other to be an *alter* ego, he must be an alter *ego*, in other words he must also be the *same*. Thus, to be truly other, the other must also truly be the same. Derrida concludes therefore that 'what the "other" means is phenomenality as disappearance' (ibid., p. 129). For to be truly other, the otherness of the other must be reduced.

Finally, having criticized Levinas's critique of Husserl, Derrida turns to defend Heidegger against Levinas's assertion that Being oppresses and dominates beings as an impersonal, tyrannical master that blocks the ethical relationship between one being and another. The kernel of Derrida's argument is this: Levinas misinterprets Heidegger's ontological difference as the ontic difference between two beings. Yet in making this error, Levinas also presupposes Being as the basis upon which Being-misconstrued-as-*a*-being can relate to other beings. '[Levinas's] metaphysics of the face therefore encloses the thought of Being, presupposing the difference between Being and the existent at the same time as he stifles it' (WD, p. 144). Thus Levinas errs in his treatment of Heidegger as he did in his treatment of Husserl: he assumes that which he rejects. Heidegger's Being is, Derrida argues, that which must be presupposed in any thought or discussion of beings, words, names or concepts. This includes the names and discourses of theology 'it [the thought of Being] precedes every relationship to God or the Gods' (ibid., p. 145). Yet – and this is very significant – it is on the basis of the thought of Being that the sacred and the divine can be thought. Being is the condition of possibility of there being any thought of God. Derrida denies that for Heidegger this amounts in any way to a positive or a negative theology. Yet his remarks are clearly not anti-theological or even non-theological. For, as Derrida concedes, '"Ontological" anticipation, transcendence towards Being, permits ... an understanding of the word God ... even if this understanding is but the ether in which dissonance can resonate' (ibid., p. 146). There is perhaps a slight disingenuousness in this withholding from theology, since to raise the possibility that talk of Being is more fundamental even than talk of God is not so much a rejection of theology as an attempt to outstrip it in its own field of operation.

In a final rearrangement of the protagonists in this essay, Derrida positions Heidegger opposite Levinas. Heidegger, the Greek 'philosopher', sees 'ontology', the ontico-ontological difference, as fundamental. Levinas, the Jewish 'non-philosopher', sees 'theology', the infinitude of the absolutely other, as fundamental. Yet despite their differences, Derrida asks whether the horizons of infinity and Being, theology and ontology, do not amount to the same thing: 'Is not God the other name of Being?' This meeting of horizons would involve a mutual deconstruction: the Levinasian God (infinity) positioned in the Heideggerian (finite) ontic field, would either require the destruction of the ontico-ontological distinction, or else the relegation of God to a finite entity. Yet, paradoxically, it is this very thought of God/Infinity, says Derrida, that unsettles *and* permits the thought of the ontological difference. Ontology and theology are in an irreducible tension which opens up the new relational dynamic of *difference*.

It is difficult to make an unambiguous reading of 'Violence and Metaphysics'. Is Derrida arguing for the impossibility of theology on the grounds that God/infinity is unthinkable without contradiction? Or is he arguing, as he will elsewhere, for the value of a possibility which is impossible and therefore, in a sense, for the value of an impossible God? Derrida's subsequent writing will support the second interpretation, as Derrida continues to use the idea of God – an impossible God – in his thinking. Although Derrida criticizes Levinas's theology, he responds to what he describes as Levinas's 'call' towards the 'unthinkable–impossible–unutterable' (WD, p. 144). In following this call, however, Derrida will take his lead not from Levinas but Heidegger.

'Violence and Metaphysics' opens up three distinct areas of investigation in which Derrida attempts to think through and beyond Heidegger's philosophy towards the conception of an impossible theology. First, Derrida strives to overcome the 'bad' theology implicit in Heidegger's thinking of Being. He remains unsatisfied both by Heidegger's Being which has not thought the 'other' of the Greek philosophy of the same, and by the impossibility of Levinas's infinite otherness. Derrida opens up the question of a position beyond or at the meeting point of Levinas and Heidegger. 'We live in the difference between Jew [Levinas] and Greek [Heidegger], which is perhaps the unity of what is called history. We live in and of the difference' (WD, p. 153). In texts published a few years later in 1967–8, Derrida tries to step behind Heidegger's conception of Being to witness to the possibility of theology grounded on 'a difference older than Being'.

Second, Derrida challenges a metaphysics of the subject ('metaphysical humanism') which he says is implicit in Heidegger's thinking of *Dasein*:

> For Heidegger, it is therefore metaphysics (or metaphysical ontology) which remains a closure of the totality, and transcends the existent only toward the (superior) existent, or toward the (finite or infinite) totality of the existent. This metaphysics essentially would be tied to a humanism which never asks itself 'in what manner the essence of man belongs to the truth of Being'. 'What is proper to all metaphysics is revealed in its "humanism".' (WD, p. 142)

Derrida announces but does not take up the issue here (turning rather to consider humanism in Levinas's metaphysics), but the question of Heidegger's humanism will soon surface again in 'The Ends of Man', in *Of Spirit* and elsewhere. Out of these discussions, Derrida will speculate about the possibility of a theology of 'heterogeneity' that is not 'gathered' around the figure of the human subject.

Third, Derrida raises the question of the constitution of ultimate phenomenological or revelatory conditions of possibility, conditions intimately tied up with questions of the 'other'. The 'other' in the case of 'Violence and Metaphysics' is always the 'other' thinker. Derrida uses Levinas as the other to Husserl and Heidegger; then Heidegger as the other to

Levinas. Finally, he gestures to the paradox of an 'other' beyond all 'others', an 'other' than cannot be 'out-othered'. But such an 'other' is impossible, because there is always scope for another 'other'. The structural condition of the 'other', Derrida argues, is 'phenomenality as disappearance', which is to say 'non-phenomenality'. Thus the 'other beyond all others' is a surd, an other which only outstrips all others by reaching its vanishing point more quickly. The question of such an 'impossible–possible' condition is one that interests Derrida greatly, particularly in his most recent writing on Heidegger. Following Heidegger, Derrida tries to describe phenomenology as an 'impossible' mode of revelation in which theological disclosure always requires the withdrawal of God.

In the sections that follow, this trilateral framework of issues will be used to structure an analysis of some of Derrida's most important writing on Heidegger. In addition to a loose thematization of the texts, there will be an attempt to retain a sense of their chronological progression since these topics also provide the structure of a loose periodization. The early texts (from 1964 to 1968) – for example, 'Violence and Metaphysics', 'Différance', '*Ousia* and *Grammē*'; and *Of Grammatology* – focus largely on the issue of the ontological difference and Derrida's assertion of a 'difference older than Being'. Texts from the 1970s and 1980s – for example, 'The Ends of Man', *Of Spirit*, 'Geschlecht' and 'Geschlecht II' – are generally preoccupied with the question of Heidegger's humanism and its motifs – of proximity, *Geist*, *Welt*, *Vorhandenheit*, *Horchen* and so on. In texts from the late 1980s and early 1990s – for example 'Restitutions', *The Gift of Death*, *Aporias*, *Sauf le nom* and 'How to Avoid Speaking: Denials – Derrida uses Heidegger's writing (in particular the concept of 'being-towards-death') as a resource for thinking through the possible–impossible structure of 'aporia' as a mystical phenomenality of disappearance. A periodization of this kind needs to be treated strictly as a heuristic device and certainly not as a rigid description of the state of affairs. But since the reader must always begin *some*where and proceed in *some* order, unstructured reading is impossible. This thematic periodization merely provides one avenue into the reading of Derrida writing on this subject.

A Difference Older than Being

Although the discussion of Heidegger in *Of Grammatology* (1967) is not a topic in itself, but part of the general argument of that book, Derrida's remarks are significant because they summarize succinctly the approach that Derrida takes to Heidegger in his early writing. Derrida considers Heidegger within a panoramic critique of Western metaphysics as logocentrism: a fundamental metaphysics most clearly evidenced by the prioritization of the spoken over the written word.

Early on in *Of Grammatology*, in a section titled 'The Written Being/ The Being Written', Derrida turns to Heidegger's attempt to undermine 'ontotheology' (a Heideggerian term for what Derrida calls 'the metaphysics of presence'). Derrida proposes that we pass through and beyond the thinking of Heidegger, radicalizing Heidegger's subversion of ontotheology and his conception of an originary difference. Derrida commends Heidegger for challenging logocentrism with the 'question of being', which examines 'the state just before all determinations of being, destroying the securities of onto-theology' (OG, p. 22). [8] But Derrida notes the paradox that in asking the question of Being, Heidegger invokes the 'voice' and the 'call' of being. Thus even as he attacks logocentrism, Heidegger employs its phonetic metaphors. Heidegger *attempts* a transgression of logocentrism, yet 'the very movement of transgression sometimes holds ... back short of the limit'. Being remains as a transcendental signified within Heidegger's discourse, even when subjected to the *kreuzweise Durchstreichung* of *The Question of Being*: 'That deletion is the final writing of an epoch. Under its strokes the presence of the transcendental signified is effaced while still remaining legible' (ibid., p. 23). Although Derrida emphasizes the significance of Heidegger's crossing-out as a crucial step in the philosophy of *writing*, he sees this deletion not primarily as an *inaugural* gesture, but the *last word* in the metaphysics of presence. Thus having situated Heidegger's phenomenology of erasure at the close of a passing era, the scene is set for the announcement of Derrida's own 'phenomenology' of writing.[9]

In his turn, Derrida famously posits *différance* as a more fundamental difference than Heidegger's ontico-ontological difference: '*Différance* by itself would be more "originary", but one would no longer be able to call it "origin" or "ground", those notions belonging essentially to the history of onto-theology' (OG, p. 23). But Derrida is insistent more than once in *Of Grammatology* that Heidegger's project cannot be side-stepped. Being and the ontological difference must be thought first, and be *crossed through*, before *différance* and writing (in Derrida's special sense) can be grasped. The concept of *différance* itself, of course, has a Heideggerian pedigree both in Heidegger's earlier conception of the 'ontico-ontological difference' between Being and beings and his later notion of a dif-ference (*Unter-Schied*) between 'world' and 'thing'.

Although in his essay 'Différance' (1968) Derrida traces the 'history' of *différance* through Hegel, Nietzsche, Freud, Saussure and Levinas, it is in Heidegger that Derrida finds the gesture at its most 'radical' and 'purposive'. 'Différance' is a complex text in which different arguments and lines of inquiry proceed concurrently and across one another: at the same time as showing how the structure of *différance* is in some ways implicit in aspects of the ontico-ontological difference, Derrida argues that *différance* is more radical or 'older' than Heidegger's difference. 'Différance' is an essay at once about the possibility and impossibility of the ontological difference, about the impossibility of presence, the (non-)phenomenality of difference, and the irreducible state of difference *as* difference for which Derrida generates a new word: *différance*. Derrida turns to Heidegger's 1946 essay 'The Anaximander

Fragment' as the material for his discussion.[10] The issue which concerns Derrida is 'the self-veiling essence of Being', in other words the *phenomenality* of the ontological difference, how difference *shows* itself in the destiny of Being. Derrida observes that Heidegger's description of the ontological difference has 'erasure' as its structure, appearing only as it disappears. Although the ontological difference has, Heidegger says, been forgotten in Western culture, traces of it remain in the Greek language. Yet these traces first show themselves in the oblivion of Being when the ontological difference itself disappears. So the trace of difference is not a presence 'but the simulacrum of a presence that dislocates itself'. The point is that although things (beings) may appear within the phenomenal field, and do so precisely on the precondition of the ontological difference, the *difference itself* between a being and Being can never become a phenomenon. This is because the phenomenality of presence is always undivided: *such-and-such a being* appears, but Being does not appear separately. The point might be made by considering the difference between an object (table) and its class (furniture): when we see a table we see all at once a table and an item of furniture, the object/class difference does not and cannot appear as such. Here is an aspect of the ontological difference which Derrida can draw upon, for as Heidegger's difference is non-phenomenal, so it is for *différance*, with its structure of differing/deferred meaning. *Différance* never is *as such*, but (to use Derrida's formula) is always otherwise, always further along in some interminable chain of possibilities.

However, at this point Heidegger and Derrida begin to part company. For Heidegger the non-phenomenality of the ontico-ontological difference can be overcome when the traces which it leaves imprinted in language speak through the functioning of language itself. For Derrida the non-phenomenality of difference is final, and language, far from rescuing the situation, only enmeshes phenomenality in an endless sequence of signs, each replacing the other in the outsideless, depthless 'play of the trace'. In 'The Retrait of Metaphor' Derrida discusses more subtly Heidegger's linguistic 'metaphysics' of Being. Despite Heidegger's apparent vigilance against what he calls 'the metaphysics' of metaphor, Derrida discerns in Heidegger a metaphysical metaphor precisely in the image of *withdrawal* (*retrait*) which erases the phenomenality of Being:

> The metaphysics which corresponds in his [Heidegger's] discourse on the withdrawal of being, tends to gather, through resemblance, all the metonymic differences into one great metaphor of Being or of the truth of Being. This gathering would be *the* language of *the* metaphysics. (Psy, p. 79)

Derrida does not oppose the metaphor as such, but points to its impossibility. In the first place the metaphor is always, he says, the metaphor of another metaphor, each one demanding another to clarify its meaning, so the meaning of a metaphor is a matter that never gets settled. Second, the idea of metaphor depends upon an idea of literal discourse. But if literal discourse is impossible, then metaphor is also impossible. There is only language, and the differences that make up language. This language is not capable of 'gathering' (*rassembler*) itself into an 'analogy' or 'metaphor' of Being.[11]

Heidegger's concept of gathering derives from his interpretation of the Greek logos which in its primitive interpretation means 'gathering'. Thus logos and speaking make possible the concatenation of language and Being.[12] By contrast with Being, its speaking and metaphors, even the *name* '*différance*' does not allow *différance* to appear:

> This unnameable is the play which makes possible nominal effects, the relatively unitary and atomic structures that are called names, the chains of substitutions of names in which, for example, the nominal effect *différance* is itself *enmeshed*, carried off, reinscribed, just as a false entry or a false exit is still part of the game, a function of the system. (M, p. 27)

For the later Heidegger in particular, language *is* phenomenality, as Heidegger puts it, 'the word is the bethinging of the thing' (OL, p. 154). And it is not just any language that permits 'showing', but the faculties of *speaking* and *naming*. In *Of Grammatology* and 'Différance', Derrida resists the privilege Heidegger gives both to the 'speaking of Being', and the unique and proper 'name of Being'. The speaking of Being, even its name, is for Derrida inevitably trapped in the relay race of *différance*, as meaning passes from signifier to signifier. Moreover, 'presence' in general suffers the same frustration as its every sign becomes nothing more than 'the sign of the sign' or 'the trace of the trace' – a dimension of veils over presence, each one lifting to reveal another, but never revealing presence itself. Since the 'trace' is always failing to be a trace of presence, it is always also 'the erasure of the trace', a phenomenality of vanishing.

In order to step forward to a post-Heideggerian position, Derrida uses the internal logic of the ontological difference to effect a deconstruction, thereby offering an interpretation in which Heidegger's text transcends itself in a way that discloses the fundamental and irreducible character of *différance*. Derrida suggests that the ontological difference is logically prior to Being itself, since it is within the ontico-ontological difference that Being appears. Thus Being is transgressed and superseded by its own process of becoming. That process, Derrida says, is *différance*. '*Différance* is what makes possible the presentation of the being-present' (M, p. 6).

This approach to Heidegger opens up the theme of death. In 'Différance', Derrida observes that the non-phenomenality of the trace, which is always a trace of a trace, means that the trace is 'simultaneously living and dead', present but always passing away (M, p. 24). In *Of Grammatology*, Derrida expands this observation to identify the deathly character of writing. Towards the end of the section, 'The Written Being/The Being Written', Derrida introduces writing as a simulacrum of death, writing becomes part of death's theme and vice versa:

What writing itself, in its nonphonetic moment, betrays, is life. It menaces at once the breath, the spirit, and history as the spirit's relationship with itself. It is their end, their finitude, their paralysis. Cutting breath short, sterilizing or immobilizing spiritual creation in the repetition of the letter, in the commentary or the exegesis, confined in a narrow space, reserved for a minority, it is the principle of death and of difference in the becoming of being. (OG, p. 25)

The arrival of writing brings with it the operation of death: 'Writing in the common sense is the dead letter, it is the carrier of death. It exhausts life' (ibid., p. 17). According to the economy that Derrida has already sketched out in his writing on Husserl, writing is to speech as death is to life, and (when conceived naïvely) the very idea of 'life' *is* metaphysics. Elsewhere in *Of Grammatology*, Derrida speaks of the operation of writing as an 'economy of death' (ibid., p. 69). Death is the supplement to *life* as writing is the supplement to *speech*, and writing-as-death, or death-as-writing, is the supplement to *living speech*. 'Death, which is neither a present to come nor a present past, shapes the interior of speech, as its trace' (ibid., p. 315). Throughout the book, the life–death metaphor is crucial. Death, as Derrida puts it, is the 'master-name' of supplementarity. And writing is, as Derrida also says, the exemplary supplement.

Derrida's later writing will illustrate how Heidegger is implicated through his humanism in this metaphysics of life, how even being-towards-death operates as the mechanism for creating a level-distinction which harbours metaphysical presuppositions.[13] Derrida will submit Heidegger's being-towards-death to what could be called a homoeopathic treatment, asking about the death (aporia) within Heidegger's discourse on death. Thus Derrida will attempt to trump Heidegger's 'non-phenomenology' of being-towards-death with his own 'non-phenomenology' of aporia.

This critique, however, will come much later in Derrida's career. What may puzzle readers of Derrida's early writing – the texts already referred to and 'The Ends of Man' – is that he hardly mentions Heidegger's being-towards-death until the mid-1970s, when he refers to it in *The Post Card* in the context of a discussion of the death instinct in Freud (PC, pp. 358ff.) and does not discuss being-towards-death as such in any depth until the 1990s. Indeed, Derrida seems to avoid engaging with the topic, deliberately (we must assume) ignoring its presence. Having effectively announced death and writing as concepts at the centre of his philosophical concerns, and having honoured Heidegger as the thinker whose *Durchstreichung* indicates a new understanding of writing, it is strange that Derrida waits so long to discuss Heidegger's analysis of death.

Metaphysical Humanism

In a number of texts from 'The Ends of Man' (1969) onwards, Derrida uncovers and deconstructs what he sees as a metaphysical humanism inherent in Heidegger's conception of *Dasein*. Through various analyses of the metaphors of *Dasein*'s self-proximity, Derrida seeks to show how 'nearness' to *Dasein* becomes the measure of *Dasein*'s propriety. Derrida applies the critique over and again in various contexts. In 'The Ends of Man' he sets out the general case against Heidegger's humanism, which is seen always to prioritize the human as that which can ask the question of its own being and is therefore most proximate both to its own being and to Being. Subsequent essays take up the theme by addressing particular metaphors of *Dasein*'s propriety, or challenging Heidegger's separation of human and animal. In 'Geschlecht' Derrida challenges the possibility of *Dasein*'s pre-factical 'neutrality' with respect to sexual difference, illustrating an original dispersion and decomposition in the foundation of *Dasein*. In 'Geschlecht II', Derrida shows how the human is elevated through a unique 'handedness' denied to animals. In *Of Spirit*, *Dasein* is shown to possess a special 'spiritual' world in which animals only weakly participate. In 'Heidegger's Ear', Derrida explores the 'listening' of *Dasein* which opens up its special encounter with Being. In 'Aporias', he deconstructs the 'nearness' of *Dasein* to its own death, which separates 'mortals' from the 'animals'. In these deconstructions Derrida's anti-Heideggerian proclivity is at its most vociferous, and cumulatively these texts constitute a formidable assault on a hidden metaphysics which is central to Heidegger's project.

It is soon apparent that the problem of the 'human' is rooted not only in the Heideggerian concept of proximity, but in a general metaphysical discrimination between what is living and what is not. It has been seen above how Derrida's early studies of Husserl and texts such as *Of Grammatology* make the case that metaphysics *per se* is identical with a carefully structured hierarchy of life from '"non-living" up to "consciousness", passing through all levels of animal organization' (OG, p. 47). Derrida will argue – notably in 'Geschlecht' and *Of Spirit* – that Heidegger's metaphysical humanism depends upon the existential analysis of *Dasein* as a living entity with a proper mode of death. In turn, the proper field of operation for the existential analysis of *Dasein* is established once the regional life sciences of biology, anthropology, psychology and the rest have been assigned their subordinate place:

> It is the whole problematic organization that is here in question, the one that subjects positive forms of knowledge to regional ontologies, which itself ... was preliminarily opened up by the existential analytic of *Dasein*. It is no accident (once more, one might say, and show) if it is in the mode of being of the *living*, the animated (hence also of the psychical) which raises and situates this enormous problem, or in any case gives it its most recognizable name. (Ges, p. 398)

A distinct economy of life and death undergirds Heidegger's metaphysics of *Dasein*. But since *Dasein*'s metaphysical priority is established not only within a hierarchy of life, but also of death, Derrida has to resist with equal vigour Heidegger's spiritualization of the life of *Dasein* and the propriety of *Dasein*'s being-towards-death.

Derrida first makes a topic of humanism in 'The Ends of Man', which is a contribution to a wider debate about humanism that was alive in French intellectual circles in the late 1960s and early 1970s and which is perhaps most famously associated with Foucault's prediction of 'the end of man' in *The Order of Things* (1967). Although in 'The Ends of Man', Derrida considers the humanism of Hegel and Husserl, the focus of the text is the problematic issue of humanism in *Being and Time*. Derrida's approach is the now familiar strategy of opening up paradoxes, in this case the paradoxes of Heidegger's critique of Western thought. Although Derrida rightly notes that the conception of *Dasein* in *Being and Time* is precisely an attempt to avoid humanism, he teases out a metaphor of distance which, he argues, reveals a presupposed humanism at the heart of Heidegger's thought:

> It is in the play of a certain proximity, proximity to oneself and proximity to Being, that we see constituted, against metaphysical humanism and anthropologism, another insistence of man, one which relays, relieves, supplements that which it destroys. (M, p. 124)

Derrida argues that *Dasein* is uniquely privileged, since it is through *Dasein*'s reflexive interpretation of its own existence that its own meaning and the meaning of Being in general are opened up. Since *Dasein* is also always discussed from the point of view of the 'we' who are asking the question of our own Being, *Dasein*'s privileges must also fall to the only entity which can constitute the 'we' of *Dasein*: man. 'We can see then,' writes Derrida, 'that *Dasein*, though not man, is nevertheless nothing other than man. It is ... a repetition of the essence of man' (ibid., p. 127). *Dasein*'s human privilege is not handed down from above, but derives from a closeness to Being which is uniquely possible for a speaking creature. *Dasein* is at once the entity which *asks* the question of being, and the exemplary entity whose being *is asked* by the question of being, and the entity which already possesses intuitively *the answer* to the question of being. This circle of inquiry creates the self-authenticating intimacy of 'self presence, the absolute proximity of the (questioning) being to itself' (ibid., p. 125). From this Derrida observes what he calls 'an entire metaphorics of proximity ... associating the proximity of Being with the values of neighbouring, shelter, house, service, guard, voice, and listening' which dominates Heidegger's thought from beginning to end (ibid., p. 130). Yet for all this complicity of metaphor with the metaphysics of presence, Derrida realizes that with *Dasein* Heidegger does attempt to make a decisive break with 'man' as hitherto conceived. So Heidegger puts an end to humanism in both senses of the word 'end':

> In the thinking and the language of Being, the end of man has been prescribed since always, and this prescription has never done anything but modulate the equivocality of the *end*, in the play of *telos* and *death*. (Ibid., p. 134)

Thus the human nearness to Being is at once the fulfilment and the erasure of humanism. Here we see in cameo Derrida's ambivalence to Heidegger. He admires Heidegger's thinking of Being in so far as it effects the destruction of metaphysical humanism. But in the very articulation of the question of Being, which must always be human, the human figure is redrawn on the crest of the destiny of Being. As Derrida will put it in *Of Spirit*, metaphysical humanism *haunts* Heidegger's efforts at its destruction. In texts which follow 'The Ends of Man', Derrida considers the 'ghosts' of humanism that haunt Heidegger's *Dasein*. It is not necessary to follow each and every aspect of Derrida's deconstruction of Heidegger's humanist metaphors and it will be enough to consider the unravelling of *Vorhandenheit* in 'Geschlecht II: Heidegger's Hand' (1987) and *Geist* in *Of Spirit* (1987).

'Geschlecht II' shows how Heidegger's metaphor of the human hand presupposes the metaphysics of the voice which he has already deconstructed in his critique of the speaking of Being. The argument is subtle and intricate, linking together a number of Derridean and Heideggerian themes. The topic of the essay is the German concept of *Geschlecht*, in the sense of the *Menschlichkeit* or human-ness of humanity. Derrida investigates Heidegger's definition of humanity based upon the uniqueness of the human hand, and strips this definition back to reveal its metaphysical presuppositions. Although talk of human handedness apparently expands Heidegger's description of the uniqueness of humanity by adding a bodily metaphor to that of the human 'voice', Derrida argues that the hand is essentially a transcendental concept which easily reduces to the metaphysics of speech. The being of Heidegger's hand, Derrida claims, is essentially that of monstration or 'showing' (*Zeichen*). It is on the basis of the phenomenal and linguistic faculty of handedness that Heidegger can distinguish between humanity and animality. 'The hand is monstrosity, the proper of man as the being of monstration. This distinguishes him from every other *Geschlecht*, and above all from the ape' (Ges II, p. 169). Derrida notes that since the hand speaks for the voice, Heidegger describes thinking as 'always (*jedenfalls*) a craft (*Hand-Werk*)' in *Was heisst Denken?*, comparing the thinker with a craftsman making a cabinet.

In Derrida's estimation, these remarks are significant for four reasons. First, Heidegger connects thinking with corporeality. Second, however, Heidegger's conception of thinking as *Hand-Werk* means that 'the hand cannot be thought as a thing, a being, even less an object'; in other words the hand is an essentially *transcendental* idea. Third, Heidegger's concept of authentic handiwork effectively rejects both the National Socialist professionalization of philosophy and the Nazi ethic of production. Fourth, the essential faculty of handedness in Heidegger is not one so much of grasping, either actually or conceptually, as one of giving. The hand's being does not belong in its literal, prehensile, function as a biological organ, but in its linguistic function as something that signs and designs, pointing out and gesturing. Thus Heidegger asserts that 'apes, for example, have organs that can grasp, but they have no hand'. As a speaker, the hand is more eloquent than the voice since it gestures in the 'perfect purity' of silence. Speech, Derrida argues, is what makes Heidegger's hand a hand since without speech the hand is merely prehensile. Having made the connection between speech and the unique handedness of humanity, Derrida is able to complete this particular deconstruction of Heidegger:

> So one sees being organized around the hand and speech, with a very strong coherence, all the traits whose incessant recurrence I have elsewhere recalled under the name logocentrism ... (L)ogocentrism ... dominates a certain and very continuous discourse of Heidegger. (Ges II, p. 181)

Thus Derrida makes the point that Heidegger's humanism belongs to Western metaphysics: the human is human because of the hand; the hand is a hand because of speech; speech is the medium of self-present meaning; and self-present meaning is the basis of metaphysics.

In a supplementary section of the essay, Derrida turns more directly to the term *Geschlecht*.[14] He argues, as indeed Heidegger does, that the word *Geschlecht* is plurivocal and cannot be fixed to a single referent. He notes an 'Aristotelian' ambivalence in Heidegger about words with unstable or plural meanings: on the one hand Heidegger appears to believe in the positive plurivocity of *Dichtung*, yet he also emphasizes the importance of gathering plurivocity into the univocal location he calls *Gedicht*. Derrida raises questions about the validity of this unified gathering of language and meaning. He notes the paradox that in order to establish the nature of the region of *Gedicht* (into which the plurality of *Geschlecht* is gathered), one has to ask about the *Geschlecht* of *Gedicht*. Thus *Geschlecht* becomes presupposed in the discourse about its own meaning. In the final paragraph of the essay Derrida poses the underlying metaphysical question which is implied by the particular issue of *Geschlecht*'s plurivocity and gathering: whether or not there is any place at which the differentiated field of language *in general* is unified. Although Derrida says that Heidegger leaves this question unresolved, clearly a critique of Heidegger is strongly implicit in the question. Derrida's first essay on *Geschlecht*, 'Geschlecht: sexual difference, ontological difference', offers a similar challenge to Heidegger's general conception of a *Dasein* which is neutral with respect to gender.

In *Of Spirit: Heidegger and the Question* (1987), Derrida extends the analysis of humanism beyond the metaphors of *Dasein*'s body into what *Being and Time* calls the basic structure of '*Dasein*' and 'world'. It is here, in the conception of 'world', that Derrida unravels 'axioms of the profoundest metaphysical humanism' (OS, p. 12). The charge of humanism made against *Being and Time* is commonplace and Heidegger is generally thought to have 'turned' from this in his later writing. Derrida, however, emphasizes the continuity of a problematic 'metaphysical humanism' across the gamut of Heidegger's work:

These difficulties ... never disappear from Heidegger's discourse. They bring the consequences of a serious mortgaging to weigh upon the whole of his thought. And this mortgage indeed finds its greatest concentration in the obscurity of what Heidegger calls spirit. (Ibid., p. 57)

To make the point, which he does with brilliant effect, Derrida conducts a survey of Heidegger's discussion of *Geist* from the 1920s through *Being and Time* (where Heidegger says he will not use the term), the 'Rectorship Address' of 1933 and *The Introduction to Metaphysics* of 1935 to the remarks of 1953 in *On the Way to Language* that *Geist* is 'flame'.

At the beginning of the analysis – and it is not insignificant that this is precisely the location, as has been shown, at which Heidegger begins to challenge Husserl – is the issue of the 'world'. Heidegger subverts the ego-world dynamic of Husserl's phenomenology by installing his own *Dasein*-world structure in its place. Derrida now subverts Heidegger's *Dasein*-world structure to uncover the superordinate operation of *différance*. In the first instance he shows how in the winter lectures of 1929–30 Heidegger uses a concept of 'world' to establish a hierarchy of animate and inanimate objects. Inanimate objects such as stones are worldless (*weltlos*), whereas *Dasein* is world-constituting (*weltbildend*). Animals are the middle term, neither fully world-constituting nor entirely worldless, but world-deprived (*weltarm*). Derrida also connects this distinction with his other (earlier) analyses, noting again the humanism of Heidegger's concept of *Vorhandenheit* and the linguistic poverty of animals who cannot ask the question which underlies the world of *Dasein*: the all-important question of Being.

Derrida makes various comments about this hierarchical scheme. First, he notes how Heidegger effectively employs a version of the *Durchstreichung* in the privative analysis of the animal experience of world-poverty. This version, which is a complete crossing through, is, Derrida argues, radically different from the *Durchstreichung* in *The Question of Being*, which only gestures at a crossing through leaving the word 'Being' showing through. It is important for Derrida to make this distinction because Heidegger's positive phenomenality of privation is a resource in the development of a Derridean non-phenomenology. Second, Derrida argues that the concepts *weltlos*, *weltarm* and *weltbildend* belong in fact to a phenomenological economy in which the world is *understood* in different degrees by animals and humans. Animals certainly can *exist* unwittingly in the world, but *having* a world requires that the world be in some sense appropriated as a phenomenon. Only humans have phenomenological access to the world *as such*. Third, Derrida repeats the observation made in 'Geschlecht' that the structure at stake here involves not just the separation of the animal from the human, but more fundamentally the separation of the living from the non-living. Fourth, in a footnote to Chapter Six, Derrida raises the difficult question of the 'life' of *Dasein*, which is never defined as such as 'living', but which nevertheless enjoys a 'spiritual' existence superior to mere animal life. But if it is unclear in what sense Dasein *lives*, 'what is being-for-death?' asks Derrida:

> What is death for a *Dasein* that is never defined essentially as a living thing? This is not a matter of opposing death to life, but of wondering what semantic content can be given to death in a discourse for which the relation to death, the experience of death remains unrelated to the life of the living thing. (OS, p. 57 n. 3)

Lastly, and this is the crucial point, Derrida develops the analysis of 'world' by noting that, in *An Introduction to Metaphysics*, Heidegger states that the 'world is always a world of spirit' (IM, p. 45). Thus Derrida argues that the whole *Dasein*-world structure at the crux of *Being and Time* should be read as a spiritual, and metaphysical, dynamic. For Derrida it is this conception of *Geist* that is most closely implicated with Heidegger's legitimation of National Socialism.

Turning to the later Heidegger, Derrida finds a different, or developed, understanding of *Geist* as 'flame', which despite its commitment to the same metaphysics of proximity in the form of 'gathering', opens up other, more interesting paths of thought. Heidegger tries to point back to a pre-Christian, pre-Platonic experience of *Geist* which is not merely the rational *psychē* or the theological *pneuma*. *Geist* thus promises the future beyond the un-concealment of pre-Christian, pre-Socratic Being: the *Ereignis*.[15] But Derrida questions the efficacy of such a promise which cannot speak itself without risking distortion in 'language', which necessarily dissembles and corrupts. Derrida also observes that Heidegger speaks of *Geist* at once as that which divides and gathers, at once forging paths into the world and at the same time drawing all together in a gathering of the One. As such, *Geist* still belongs to the Heideggerian metaphysics of proximity. However, these last observations give Derrida the material for a more ambiguous and suggestive conclusion. On the one hand Heidegger's *Geist* points to a heterogeneous origin prior to the Christian–Platonic myth of a pure beginning. On the other hand, in Derrida's estimation, Heidegger never properly disentangles *Geist* from the spirit of Christianity. This implies the possibility of a heterogeneous essence to Christianity itself. In an imaginary dialogue which concludes *Of Spirit*, Derrida depicts a tension which cannot be resolved between Heidegger's assertion of a heterogeneity which makes possible all (religious) discourse and the imaginary (but not improbable) assertion of 'certain Christian theologians' that this heterogeneity constitutes the very identity of an all-embracing Christianity. The unspoken issue here is whether *différance* must *necessarily* be thought *before* every philosophy and theology. Of course in many places Derrida offers a fierce defence of the province of *différance* against attempts at philosophical and theological thematization. But it is precisely the discourse of such a defence which, despite itself, thematizes *différance*. So it is not unreasonable to ask whether this theme of *différance*, however reluctantly assembled, also belongs to the essence of a theology, whether Christian or otherwise.

Revelation as Disappearance

The foregoing analyses have started to expose just how central the question of
phenomenology is to an understanding of Derrida's reading of Heidegger.
The point of the early essays is to show the impossibility of the 'presencing'
of the ontico-ontological difference and to reveal an older difference, a non-
presencing *différance*, which exists soundless and invisible beyond our gaze,
even slipping through the mesh of philosophical language and concepts. The
paradigm of a non-phenomenality is already present in Heidegger's text, but
mixed imperfectly with other Heideggerian voices, and contaminated with a
Heideggerian metaphysics of presence. Thus Derrida invokes *différance* at
once to fulfil Heidegger's phenomenology and to transcend its errors.

What is the nature of Heidegger's error? At the core of Heidegger's mistake
is the grounding of phenomenality in the intimacy of self-presence – the
privilege Heidegger gives to Being's self-proximity, to the 'ownmost'
properties of *Dasein* and to the quality of nearness itself. All this amounts to a
version of the very metaphysics of self-sameness which Heidegger is
elsewhere striving to overcome. In 'The Ends of Man' Derrida puts the
problem in a nutshell:

> The prevalence granted to the *phenomenological* metaphor, to all the varieties of
> *phainesthai*, of shining, lighting, clearing, *Lichtung*, etc. opens onto the space of
> presence and the presence of space, understood within the opposition of the near
> and far – just as the acknowledged privilege not only of language, but of spoken
> language . . . is in consonance with the motif of presence as self-presence. The near
> and the far are thought . . . before the opposition of space and time, according to the
> opening of a spacing which belongs neither to time nor to space, and which
> dislocates, while producing it, any presence of the present. (M, p. 132)

The conception of Being itself falls foul of the metaphysical privilege that
Heidegger gives to the speaking of Being. And Heidegger's metaphysical
humanism is the same mistake in another guise since the phenomenological
problem with Heidegger's body of metaphors is illustrated nowhere better
than in *Dasein*'s various metaphors of body:

> I have tried to problematize Heidegger's analyses . . . I shall underscore and
> generalize here only this remark: whether a matter of the hand, of feet, eye, sex or
> ear, the Heideggerian phenomenology of *Dasein*'s body, in what is more original
> and more necessary in that phenomenology, supposes precisely the
> phenomenological as such or the phenomenological 'as such'. The structural
> difference between *Dasein* and non-*Dasein*, for example the animal, is the
> difference between a being open to the as such and a being that is not. (Ges IV,
> p.173)

Derrida's phrase here – 'the phenomenological as such or the
phenomenological "as such"' – begs the question of another
'phenomenology': phenomenology 'not-as-such', a phenomenology not of

self-presence, but of non-self-presence, in other words a 'phenomenology' of the 'other'. This is what Derrida in 'Violence and Metaphysics' calls 'phenomenality as disappearance' or in *Signéponge* as 'remaining in order to disappear or disappearing in order to remain' (S, pp. 56–7). The path to this phenomenological 'not-as-such' involves asking a particular kind of question:

> What the thought of the other *as* other means, and whether or not the light of the 'as such' is dissimulation in this unique case. Unique case? No, we must reverse the terms: 'other' is the name, 'other' is the meaning of the unthinkable unity of light and night. What 'other' means is phenomenality as disappearance. (WD, p. 129)

There is no end to such a line of inquiry; indeed, any attempt even at the 'philosophical elucidation' of such a path 'will ceaselessly call upon "contradictions"'. The outcome is non-phenomenology which is not so much the absence of revelation as a mode of revelation which is always revealing its own failure.

Heidegger's text not only carries the voice of the 'phenomenological as such', but it also speaks powerfully of this 'other' phenomenology as disappearance. As Derrida puts it (elsewhere and in a different context), there are in Heidegger 'two texts, two hands, two visions, two ways of listening, together simultaneously and separately' (M, p. 65). Turning to the second voice, we see how even in his description of nearness, Heidegger implies another phenomenological procedure: privation, a cancelling out which discloses. Thus the process of bringing objects close into the spatial vicinity of *Dasein* and its body is described by Heidegger as 'ent*fernen*' (translated by Robinson and Macquarrie as 'de-severing'). Using Heidegger's privative construction, *entfernen* is a de-distancing, a removal from afar in order to bring something near:

> 'De-severing' amounts to making the farness vanish – that is, making the remoteness of something disappear, bringing it close. *Dasein* is essentially de-severant: it lets any entity be encountered close by as the entity which it is ... *In* Dasein *there lies an essential tendency towards closeness*. (BT, pp. 139–40)

We find a modified, but essentially similar procedure in the later Heidegger. In 'The Thing' Heidegger argues this time not for the privation of distance to disclose nearness, but for the privation of *nearness* to disclose nearness. Nearness, says Heidegger, is not a question of a merely physical space, but of *phenomenological* space, of 'the thinging of the thing', the showing of the thing in our existential–perceptual field. In this process, 'nearness *preserves* farness. Bringing near in this way, nearness conceals its own self and remains, in its own way, nearest of all' (PT, p. 178). It is the potential of this 'other' phenomenology that Derrida seeks to explore in his more recent writing on Heidegger. The focus of these texts is Heidegger's being-towards-death, the 'possible–impossible' phenomenological structure, which provides the stepping stone to Derrida's own aporetic phenomenology.

It is not easy to see where the shift to this later phase in Derrida's writing begins, since the concern with non-phenomenology goes right back to the earliest essays and the deconstruction of Husserl. Yet the discussion clearly does move into a new field, because (to take one example of change) being-towards-death is hardly touched upon in the early texts, but becomes a central preoccupation of the later writing. There is the clear hint of this change in 'Restitutions' from *The Truth in Painting* (1978), an interesting but neglected essay which considers the respective opinions of Heidegger and Meyer Shapiro on the ownership of the shoes in a painting by Van Gogh entitled *Old Shoes with Laces*. Although apparently an exercise in art criticism, this essay is more properly a philosophical discussion which repeats and develops themes from elsewhere in Derrida's writing. 'The philosophy of art', argues Derrida in another place, 'presupposes the art of philosophizing' (TP, p. 41).[16] Art is the pretext of the essay, but Heidegger's philosophy is the subject. Derrida uses Heidegger's remarks in 'The Origin of the Work of Art' as a point of access into a series of philosophical questions of general significance, not least among which is the question of 'reference' and 'the truth of that which is an indispensable condition for knowing what reference means' (ibid., p. 322). This takes Derrida towards the discussion of the grounds of truth itself and Heidegger's understanding of the condition of truth as *aletheia*.

For the purposes of this book, the most significant aspect of Derrida's discussion is his consideration of Heidegger's concept of *Verlässlichkeit*, a word which does not have a ready translation, but which concerns reliability, dependability or trustworthiness. (Derrida rightly resists the translation of *Verlässlichkeit* as 'solidity', which removes all sense of 'trust' from the term, and proposes 'fidelity' as a possible alternative.) Heidegger uses *Verlässlichkeit* to describe the basis upon which any form of correspondence or reference can be made. Thus for Derrida, the notion of *Verlässlichkeit* is anterior to the discussion about ownership or reference. It is only on the *condition* of the shoes' *Verlässlichkeit*, their reliability or faithfulness as a property of their *being*, that any form of judgement can be made. Knowing is for Heidegger, as has been illustrated elsewhere, always subordinate to being. *Verlässlichkeit* concerns the pre-original belonging of objects to 'the earth', what Derrida calls the 'precontractual ... marriage with the earth'. In this way the whole question of 'reference' is suspended from the question of the being of the shoes. If *Verlässlichkeit* is translated as 'trustworthiness' it can be said that reference is possible only on the basis of a certain *trust* or *faith*. This faculty of faith, as the following chapter will elaborate, is crucial in Derrida's theology and in his theory of truth.

A most interesting aspect of Derrida's analysis at this juncture is not so much an argument or even a point, but more of a hint or gesture. *Verlässlichkeit* is a cognate of *Verlassenheit*, a term of great significance not only to Heidegger but also to Derrida. Whereas *Verlässlichkeit* implies a drawing together of things through dependability, *Verlassenheit* means abandonment or letting go. Thus *Verlässlichkeit* 'laces *and* lets loose at the same time', it is a 'preoriginary gift *or* abandon', a 'drawing ... toward ... *and* then making ... go away' (TP, pp. 354 and 356, italics added). This raises for Derrida the question of Heidegger's 'whole path of thought' which 'leads back, by a de-distancing, to a *Da* (the *Da* of *Sein*) which is not merely close, but whose proximity lets the distance of the *fort* play within it' (ibid., p. 357). Here Derrida touches upon the paradox of Heidegger's privative strategy, which he addresses more fully in a later text. It is through a *privation* of fidelity, of intimacy, or dependency (that is to say, through infidelity, distance or independence, in short *abandonment*) that fidelity itself is disclosed or uncovered. This is Heidegger's understanding of truth as *aletheia*, the truth which is granted by taking away. Although Derrida does not explore this notion in depth here, the idea of phenomenality as disappearance resonates powerfully at the end of the essay:

– It's just gone.
– It's coming around again.
– It's just gone again. (Ibid., p. 382)

Phenomenality is caught in a revolving door which is always coming round to the same point. This is the 'other' phenomenology: phenomenology not-as-such.

It was not until the 1990s – in *The Gift of Death* (1992) and *Aporias* (1993) – that Derrida sought to develop the theme of non-phenomenality through a consideration of Heidegger's being-towards-death. For Heidegger, of course, the reality of *my* death necessarily stands outside living consciousness and provides an exit from the sphere of Husserlian phenomenology. For Derrida, being-towards-death is the *topos* for considering an aporetic phenomenality which is already present in Heidegger, but which requires further development and clarification. *The Gift of Death* approaches the issue of being-towards-death at the edge of a discussion of the possibility of a responsible ethical subject. In *Aporias* Derrida tackles the issue much more directly by asking the very question of the phenomenality of being-towards-death.

Derrida begins *The Gift of Death* by considering Jan Patočka's attempt to write a history of 'responsibility' in European religion.[17] Patočka sees the birth of responsibility as a secondary moment which follows a primal state of demonic, orgiastic religion which is essentially 'irresponsible'. Proper religion begins when the demonic sacred is destroyed in favour of responsibility. This journey to responsibility involves, above all, the genesis of an ethical subject who is required not only to carry the burden of responsibility, but who is required so that there is even the possibility of responsibility. At stake also is the genesis of history itself, as the history of responsibility or a narrative of human decisions. Derrida calls the two moments of religion (the demonic and the responsible) 'two heterogeneous types of secret'. By this he means that both the *condition* of the demonic state itself and the *transition* to the responsible state remain mysterious. Between these two types of secret, and superseding them, is the Christian secret or *mysterium tremendum*, Christian responsibility as self-giving love, which Patočka sees breaking with the ethical self of Platonism. These three secretive or mysterious transformations which form the genealogy of Western 'responsibility', can only be understood within the 'economy of sacrifice'. Setting along a path already well prepared in *Given Time* Derrida considers this economy of sacrifice under the title of the 'gift of death'.

Derrida contrasts Patočka, Heidegger and Levinas on the question of what creates a responsible ethical subject. For Heidegger, it is 'being-towards-death', a state to which *Dasein* is called by the voice of 'conscience', and which individuates *Dasein* to create the condition for responsibility. For Levinas, Heidegger's emphasis upon the death of the *self* implies responsibility for oneself, the privilege of one's own death, and blocks what he sees as the essential priority of the Other, without which responsibility is impossible.[18] For Patočka it is *God* who individuates the self with his gaze, granting mysteriously a sense of responsibility which forces us to tremble. Patočka does not acknowledge Heidegger but uses concepts which are 'Heideggerian', such as the orientation towards death which he sees as essential to responsibility. Aligning himself essentially more with Patočka than with the other two, Derrida reverses from the questions of responsibility and 'being-towards-death' to take the discussion to a more fundamental level: a consideration of the *condition* of the possibility of death, in other words *the gift* of death:

> On what condition is responsibility possible? On the condition that the Good no longer be a transcendental objective, a relation between objective things, but the relation to the other, a response to the other; an experience of personal goodness and a movement of intention ... On what condition does goodness exist beyond all calculation? On the condition that goodness forget itself, that the movement be a movement of the gift that renounces itself, hence a movement of infinite love. Only infinite love can renounce itself and, in order to *become finite*, become incarnated in order to love the other, to love the other as finite other. This gift of infinite love comes from someone and is addressed to someone; responsibility demands irreplaceable singularity. Yet only death ... can give this irreplaceability, and it is only on the basis of it that one can speak about a responsible subject, the soul of a conscious self, myself, etc. ... But the mortal thus deduced is someone whose responsibility requires that he concern himself not only with an objective Good but with a gift of infinite love, a goodness forgetful of itself. There is a structural disproportion or dissenter between the finite and responsible mortal on the one hand and the goodness of the infinite gift on the other hand. One can conceive of this disproportion without assigning it to a revealed cause or without tracing it back to the event of original sin, but it inevitably transforms the experience of responsibility into one of guilt: I have never been and never will be

up to this level of infinite goodness nor up to the immensity of the gift, the frameless immensity that must in general define (*in*-define) the gift as such. (GD, pp. 50–1)

Here Derrida, using Patočka's scheme, effectively incorporates the Heideggerian analysis of death within a Christian structure. The register of Derrida's voice in this passage is uncertain. Is he speaking for himself or for Patočka or both? Perhaps it should only be said that Derrida *entertains,* without criticism, Patočka's radical-Christian economy of death.

Derrida thus shifts discussion towards the question of the Other with a capital 'O', the wholly Other, in any language: God. Taking up Kierkegaard's vocabulary, it may be said that we stand in fear and trembling before this Other as infinite love, both as that which clarifies our death by contrast with its infinitude, and as that which opens up a responsibility for which we are never adequate. The impossibility of ethical adequacy is summed up in the story of Abraham's sacrifice. To enter into absolute responsibility, Abraham must give up what he most loves. But the sacrifice of his son, which is what God requires, paradoxically amounts to irresponsibility:

As a result, the concepts of responsibility, of decision, or of duty, are condemned a priori to paradox, scandal and aporia. Paradox, scandal and aporia are themselves nothing other than sacrifice, the revelation of conceptual thinking at its limit, at its death. (GD, p. 68)

This paradox of responsibility stands behind all the 'Religions of the Book' and is therefore not specifically Christian. Absolute responsibility in one direction, whether to God or to another person, requires neglect of one's responsibilities to others. A secret and ultimately unjustifiable decision must be taken to choose particular responsibilities and sacrifice others. This decision, which cannot appeal to responsibility for its justification, takes us beyond ethics and duty to what Derrida sees as the utterly secret dimension of sacrifice. Derrida is not seeking to justify Abraham's decision to sacrifice Isaac, merely to assert that something/someone always gets sacrificed in the exercise of responsibility. Day-to-day responsibility requires that the gift of death be made, that sacrifices be made, that something be given up. This reinserts passion into the realm of responsibility. Thus Patočka's dimension of the demonic, orgiastic religion of the sacred, having been repressed in the development of responsibility, returns at the moment when responsibility finds its absolute expression.

This economy of responsibility and sacrifice 'implies that God, as the wholly other, is to be found everywhere there is something of the wholly other' (GD, p. 78). Invoking Husserl by name and Levinas by implication, Derrida argues that since other people are *other* people, whose otherness is guaranteed by not-being-*oneself*, every other person is a part of the abstract sacredness of the wholly other. He sums up this play of alterity between God, self and other people in the phrase 'tout autre est tout autre' ('every other (one) is every (bit) other'), a phrase which can in Levinasian fashion be re-expressed in theological terms as 'every other (one) is God' or 'God is every (bit) other'.

It is this phrase, 'tout autre est tout autre', which forms the title of the final chapter of *The Gift of Death*. Here, in a long analysis of passages from St Matthew's Gospel, Derrida contrasts the 'calculating' Christian economy of sacrifice (where humans give up something in order to receive in return from God the greater rewards of the Kingdom of God) with the pure giving of sacrifice, a giving which gives secretly outside the circulation of exchange. The pure giving, the infinite gift, the infinite love is a divine act, pure grace, what Nietzsche calls 'that stroke of genius called Christianity' in which God himself, in complete self-sacrifice, pays off the debt owing to him.

In this essay we also see Heidegger's being-towards-death against the background of Derrida's theological position. Derrida is not satisfied with Heidegger's reduction of responsibility and selfhood to the horizon of *Dasein*'s mortality. *Dasein*'s death takes place on the basis of a more general economy of death and sacrifice. *Dasein* finds itself by losing itself because in general there is, in the first place, such an economy of finding and losing: the economy of sacrifice. Furthermore, for sacrifice to be thought of as a possibility, God must be raised as a possibility – or if not God, at least Godness, givenness, grace or the gift.

In *Aporias: dying – awaiting one another at the limits of truth* (1993), Derrida launches a more determined and penetrating study of being-towards-death. Derrida's discussion proceeds in two directions at once: first he deconstructs the metaphysics of death that he finds implicit in Heidegger's being-towards-death; secondly, he develops the theme of non-phenomenality by drawing upon the possible-impossible structure of Heidegger's phenomenology of death. Both aspects of *Aporias* are important, illustrating as well as any other text Derrida's ambivalence towards Heidegger. What is shown here too, is the way that Derrida negotiates a passage through and beyond the Heideggerian analysis of death.

Having established that 'death' may be thought of as a 'limit' or 'border' at the unknown edge of life, Derrida sets out in the first section, 'Finis', a fairly schematic framework, separating out three categories of 'border': first, cultural borders between geographical or ethnic regions; second, borders between discourses or faculties; and third, borders between words and concepts. Derrida applies this framework to Heidegger's existential analysis of death, showing how Heidegger seeks to position his concept of death prior to any cultural, discursive or conceptual differences. Derrida explains how Heidegger's interpretation is based upon a metaphysical level-distinction between *sterben*, *verenden* and *ableben* (which there is no need to discuss again here – see Chapter 3 above). Since the death of *Dasein* defines the fundamental identity of humans as those who know death *as such*, the existential interpretation of death must precede all *cultural variations* in human death, all other *sciences* of death (biology, anthropology, psychology, theology and so on) and all other *categorical distinctions* between ' kinds' of death. In this way Heidegger attempts to establish a *proper* idea of death, as it were to phenomenalize death clearly and distinctly. This awareness of death as a phenomenon is *Dasein*'s ownmost property.

Derrida's deconstruction of the propriety of *Dasein* in *Aporias* largely follows his earlier dismantling of Heidegger's humanism. But here Derrida treats Heidegger's approach as an instance of a wider and more powerful tradition:

> Heidegger not only says that the existential interpretation of death precedes, is presupposed by all other discourses on death, but also founds (*fundiert*) them ... This order of orders belongs to the great ontologico-juridico-transcendental tradition, and I believe it to be undeniable, impossible to dismantle, and invulnerable (at least this is the hypothesis that I am following here) – except perhaps in this particular case called death, which is more than a case and whole uniqueness excludes it from the system of possibilities, and specifically from the order that it, in turn, may condition. What I mean here is an entirely other 'logic' of the order: if there are legitimate and powerful questions about the foundation and the 'already' of the condition of possibility, then they are themselves made possible and necessary by a relation to death, by a 'life–death' than no longer falls under the case of what makes it possible. That is what I will call the aporia. (A, pp. 45–6)

The issue of being-towards-death is not just one for students of Heidegger. At stake here is the possibility of disrupting the structural scheme of modern metaphysics. *My death* constitutes a phenomenological void, being at once the absolute human possibility and absolutely humanly impossible to realize as an event *as such*. Derrida recognizes what Heidegger has already realized: *my death* is *sui generis*, the exemplary aporia – once it is approached from the point of view of the subject, and as Derrida notes (only grudgingly acknowledging the debt to Husserl), I as *subject* have the only possible perspective on *my* death (ibid., p. 56). Thus *my death*, or my 'life–death' – however paradoxical and impossible – functions as the irreducibly 'other' to any phenomenology (or theology):

> The impossibility of existing or of *Dasein* that Heidegger speaks of under the name of 'death' is the disappearance, the end, the annihilation of the *as such*, of the possibility of the relation to the phenomenon *as such* or to the phenomenon of the '*as such*'. (Ibid., p. 75)

So, standing at the limit of what is 'as such', Heidegger's conception of death provides the avenue into thinking that other phenomenality: phenomenality not-as-such, phenomenality as disappearance: aporia. Unlike Aristotle's 'blocked paths', which are overcome with dialectics, the Derridean aporia must simply be endured. Thus the aporia is not endured as a phenomenon, but rather as the impossibility of the phenomenon. There is, Derrida asserts, no aporia *as such*:

> The ultimate aporia is the impossibility of the aporia *as such*. The reservoir of this statement seems to me to be incalculable. This statement is made with and reckons with the incalculable itself. Death, as the possibility of the impossible *as such*, is a figure of the aporia in which 'death' and death can replace … all that is only possible as impossible, if there is such a thing: love, the gift, the other. (A, pp. 78–9)

One of the consequences or corollaries of the impossibility of aporia is the fact that even the fundamental analysis of death (which Derrida also sees in Freud and Levinas) cannot avoid 'a hidden bio-anthropo-thanato-theological contamination'. Thus the paradox of aporia is confounded at another level by the indelible mark of theology. Consequently the theological space of aporia is still an issue.

In *Aporias*, Derrida mentions only in passing the concept of the 'gift', which also shares the possible–impossible structure of aporia. In an earlier text, *Given Time 1: Counterfeit Money* (1991),[19] Derrida explores more fully the idea of the 'gift' as an instance of an impossible phenomenality as disappearance:

> The gift, like the event, must *remain* unforeseeable, but remain so without keeping itself. It must let itself be structured by the aleatory; it must *appear* chancy or in any case lived as such, apprehended as the intentional correlate of a perception that is absolutely surprised by the encounter with what it perceives, beyond its horizon of anticipation – which already appears phenomenologically impossible. Whatever the case may be with this phenomenological impossibility, a gift or an event that would be foreseeable, necessary, conditioned, programmed, expected, counted on would not be lived as either a gift or an event, as required by a necessity which is both semantic and phenomenological. That is why the condition common to the gift and the event is a certain unconditionally. (GT, pp. 122–3)

The pure gift, as an instance of pure impossibility, contains another model of a Derridean impossible phenomenology: 'The gift does not *exist* and does not *present* itself. If it presents itself, it no longer presents itself' (ibid., p. 15).

Although Derrida owes a debt to Heidegger for the philosophical idea of the gift, *Given Time* is a general study of giving and Derrida offers only what he calls a 'preliminary and minimal' consideration of Heidegger on the subject of the gift and time. What intrigues Derrida here is the sense of the '*es gibt*' in Heidegger's assertion in *On Time and Being* that 'there is/there gives Being' and that 'there is/there gives time'. Heidegger states that time and being are given to each other and held in a relation. Following Heidegger further, Derrida notes that this giving takes place as a kind of play within the quadrilateral space of the fourfold. As play, the giving does not get caught up in an economy of exchange. The question Derrida seeks to explore is whether any pure gift is possible or whether all giving is a form of exchange which expects something in return. In order to give purely one must expect nothing in return, there must be no exchange or payment.

It is easy to miss the point of such a discussion and see it as a minor topic of little general significance. However, in more conventional philosophical language, Derrida is asking about the possibility *in general* of the *a priori*, something purely and necessarily *given* which can be *taken for granted*. The theme of the gift was first clearly articulated by Derrida in the Hegel column of *Glas* (1974), but is nascent in Derrida's earliest work.[20] In *Glas*, Derrida is more candid about the philosophical and theological significance of 'gift':

> The gift can only be a sacrifice, that is the axiom of speculative reason. Even if it upsurges 'before' philosophy and religion, the gift has for its destination or determination ... a return to self in philosophy, religion's truth. (G, p. 243)

Thus the question of 'the gift' is the question of grounds, of a starting-point in philosophy, of what can be taken 'as read' and from which a philosophical or religious discourse can flow.

This is an absolutely crucial question for deconstruction which deconstructs precisely the notion that there are any grounds from which to launch philosophy or religion. But a *tu quoque* objection lurks within the activity of deconstruction: on what *grounds* is the critique of grounds possible? Has not deconstruction presupposed the very thing that it seeks to deconstruct? How can deconstruction begin without a starting-point? And how could deconstruction legitimate any starting-point? What is taken for *granted* in deconstruction; what *gives* it a point of departure; what is 'the gift' that makes deconstruction possible? In the consideration of 'the gift' Derrida explores this reflexive dilemma. His conclusion is characteristically undecided: there must be a ground from which to begin deconstruction, a starting-point; but since that ground is language, the starting-point is not a (temporally or spatially) fixed platform, but a fluid, unbounded zone of differences and deferred meaning. 'The gift' which inaugurates deconstruction is at once given and taken away: given in that *it happens*, taken away in that it amounts to nothing in particular. It would be wrong to think that Derrida is asserting the impossibility of the *a priori*, still less its absolute possibility. What he tries to open up in the consideration of the gift is the condition of there being a possibility of an *a priori*. Using the Heideggerian formula, this possibility is paradoxically characterized as an impossibility. The argument that Derrida effectively offers is that the contingent *is* the necessary, that the aporetic condition of language offers nothing more certain or necessary than its own contingency. This necessary contingency is emblematized in the concept of 'gift'.

The difficulty with a pure gift is that it can never be recognized because recognition would bring it into the circle of exchange, it would become 'counterfeit money', appearing to be a gift, but really working to exact profit. The pure gift cannot be given *from* someone *to* someone without entering the circle of exchange of subject and object, sender and receiver. So 'the gift is another name for the impossible'. Yet still 'we think it, we name it, we desire it. We intend it. And even if or because or to the extent that we never encounter it, we never know it, we never verify it, we never experience it in its present existence' (GT, p. 29). Only through an 'economy of death' can the gift, as such, be made:

> The death of the donor agency (and here we are calling death the fatality that destines a gift *not to return* to the donor agency) is not a natural accident external to the donor agency; it is only thinkable on the basis of, setting out from, the gift. This does not mean simply that only death or the dead can give. No, only a 'life' can give, but a life in which this economy of death presents itself and lets itself be exceeded. Neither death nor immortal life can give anything, only a *singular* surviving can give. This is the *element* of this problematic. (Ibid., p. 102) [21]

If the *a priori* is possible as a pure gift, then, it is an *a priori* that destroys itself in granting itself. Thus the *a priori* is possible only as an impossibility, it can grant only what it takes away.

Shifting the discussion into the region of history and narrative, Derrida argues that 'the gift' and narrative are linked in the concept of 'the event'. For there to be a narrative or history something must occur or be *given*. An event must *happen* either to inaugurate or interrupt the sequence of events that makes a narration:

> There must be an event – and therefore appeal to narrative and event of narrative – for there to be a gift, and there must be gift or phenomenon of gift for there to be narrative or history. (Ibid., p. 122)

In case we make the mistake of thinking of the event of the gift as anything certain, Derrida makes it clear that

> the gift and the event obey nothing, except perhaps principles of disorder, that is principles without principles. In any case, if the gift of the event, if the event of the gift must remain unexplainable by a system of efficient causes, it is the effect of nothing. (Ibid., p. 123)

Concluding Remarks

Having opened up an avenue into and through Derrida's writings on Heidegger, it is necessary now to see whether, taken in sum, there is an overall shape to Derrida's discussions and their development. A useful first step is to consider the *spirit* in which Derrida reads Heidegger. In the early essays, Derrida is explicitly trying to write himself into the narrative of Western philosophy, even as he proclaims the need to break with it. (Yet as Gasché observes, the attempt to make a break with all previous philosophy is one of philosophy's most constant characteristics.) By depicting Heidegger as the anti-metaphysician who cannot quite escape metaphysics, Derrida prepares the story of philosophy for his own entrance.[22] He is able to supply the philosophical apparatus which will purify Heidegger's project, saving it from its own metaphysical predilections. In a similar fashion, Derrida positions himself in relation to Hegel. Hegel is 'the last philosopher of the book and the first philosopher of writing', who *almost* thinks *différance* in the *Aufhebung*, but becomes stuck in his own metaphysical conception of the totalization of history. Derrida tries to untie the knot that seals Hegel's infinity, suggesting the traces of the other, the *différance*, which remain outside the envelope of *Geist*'s self-sufficiency.

In the later essays, however, Derrida's engagement is much more complex, more thorough, more than just an attempt to radicalize and surpass Heidegger in the critique of metaphysics. In his more recent writing, Heidegger's texts are used less as a stepping-stone or foil, and more as matrices within which to explore philosophical problems. By way of example, compare two short passages: The first is from *Of Grammatology*:

> Entity and being, ontic and ontological, 'ontico-ontological', are in an original style *derivative* with regard to difference; and with respect to what I shall later call *différance* ... The ontico-ontological difference and its ground (*Grund*) ... are not absolutely originary. Difference by itself would be more 'originary', but one would no longer be able to call it 'origin' or 'ground'. Those notions belonging essentially to the history of onto-theology. (OG, p. 23)

The tone is pioneering: Heidegger is an essential, perhaps *the* essential, rung on the ladder to the articulation of *différance* and arche-writing. But Heidegger's fundamental concepts, particularly the ontological difference, have still to be 'passed through' or 'transgressed'; one must think not within but '*on* the horizon' of Heidegger's paths of thought. This is all of a piece with the fiercely eschatological tone of *Of Grammatology*, which announces the 'closure' of what Derrida variously calls 'the historico-metaphysical epoch' and 'the age of the sign'. Beyond this collapsing era lies the 'end of the book and the beginning of writing' and the 'ineluctable world of the future' of which there are 'signs of liberation all over the world'. Derrida's tone is never as bold or crude elsewhere, but the gesture is not restricted to *Of Grammatology*. *Dissemination*, for example, opens with prophecies about the end of the 'book'; and Derrida's discussion of the 'destiny' of philosophy in 'Violence and Metaphysics' has, albeit muted, the same eschatological tone. Having set up an epochal, eschatological framework (one which, ironically, owes more than a little to Heidegger), Derrida locates Heidegger on the horizon between two epochs, rather as Heidegger silhouettes Nietzsche against the sunset of metaphysics.

Leaping across twenty-five years, the second passage comes from *Aporias*. In this text Derrida claims to inherit from Heidegger 'a style of questioning' which traces and retraces Heidegger's paths, not aiming to step, or even stare, beyond their horizon, but seeking to think through certain problems raised within Heidegger's texts:

> I hope I have convinced you my purpose was not to justify a passage ... toward a more radical, originary, or fundamental thought ... On the contrary, based on the example of Heidegger ... my discourse was aimed at suggesting that this fundamentalist dimension is untenable. (A, p. 79)

Derrida's tone is no longer that of a *post*-Heideggerian thinker who has overcome the inadequacies of Heidegger's philosophy, but that of a fellow traveller. In *Aporias*, the Heideggerian aporias are something we must 'endure', stuck in their possibility of the impossible, whose depth is 'incalculable'. Derrida sees himself caught in the network of Heidegger's paths. It is not that eschatology has disappeared in these later texts, indeed it is arguably more potent. But Derrida may be said to have developed an *immanent* eschatology in which the *eschaton* takes the form of the ever-impending aporia. In such an eschatology finitude is always with us in the form of its impossibility. Thus from *Of Grammatology* to *Aporias*, the 'apocalyptic tone' shifts register from prophecy to mysticism.

This modulation of voice accompanies a development in the theme of death. In the early texts, *Speech and Phenomena*, *Edmund Husserl's Origin of Geometry: An Introduction* and *Of Grammatology*, Derrida deploys what he terms 'the principle of death' (OG, p. 25) in a dramatic confrontation with the entire gamut of Western thought. 'Death' (or 'writing', or 'difference' – the words are loosely interchangeable here) is positioned as the 'other' of Western European thought. 'Life' and 'living speech' – whether in living presence, Being or *Geist* – are the essence of the passing epoch of metaphysics: the age of the sign. Life is another name for the 'logos' of 'logocentrism'; death is its excluded other. In view of the fact that the age of the sign is 'essentially theological', theology too is seen within the metaphysics of life. In this early eschatological scheme of changing epochs, 'death' is, for Derrida, an anti-theological principle. This relationship between death and theology depends upon a particular determination of the meaning of 'theology'. Derrida uses 'theology' as a more or less undifferentiated slogan for the metaphysics of the passing epoch. Although the talk of 'epochs' soon drops out of Derrida's philosophy, the designation of 'theology' as metaphysics continues throughout. This is true even in the case of negative theology.

There is, however, another complementary path of thought in Derrida's early writing. 'Violence and Metaphysics' hardly mentions 'theology' but Derrida does talk about *God*. This distinction becomes crucial (although there are difficulties with it, as the earlier discussion of 'Violence and Metaphysics' shows). Derrida reserves the term 'theology' as a pejorative, to designate the attempt to uphold metaphysics. But he uses vocabulary about 'God' to assist exploratory discussions about final causes and grounds. Thus when 'death' is used in *Of Grammatology*, the effect is to signal the deconstruction of the various discourses which Derrida calls 'theological'. Yet when, in 'Violence and Metaphysics', Derrida considers the confrontation of 'death' with a 'God' of the Hegelian type the outcome is rather more interesting:

> Infinite alterity as death cannot be reconciled with infinite alterity as positivity and presence (God) ... Unless God means Death, which after all has never been *excluded* by the entirety of classical philosophy ... But what does this *exclusion* mean if not the exclusion of every particular *determination*? And that God is *nothing* (determined), is not life because he is *everything*? and therefore at once All and Nothing. Life and Death. Which means that God is or appears, *is named*, within the difference between All and Nothing, Life and Death. Within difference, and at bottom as Difference itself. (WD, p. 115)

The possibility which is opened up here is of God as 'the effect of the trace ... the movement of erasure of the trace in presence' (ibid., p. 108). The possibility of God is tied up with his death: God's death is what makes God (im)possible. Here Death remains permanently intersected with Life (conceived as God or full presence). In a move that he repeats again and again, Derrida employs 'God' (later the gift, aporia, chiasmus, *khora*) in the attempt to describe the opening of language and difference. The tone here is not so much that of a prophetic voice at the end of the epoch of theology, but rather a mystical voice speaking from the theological space of God's erasure.

Death in some of these early texts is a highly abstracted and general concept. The Heideggerian procedure which interests Derrida in *Of Grammatology* is the abstract *Durchstreichung* of Being. Yet in later texts, Derrida considers death from the personal perspective: the deaths of Roland Barthes; mourning for Paul de Man; *my* death as a metaphor for the death of 'what I mean' in communication; one's *own* death as that which guards one's own life ('To Speculate – On Freud'); *my* death as an impossibility (*Aporias*); *my* death as sacrifice (*The Gift of Death*). Derrida's viewpoint shifts from the impersonal to the personal, away from a vantage point that views at a distance the closing of an epoch, to the perspective of personal mortality: my death seen from within my horizon.[23] This personal death is a problem, of course, as is the horizon within which it occurs. The matrix for this problem and the model for such a perspective is Heidegger's being-towards-death. Having withheld a discussion of being-towards-death in the early texts, Derrida becomes preoccupied with the idea, seeing in it not so much an answer but a point of access to the question of aporia. The meditation on being-towards-death, the impossible possibility, takes Derrida's thinking to the aporetic zone at the heart of language and philosophy, the point where the *eschaton* crosses over itself in the death of death. But this zone is not 'beyond' Heidegger's paths of thought. To take up Derrida's phrase, Heidegger and he await each other at the limits of truth.

This 'anthropological' or 'anthropo-thanatological' turn in the theme of death is an interesting development. Ironically it is the reverse of Heidegger's *kehre*, which took him away from the phenomenologically particular sense of being-towards-death to the more abstract concept of 'mortals' and the oblivion of Being. But Derrida turns away from the question of an abstracted epochal death of presence towards the question of that death which impinges on human life: my death. There is something of a transcendental flavour about this manoeuvre, and this is perhaps where an explanation lies. As Derrida observes from the outset, phenomenology involves a direct appeal to perception and experience, in order to expose a dimension which cannot be falsified. Is it not inevitable that in order to make apparent a claim of any kind – even the claim of a disavowal-of-a-claim – deconstruction must enter the phenomenological arena, working within its language and structures? Of course Derrida resists the privilege both of Husserl's *epochē* and the phenomenological priority Heidegger gives to the 'existential' analysis of death, but these procedures clearly interest him greatly. In particular, Derrida sees *my* being-towards-death as a moment of exemplary non-phenomenality, an orientation towards that which, by definition, can never appear *for me*. Yet even in its very non-phenomenality, the aporia of my death is still *mine*. In *Aporias* Derrida argues that the Heideggerian consideration of death (which Derrida himself pursues) must necessarily *begin* on 'this side' of consciousness even if the phenomenality of *my* death turns out in the end to be impossible (A, p. 56).

Moreover, it is along the path of a deconstruction of Husserlian and Heideggerian phenomenology that Derrida's own phenomenological gesture is made, as he appeals to the (impossible) perception and experience of aporia. This aporia is intended as the ruin of phenomenology. But the spoilation of phenomenology needs to be 'shown', and in that showing, phenomenology survives. So the alliance of deconstruction with phenomenology is inevitable. Derrida's recent concern with Heidegger's attempt to subvert phenomenology through being-towards-death is perhaps a product of this inevitability. If so, this would confirm Habermas's thesis that 'Derrida does not extricate himself from the constraints of the paradigm of the philosophy of the subject.'[24]

In many ways this constitutes a return to the issue raised in *Speech and Phenomena* and *The Origin of Geometry*: 'the play of life and death in the *I*'. In these earliest texts Derrida latches on to the apodicity of the subject, in the form of the 'living present', as an exemplary metaphysics. (In *The Origin of Geometry* Derrida repeatedly underscores the point that the 'living present' is essentially subjective: '*my* living present'.) The idea of 'my death' is not the problem that it is in *Aporias*, but an exemplary aporia deployed to deconstruct the metaphysics of Husserl's absolute living transcendental ego. 'My death' is what is excluded and repressed by 'my living present'. It is to this location, which he calls 'the theatre' of phenomenology, that Derrida returns in his later writing (SP, p. 89). Derrida continues the deconstruction of phenomenology, arguing that death remains outside phenomenological analysis since it cannot show itself 'as such'. Yet this time the deconstruction of phenomenology is taken a stage further, beyond Husserl into Heidegger's phenomenology of 'privation' in *Being and Time*. The target is the phenomenological gesture in Heidegger's reduction to the 'ownmost' sphere of *Dasein*. Derrida argues that there is no such thing as a 'proper' human form of death through which *Dasein* can obtain clarity of identity. Thus Heidegger's phenomenology fails, like Husserl's, to provide a certain ground for human experience. But there is another aspect to Heidegger's phenomenology that Derrida finds much more significant – the condition of possible–impossible which is opened up by being-towards-death. This is the Derridean aporia which deconstruction discloses and exploits.

This common 'phenomenological' impulse in Husserl, Heidegger and Derrida has been mentioned already, but is worth restating here. In his reading of Heidegger, Derrida's impulse (as with Husserl) is to seek to disclose an unconsidered anteriority beyond or within Heidegger's project. The ontological difference presupposes an older difference; *Dasein*'s being-towards-death presupposes a more general condition of aporia; *Dasein* presupposes a particular determination of human life; *Dasein*'s *Vorhandenheit* presupposes a linguistic structure of signification; *Gedicht* presupposes the plurivocity of *différance*; being-towards-death presupposes a more primal concept of sacrifice; the *es gibt Sein* presupposes an economy of giving. In each case, Derrida seeks to *show* a dimension which has in some sense been overlooked or inadequately described by Heidegger. What we see in Derrida's writing is not a philosophy *sui generis*, but another philosophy in the broadly 'phenomenological' tradition which also embraces Husserl and Heidegger. To be sure, Derrida's 'phenomenology' is not of the classic variety which seeks to establish the conditions that make knowledge possible. But it would not be at all hard to argue that deconstruction is a form of *epochē*, and that Derrida seeks to uncover something more 'true' or 'real' than that uncovered by, say, Husserl.[25] Notwithstanding the fact that what Derrida claims to uncover is precisely the impossibility of the sort of knowledge dreamed of by Husserl, Husserlian procedures do belong to the genealogy of deconstruction. Between Husserl and Derrida in that genealogy is Heidegger's phenomenology of privation: truth as *aletheia*. Whereas the *epochē* crosses out or sets aside those things that block the transcendental perspective, privation crosses out the distance that blocks existential closeness. Deconstruction in its turn seeks to improve the veracity of our perspective by pointing out that veracity is blocked by an infinite complexity and self-contradiction. Thus Derrida tries to make a phenomenon of the impossibility of a phenomenology. This whole enterprise takes place on the presupposition that we will be *wiser* for reading the philosophers concerned. No one can doubt that Derrida's philosophy is a tremendously complicated and paradoxical turn in the development of phenomenology. Yet who could suppose that Derrida is not trying to *show* us the truth, however problematized, and that his writing does not belong to this history of *showing*?

Certainly this showing is of the most uncertain kind, as Derrida well knows: 'This "meaning-to-say-nothing" is not, you will agree, the most assured of exercises' (P, p. 14). Against phenomenology, Derrida tries to show the impossibility of showing. Yet how can one *show* that showing is a problem without presupposing the very faculty that is in question? This paradox of phenomenality, where phenomenology and non-phenomenology pass over each other in a double gesture of negation and affirmation, is the chiasmus or cross at the heart of Derrida's philosophy.

Notes

1 H. Ott, *Martin Heidegger: A Political Life* (HarperCollins, London, 1993).
2 Derrida cites Heidegger's reference not only to the 'spirit' of the German people, but his reference to them as 'das metaphysische Volk' (OS, p. 45).
3 Derrida treats *Geist* at two levels: on the one hand as a crude slogan in the rhetoric of fascism; on the other as a significant philosophical concept in Heidegger's pre-Socratic and pre-Christian understanding of Being and its destiny. Thus Derrida at once uses the issue of *Geist* to localize the 'problem' of Heidegger's Nazism, and at the same time to assert that *Geist* is not a local issue at all but a fundamental aspect of Heidegger's philosophy. It is hard to tell what conclusion Derrida reaches: is he letting Heidegger off the hook by implying that his Nazism is an aberration in a philosophy which is otherwise blameless? Or is he (since the metaphysical problems with Spirit remain throughout Heidegger's work) implicating the whole of Heidegger's project in the errors of the 1930s? Derrida appears to say both things at once. However, he does refuse to write off Heidegger's philosophy at a stroke on account of fascist components within it. Derrida describes his own approach as an 'opening up' of Heidegger's writing. He acknowledges the *'fact* named Nazism and what Heidegger had taken on of this', but resists what he calls the 'foreclosure' of Heidegger's thought by the 'card-carrying anti-Heideggerians' (Poi, pp. 192ff.).
4 There are in Derrida's writing so many discussions of, remarks about and references to Heidegger that an exhaustive survey is neither practicable nor profitable. What follows is an analysis which aims to illustrate the range of Derrida's discussions. Some other texts on Heidegger and negative theology will be discussed in Chapter 5.
5 Graham Ward offers a different interpretation in *Barth, Derrida and the Language of Theology* (Cambridge University Press, Cambridge, 1995), pp. 178–90. Ward sees 'Violence and Metaphysics' as an attempt by Derrida to 'modify' Levinas's project by adding a 'supplement' of his own. The notion of 'modification' or as Ward also calls it, 'negotiation' is interesting, but it understates both the strong element of critique in this essay and Derrida's affirmation of Heidegger. If a modification takes place, it is primarily the modification of Heidegger's ontological difference by Levinas's idea of absolute and infinite alterity.
6 E. Levinas, *Totality and Infinity*, cited by Derrida in 'Violence and Metaphysics' (WD, p. 108).
7 Levinas has replied in a general way to 'Violence and Metaphysics' in an essay called 'God and Philosophy', first published in *Le Nouveau Commerce*, 30–1 (1975), pp. 97–128 and translated by R. Cohen in E. Levinas, *Collected Philosophical Papers*, (Martinus Nijhoff, Dordrecht, 1987), pp. 153–73.
8 However, in a later essay, Derrida complains that 'fundamental ontology' erases the particularity of gender in *Dasein*. In 'Geschlecht: sexual difference, ontological difference' (1983) Derrida argues that one of the consequences of Heidegger's separation of the analytic of *Dasein* from 'the sciences of life' is that the themes of sexual difference and sexuality are not treated by Heidegger: *Dasein* is apparently both genderless and asexual. *Dasein* has, for Heidegger, an originary structure which precedes its spatial distribution into particular gendered human lives and its temporal distribution across its own lifetime, from birth to death. To understand this, argues Derrida, we must return to Heidegger's 'privative strategy' in *Being and Time* which defines 'life' negatively as an abstraction from *Dasein*. This discloses, for Derrida, a fundamental difficulty with Heidegger's philosophy: the 'problematic organization' of ontological difference into regional and fundamental ontologies.
9 Although this is the mood of early Derrida, the position changes significantly in later texts. In fact Derrida effectively reappropriates Heidegger's crossing through of Being in his own figure of the chiasmus. See pp. 157–163 below.

10 Originally published in *Holzwege* (Klostermann, Frankfurt, 1957). Translated by G. Aylesworth as 'The incipient Saying of Being in the fragment of Anaximander', in *Basic Concepts* (Indiana University Press, Bloomington, 1993).
11 In another essay ('Envois') Derrida argues that Heidegger's speaking of Being is an attempt to gather Being into the very kind of epochal 'world picture' that Heidegger criticizes in his lecture 'The Age of the World Picture'. Derrida argues that the very destiny of Being forbids this gathering and points beyond what he sees as Heidegger's 'différence comme ... *un envoi de soi*' to a difference which is 'un envoi de l'autre, des autres. Des inventions de l'autre' (Psy, p. 137). Derrida's resistance to the Heideggerian motif of 'gathering' is a frequent feature of his writing.
12 *Legein* is a cognate of logos. For Heidegger's analysis of this, see *Introduction to Metaphysics*, tr. R. Manheim (Yale University Press, New Haven, 1987), pp. 123ff.
13 See for example OS, p. 55, or A, p. 29.
14 Derrida calls this section 'Geschlecht III'.
15 *Das Ereignis* literally means 'the event', but is used by Heidegger to mean the mutual self-appropriation of the fourfold: earth, heaven, divinities, mortals. This appropriation is also a form of showing (deriving an additional sense from *eräugnen*, 'to put before one's eyes'), leading Hofstadter to offer the translation 'the disclosure of appropriation' (see his introduction to *Poetry, Language, Thought*, pp. xviii–xxii).
16 Derrida's criticism of Shapiro in the essay concerns his ignorance of 'the philosophical context' for Van Gogh's painting and its interpretation. Shapiro does not investigate the presupposition of subject–object relationships inherent in his accusation of Heidegger's 'projection' (TP, p. 367). The consideration of nothingness, which Derrida sees as part of the interpretation of the painting, can only be achieved in philosophy or poetry (ibid., p. 378). Shapiro underestimates the 'more philosophical scope' of 'The Origin of the Work of Art' (ibid., p. 358). Finally, Shapiro does not go beyond the 'determinable frontiers' of the painting – 'beyond these frontiers lies, for example, the philosophical context' (ibid., p. 353).
17 J. Patočka, *Heretical Essays in the Philosophy of History*, tr. E. Kohác (Verdier, Lagrasse, 1981).
18 Derrida contests this reading of Heidegger, quoting a passage from *Being and Time* which shows that one may sacrificially 'go to ... death for another' (GD, p. 42).
19 Published in 1991, but based upon a theme explored in lectures and seminars from 1977–8.
20 For example, 'Violence and Metaphysics' (WD, p. 148).
21 The suggestion that death provides the opportunity for a disinterested form of giving is not original to Derrida. See Søren Kierkegaard, 'The Work of Love in Remembering One Dead', *Works of Love* (Collins, London, 1962). Kierkegaardian themes of sacrifice and death are prominent in Derrida's writing of the 1990s.
22 'To the extent that such a logocentrism is not totally absent from Heidegger's thought, perhaps it still holds that thought within the epoch of onto-theology, within the philosophy of presence, that is to say within philosophy *itself*. This would perhaps mean that one does not leave the epoch whose closure one can outline. The movements of belonging or not belonging to the epoch are too subtle, the illusions in that regard are too easy, for us to make a definite judgement' (OG, p. 12).
23 Derrida's intention in turning to the sphere of personal mortality is not to escape the general questions of finitude, but to find a better milieu for them. He explains in an interview from 1976 that 'the scene of "I am dead" – with all its investments – maintains for a long time a general value. Universal structures are interpreted through it' (Poi, p. 21).
24 *The Philosophical Discourse of Modernity* (Polity Press, Cambridge, 1987), pp. 166f.
25 From the late 1990s on, Derrida becomes more and more explicit in calling deconstruction a form of *epochē*. For example, see Adi, p. 20.

Chapter 5

Theological Impossibility

God sees from your side and from mine at once, as absolute third; and so there *where he is not there, he is there;* there *where he is not there, is his place.*
(TS, p. 71)

It's to death that already I owe everything I earn, I have succeeded in making of it, as I have with god, it's the same thing, my most difficult ally, impossible but unfailingly faithful once you've got him in your game.
(Cir, p. 172)

It is well known that if there is one word that remains absolutely unassignable or unassigning with respect to its concept and thingness, it is the word 'death'. Less than for any other noun, save 'God' – and for good reason, since their association . . . is probably not fortuitous – is it possible to attribute to the noun 'death' and above all to the expression 'my death' a concept or a reality that would constitute the object of an indisputably determining experience.
(A, p. 22)

The constancy of God in my life . . .   (Cir, p. 155)

Do as I do and learn faith.   (PC, p. 116)

Between Negative and Positive Theology

There is a striking congruence and interrelation of approach in Husserl, Heidegger and Derrida. Heidegger's privative strategy of *Destruktion* is a radicalized form of the Husserlian reduction. Derrida's strategy of deconstruction is a radicalized form of the Heideggerian 'privative strategy'. In each case some essentially *negative* procedure is used to effect the disclosure of a ground. Husserl negates/brackets the false certainties in the field of perception to open up the true certainty of phenomenological perception. Heidegger negates the false certainty of ontic perception to open up the ontological certainty of the Being of beings. Derrida negates certainty itself to open up the radical uncertainty of *différance*. Each operates by identifying and dismantling a false apodicity, showing the play of shadows for what it is, like the prisoner in Plato's cave who releases the blinkers on the others.

This strategy of negation raises the question of whether deconstruction, in effect, is a negative theology, securing by denials an essentially theological ground which cannot be outstripped or undermined. As Mark C. Taylor puts it, 'is his [Derrida's] nonsaying nonetheless a saying? A denegation?'[1] This question provides a beginning for the discussion of Derrida's theology: an investigation into deconstruction itself to determine the possibility of its character as a form of theological discourse.

A number of critics have made the case that Derrida is indeed a negative theologian. John Caputo, for example, sees Derrida as a negative theologian who goes beyond the name of 'God' to a wholly other who is beyond names.[2] Arguably the most interesting analysis of Derrida and negative theology is offered by Kevin Hart in *The Trespass of the Sign*. Hart makes the case that Derrida is an anti-metaphysician who enables negative theology to break its residual metaphysical restrictions and develop into a 'general negative theology' which 'can resist the illusions of metaphysics'.[3] Derrida does this, Hart argues, by identifying the complicity of discourse and metaphysics. Derrida's exploitation of *différance* in deconstruction allows negative theology to make its final gesture by unsettling this complicity and opening up the possibility of a non-metaphysical theology.

The basis for Hart's theory is an interpretation of Derrida's relationship to Kant. Hart goes beyond the generally accepted view that Derrida belongs to the 'great Kantian tradition' in so far as he addresses certain 'Kantian' questions about knowledge. Hart locates Derrida within 'a hidden genealogy relating Heidegger and Derrida to Kant'.[4] This and other relationships that Hart explores are complex and subtle. However, in summary, Hart sees Derrida and Heidegger in the Kantian anti-metaphysical tradition. Although Derrida deconstructs Kant, deconstruction itself is still framed by a *parergon* of Kantian structures: the critique of metaphysics, the impulse to develop a 'new transcendental aesthetic' of conditions of possibility of knowledge, and philosophical concerns that are semiological, and therefore essentially epistemological. Thus Derrida's deconstruction is seen to be akin to negative rather than positive theology, establishing by means of rigorous critique the limits and conditions of what can be known about God.

A great deal hangs on the accuracy of Hart's description of Derrida's relationship to Kant, which is problematical. In this respect there is a significant, and arguably insurmountable, objection to Hart's view of Derrida. The upshot of Hart's argument is the view of Derrida as a Kantian idealist, concerned only with discourses and with the conditions of knowledge. Thus Hart argues that Derrida's theological interests are also essentially idealist, effectively radicalizing Kant's 'religion within the limits of reason' to 'religion within the limits of deconstruction'. Yet deconstruction is not a new idealism, indeed Derrida sees 'the critique of idealism' as a possible title for his entire philosophy (P, p. 62).

Some remarks by Don Cupitt are helpful here. Cupitt recognizes that Derrida's early 'transcendental' philosophy of arche-writing is at risk of being read, in Hart's manner, as an 'idealism-of-the-sign'. Consequently, Cupitt argues for a 'semiotic materialism' that saves linguistic philosophy from transcendentalism.[5] This helps us to draw the boundary between Kant and Derrida. Derrida speaks of two sorts of writing: writing proper as marks on the page, and an 'idea' of writing in general: arche-writing. Such talk of a general idea of writing would seem to place Derrida firmly in the transcendental tradition. However, his use of the quasi-transcendental concept of arche-writing is, as Gasché explains, an attempt to 'breech' transcendental philosophy from 'within'.[6] Arche-writing is a transcendental Trojan horse, which colludes with the Kantian tradition in order to subvert it. In fact it is precisely Derrida's general philosophy of *writing* (as distinct from a philosophy of language) that marks his most decisive break with idealism, Kantian or otherwise. Although Derrida insists that arche-writing cannot be reduced to writing in the ordinary sense, it is none the less *writing*, and it 'essentially communicates with the vulgar concept of writing' (OG, p. 56). Moreover, Derrida is emphatic that 'corporeal exteriority undoubtedly does not *constitute* the sign as such but, in a sense that we must make clear, is *indispensable* to it' (EH, p. 94). Thus arche-writing cannot, and should not, be divorced from the 'semiotic materialism' of physical writing: inscription, a 'body of signs', a scribbling, a physical marking or tracing. However, this requires some qualification. Derrida cautiously states that what he writes 'can be considered "materialist"' (P, p. 64), yet he insists that *matter*, in this context, must indicate a general economy of 'radical alterity' if idealism is not to be reinstated in the guise of a 'metaphysical materialism'. Derrida is also anxious to stress that deconstruction is concerned with the concrete institutions within which particular discourses are sustained.[7] Thus in an essay on Kant, Derrida specifically states that

> it is because deconstruction interferes with solid structures, 'material' institutions, and not only with discourses or signifying representations, that it is always distinct from an analysis or a 'critique'. (TP, p. 19)

This emphasizes Derrida's insistence elsewhere that deconstruction is not a critique 'in the general sense or in a Kantian sense' (Psy, p. 390).[8] By contrast, we have argued that deconstruction is better understood as a radicalized form of the phenomenological *epochē*, as Derrida himself has made explicit: 'It is true that for me Husserl's work, and precisely the notion of epochē, has been and still is a major indispensable gesture. In everything I try to say or write the epochē is implied' (Hos, p. 81).

Although Hart argues that deconstruction is not simply a form of negative theology, he believes that it is in the realm of negative rather than positive theology that Derrida has a contribution to make. Deconstruction helps negative theology understand its mission to subject all conceptions of God – negative and positive – to radical critique. Although this is a useful insight, it underestimates the way in which Derrida repeatedly and over many years has distanced 'deconstruction' and '*différance*' from negative theology on the one hand and critique on the other.[9] '*Différance*', he writes, is 'not theological, not even in the order of the most negative of negative theologies' (M, p. 6). And elsewhere, he deconstructs the logic of negative theology: 'Imagine the God of a negative theology', ponders Derrida, 'attempting by himself to describe himself, to catch himself in the grid of a determining discourse: he will almost annihilate himself' (M, p. 282). The point of these refutations and deconstructions is to clear the path not for a new kind of negative theology – still less a new positive theology – but a theology of impossibility.

This book argues that Derrida is best understood in a genealogical line following Husserl and Heidegger. Derrida's extensive writing on Husserl provides the essential *documentary* link with Enlightenment philosophy, which Hart struggles to make through Kant.[10] We have seen how Derrida engages with Husserl precisely on the topics of metaphysics and theology. Since Husserl's *epochē* and Heidegger's being-towards-death are both negative procedures, Derrida argues that both can be interpreted as forms of negative theology: 'Transcendental phenomenology, insofar as it passes through the suspension of all *doxa*, of every positing of existence, of every thesis, inhabits the same element as negative theology' (ON, p. 67). Elsewhere Derrida argues that Heidegger's being-towards-death (itself an existential version of the phenomenological reduction) also sets him in the tradition of 'the apophatic mystics' (ibid., p. 67). It is out of his interaction with Husserl and Heidegger that Derrida will step forward beyond negative theology to a new non-real theological understanding in which the old theological concepts and structures are at once negatively deconstructed and yet still glowing with a positive afterlife. This theology is able, in Derrida's phrase, 'to put the old names to work' (D, p. 5) in a non-theological space 'between God and God' (WD, p. 294).

In two essays written in the late 1980s and early 1990s, Derrida has discussed in some greater depth both the identity of negative theology and his criticism of it. It is helpful briefly to examine these texts before proceeding to discuss the more general question of deconstruction and negation. 'How to Avoid Speaking: Denials' (1987), in which Derrida explores the relationship between the 'trace' and 'negative theology' is, with 'Sauf le nom' (1992/3), Derrida's most complete discussion of the subject.

'How to Avoid Speaking: Denials' offers three 'paradigms' for negative theology: the first Platonic, the second Christian and the third Heideggerian. The Platonic negative theology aims to stake out the two separate regions: that of the Good, and that of the *khora*. The apophasis of the Good is a transcendental or hyperbolic movement striving to go 'beyond' the determinations of being, essence or existence towards that which is the unintelligible (*alogon*) source of intelligibility. By contrast, the apophasis of *khora* tries to gesture towards that fundamental place or origin which grants the formal conditions of being, but which is neither sensible nor intelligible and can only be addressed through 'bastard reasoning' (*logismo tini notho*). The Christian apophases are a development of the transcendent apophasis of the Good but with the added apostrophic dynamic of prayer, that is, an address to the Other, who is beyond being. The Heideggerian apophasis concerns the articulation of Being. Derrida notes various moments of apophasis in Heidegger, including his description of 'the Nothing' in *What Is Metaphysics?*, and his rethinking of *khora* in *What Is Called Thinking?* But what interests Derrida in this essay are two instances in which Heidegger tries to 'avoid speaking' of Being: first in *The Question of Being* and second in his reported remark of 1951 that were he to write a theology he would not speak of Being. Derrida argues that there is, in Heidegger's separation of the discourses of God and Being, a point where they meet and become one. After all, the discourse of Being and the discourse of God *both* require the crossing-out of Being. 'What difference is there between writing a theology and writing on Being? ... Most of all when he [Heidegger] writes the word "being" under and in the place (*Ort*) of the cancellation in the form of a cross?' (H, p. 128).

The essay is, in effect, an argument for the impossibility of a 'classic' negative theology. Derrida argues that discourses of negation are always *also* affirmative, either echoing or presupposing the positivities they seek to describe by denials. In each paradigm, Derrida establishes that a purely negative discourse is not possible:

> The possible absence of a referent still gestures, if not towards the thing spoken about (such as God who is nothing because he takes place *without place, beyond Being*), at least towards the other (other than Being) who calls or to whom this speech is addressed, even if it speaks to him for speaking's sake or to say nothing ... The most negative discourse, even beyond all nihilisms and negative dialectics, preserves the trace: The trace of an event older than it *or* of a 'taking-place' to come, the one *and* the other: there is here neither an alternative nor a contradiction. (H, p. 97)

Thus in Plato's paradigm, the Greek conception of the Good is not the opposite of being (that is, 'Nothing'), but the other of being, thus the apophatic discourse of the Good gestures towards the positive rather than the negative. In a similar way, *khora* is neither being nor non-being, so therefore never a 'void'. Furthermore *khora* invites discourse, which (if that discourse is to be meaningful) presupposes the trace of *khora* somewhere in language. In the Christian paradigm Derrida observes that negations are always held and contained within the positive apostrophe of a prayer. Finally he notes that Heidegger's erasure of Being is not essentially negative, but positive, using concealment to effect a positive disclosure. In sum, Derrida tries to demonstrate that there is an inescapable apostrophe which unsettles, or deconstructs, the self-sameness and identity of negative theology. Derrida calls this 'the promise':

> I will speak of a promise, then, but also within the promise. The experience of negative theology is perhaps connected *to* a promise, that of the other, which I must keep because it commits me to speak at that juncture where negativity ought to take discourse to its point of absolute rarefaction. (H, p. 84)

This promise also takes the form of prayer. This double gesture within all negative theology – apophasis and apostrophe, denial and promise, silence and prayer – is also the double gesture of the trace, simultaneously marking and erasing. However, the trace is *not* negative theology but the moment of its de-negation, the point where negative theology crosses itself out. In this twilight of the trace Derrida asks, at the end of the essay, 'would a theology be possible?' He does not offer an answer, either here or elsewhere. His 'theology', in so far as we can speak of such a thing, is the articulation of the possibility of theology which is also its impossibility: the crossroads at which a theology becomes both possible and impossible.

In 'Sauf le nom' Derrida takes up again this theme of the (im)possible character of theology, making a trilateral comparison between (i) the 'impossible' idea in Angelus Silesius that 'to become Nothing is to become God'; (ii) the possibility of the impossible in Heidegger's being-towards-death; and (iii) deconstruction, also conceived as an impossible possibility.

> This thought [that to become Nothing is to become God] seems strangely familiar to the experience of what is called deconstruction. Far from being a methodological technique, a possible or necessary procedure, unrolling the law of a programme and applying rules, that is unfolding possibilities, deconstruction has often been defined as the very experience of the (impossible) possibility of the impossible, of the most impossible, a condition that deconstruction shares with the gift, the "yes", the "come", decision, testimony, the secret, etc. And perhaps death.
> . . .
> The possibility of the impossible, of the 'most impossible', of the more impossible than the most impossible, that recalls, unless it announces, what Heidegger says of death: '*die Möglichkeit der schlechthinnigen Daseinsunmöglichkeit*' ('the possibility of the absolute impossibility of *Dasein*'). What is, for *Dasein*, for its possibility, purely and simply impossible is what is possible, and death is its name. I wonder if that is a matter of a purely formal analogy. What if negative theology were speaking at bottom of the *mortality* of *Dasein*? (ON, p. 44)

Here Derrida makes some of the connections which mark the basis of his own theological view: *Dasein*'s individuation through mortality (being-towards-death) is suggested as a kind of negative theology, and death, as the 'possible impossible', is put forward as a name for the 'condition' of deconstruction. Although nothing definite is asserted in these suggestions, a dimension of theological opportunity is opened up.

Further on in 'Sauf le nom', Derrida clarifies this dimension of possibility by offering a deconstruction of negative theology. He posits the question of the 'other' of negative theology, that which is excluded or 'structurally exterior' to its discourse. This other is, naturally, the possibility of a positive theology, or as Derrida cautiously puts it, 'positivity de-negated' (ON, p. 51) 'Emptiness', argues Derrida, is essential to the 'vocation' of negative theology, since its aim is to say *nothing*. Yet this aim constitutes a negation of saying *something*, a resistance of, or protection against, 'actual or full intentional meaning'. Thus the possibility of plenitude is excluded by, but therefore also structurally necessary to, the discourse of negative theology (rather in the way that in reverse, emptiness (death) is excluded by Husserl's plenitude of living presence).[11] Negative theology is therefore *relational*, standing between two poles: on the one hand there is the *kenotic* emptiness of its vocation; on the other hand there is the return of what is repressed by *kenosis*, namely a de-negated positivity. The idea of a 'de-negated positivity' is well illustrated in Heidegger's *kenosis* of *Dasein* in being-towards-death. Derrida makes the point here – as he does more fully elsewhere (GD, p. 47) – that *Dasein*'s self-negation in death is a defining moment, the moment that gives *Dasein* its boundary, its clarity as a self, its positivity as the life of an 'I'. (Later in the essay, Derrida cites further examples of denegated positivities: Heidegger's cruciform *kreutzweise Durchstreichung* of Being, the *Gevier* of the late writing on language, and the notion of God under erasure which is proposed in Jean-Luc Marion's *God without Being*.)

At this point Derrida tries to position more precisely this 'without being', the Platonic *epikeina tes ousias*, in relation to Heidegger's project. He notes that Heidegger's appeal to *existence*, rather than the egological concepts of subject or soul, is a movement of transcendence. But whereas Heidegger's transcendence stops at the Being of beings, the 'hyperbolic' tendency in the Platonic tradition points further and further into the 'beyond' of a space surpassing both God and Being. In this utterly indeterminate region, where discussion (dialectics) ceases, Silesius is able to conflate his own voice with that of God, asserting that 'I am as God and God as I'. Derrida sees this as a dangerous moment, because negative theology ceases to function as radical critique and assumes 'a sententious voice that produces or reproduces mechanically its verdicts with the tone of the most dogmatic assurance: nothing or no one can oppose this' (ON, p. 67). The problem, as Derrida sees it, is that negative theology operates ultimately in 'the name of a way of truth' with the 'desire to say and rejoin what is proper to God' (ibid., p. 69). Or as he has put it elsewhere, 'the negative movement of the discourse of God is only a phase of positive ontotheology' (WD, p. 337, n. 37).

The 'proper' of God for Silesius is the playfulness of creation. This playfulness is possible through the abandonment (*Gelassenheit*) of God. God must be abandoned in order to be grasped. (Here Silesius resonates again with Heidegger and the abandonment of *Dasein*.[12]) After abandonment, the self enters into the play of God in creation. Taking the logical regression a step further, Derrida asks what precedes God's play and makes it possible. Is there a place which is the precondition of the play in which God appears? Is this place God himself? Derrida poses two possibilities: first, that God calls the dimension of play into being; second, that this place is prior, and alien, to God and creation – in other words the *khora*, a site that cannot even be properly determined as a place or even as life or death. These possibilities exclude each other and, since it is not possible to determine which is the case, they form an 'absolute heterogeneity'. The gap of knowledge which opens up here constitutes one of 'the aporias of negative theology'. It is a gap which is created by what Derrida calls the problem of the 'without', that is to say, the question of what lies 'without' or beyond every 'determined concept'. What is being spoken of here is, in other words, the question of the 'other' which deconstruction relentlessly pursues in every text.

Derrida does not provide a tidy solution to the aporia of theology, but towards the end of the essay, he cites approvingly two maxims of Silesius: 'No death is without life'; and 'nothing lives without dying / God himself, if He wants to live for you, must die'. There is only the vaguest suggestion here – but it is one that will also be found elsewhere in Derrida's writing – that aporia itself would constitute the basis of an 'other' theology which is neither positive nor negative, between the death and the life of God.

Deconstruction and Negation

The rejection of the view of Derrida as a negative theologian does not dispose of the question of his use of negation in the procedures of deconstruction. Clearly Derrida *is* using negation and his discourse does *resemble* negative theology even at times to the point, as he says, of being 'indistinguishable' from negative theology. But if the title 'negative theology' does not sit well on deconstruction, what then *is* the correct understanding of deconstruction and its relationship with the concerns of theology? It is necessary at this point to consider more fully the nature of the discourse of deconstruction.

An inquiry into deconstruction can be perplexing. Derrida's own writing about deconstruction tends to consist of a series of denials. He is emphatic that deconstruction is not a critique, not an analysis, not a method. However, he becomes still more mysterious when he says that 'all phrases of the type "deconstruction is X" or "deconstruction is not X" *a priori* miss the point, or let's say they are at least false ... What isn't deconstruction? everything of course! What is deconstruction? nothing of course!' (Psy, p. 392). This certainly has the grammar and tone of a negative theology, as Derrida admits elsewhere: 'the detours, locutions, and syntax in which I will often have recourse will resemble those of negative theology, occasionally even to the point of being indistinguishable from negative theology' (M, p. 6). Yet negative theology, unlike deconstruction, is concerned to disclose what Derrida calls a 'superessentiality' beyond 'finite categories', whereas deconstruction, unlike negative theology, is concerned to avoid essentiality. Thus in the resistance of essentiality, deconstruction must try to avoid even the metaphysical shadow of its own essentiality.

The point that Derrida is making – the point that will be missed if the identity of deconstruction is fixed by definition, even by the definition 'negative theology' – is that deconstruction gestures beyond the metaphysics which is implicit in every attempt to assert identities. The 'instituting question of philosophy' is, Derrida explains in *Of Grammatology*, the question of identity, the question *'ti esti'*, 'what is . . . ?' (OG, p. 19). This question is also the inaugural question of metaphysics, the invitation to assert the essence of a thing and begin the construction of a distinction between the thing itself and its essential form. Deconstruction aims to challenge 'the very form of the question', evading the response 'X is . . .'. Thus deconstruction itself must be vigilant in keeping its distance from the answer to the question of its own propriety and identity. For deconstruction is 'above all else the search for the "other",'[13] and as a *search* deconstruction is an activity rather than a doctrine. Thus the deconstructive measure of deconstruction is the extent to which it can contemplate its own 'other', resisting the temptation to settle into an identity of itself as this or that.

The rationale of deconstruction, then, belongs within the logic of resistance. To use the language of the New Testament, deconstruction is perhaps the discourse of the *skandalon*, a discourse against the proud, laying stones to be tripped over by those who are too certain. Faced with a tradition of metaphysics which is not only part of Western culture, but is written, as Nietzsche puts it, into its *grammar*, how is Derrida to oppose this tradition without somehow getting caught up in the cloying web of its language? If Derrida were to allow the determination of deconstruction as *this* or *that*, deconstruction would all too easily become absorbed into the conditions of possibility of the very tradition that it aims to oppose. Kierkegaard faced the same difficulty when trying to resist the omnivorous dialectical reason of Hegel. Kierkegaard could give no concession to the dialectic of world history without being absorbed by it. Kierkegaard's only recourse – turning Hegelian pejoratives to his own advantage – was to declare the basis of his own philosophy to be irreducibly subjective. Nietzsche, in opposing the spiritual, rational history of philosophy made similar gestures of resistance by 'philosophizing with a hammer' and declaring true thinking to be a form of dancing. Most notably, Heidegger, recognizing the need for a 'different language', placed 'Being' under erasure B̶e̶i̶n̶g̶ 'in order to resist 'the almost ineradicable habit of conceiving Being as something standing by itself and only coming at times face to face with man' (QB, p. 81). Derrida's deconstruction needs to be understood in this context, as a strategic attempt to criticize a tradition which has almost everything stacked in its favour: apparent control of the medium of all possible discussion; hegemony over all established forms of structure and concept; and the authority to say what counts as legitimate criticism.

Derrida's argument is that every question we ask about deconstruction and every possible answer we try to give, belong within the discourse of Western metaphysics. Everything that appears absurd about deconstruction appears absurd from the vantage point of logocentrism, every objection to deconstruction is made on the grounds of its violation of the metaphysics of presence. Thus deconstruction can not, *a priori*, offer any satisfactory rationale for, or legitimation of, itself. All that may be said of the purpose of deconstruction is that it resists metaphysics. As to the *ultimate* value or justification of that project, nothing can be said.

It would therefore be quite unjust to take the refusal to define deconstruction as deliberate obscurantism on the part of Derrida. What he is refusing are those *definitive* and *totalizing* predicates which attempt to fix the identity of deconstruction absolutely and take the play of the word out of circulation. The function of deconstruction is to open up the irreducible play of difference in every text. Deconstruction can be described, but always *within* the play of language. Thus Derrida, in the course of his 'Afterward' to *Limited Inc.*, is able to speak about 'denials, lies, defamations, insinuations against deconstruction', and about 'errors' and 'dishonesty' in the presentation of deconstruction (LI, pp. 151–3). It does not follow from the fact that Derrida will not allow deconstruction to submit to a *closed* interpretation that deconstruction therefore resists *all* interpretation. Derrida is able to offer an explanatory discourse about deconstruction (and he does), he can defend deconstruction against its critics and he is able to correct errors in its interpretation.

Although deconstruction resists closure, it is none the less the case that deconstruction falls prey to the very metaphysics it opposes. The reason for this is by now clear. Deconstruction must operate within the onto-theological discourses of philosophy, it must 'inhabit' metaphysical structures. No matter how effectively these structures are resisted, there is always a complicity between deconstruction and metaphysics, a complicity moreover that does not arise accidentally, but as one of the structural features of deconstruction itself.

Derrida, as has been noted, distinguishes deconstruction from critique. A critique must assert a ground from which to operate. Deconstruction does not have any ground in this sense, or rather the ground it uses is the internal or immanent ground of the texts it deconstructs. Thus Derrida's ground for the criticism of phenomenology is phenomenology itself. Derrida's deconstruction is a reduction of the reduction, an *epochē* of the *epochē*, phenomenology with a vengeance. He takes Husserl's three-stage phenomenological method, adding as it were a fourth (deconstructive) reduction of his own, 'bracketing' living presence to disclose the play of life and death.

It has been seen that in making his deconstruction of phenomenology, it is not Derrida's intention simply to falsify the truth-claim of Husserl's living present. Derrida's approach is altogether more subtle and interesting. In the treatment of the living present, we note Derrida's careful and deliberate attitude: He does not attempt to negate utterly the idea of a 'living present', but to problematize the apodictic claims that Husserl makes for it. For Husserl the living present bears the character of simplicity and priority. Derrida argues that when the living present is set before us to be tested against its own criterion of living presentation – when we look, in other words, at the extent to which the living present really is present and immediate – it always appears like the so-called 'live' broadcast, a delayed or transmitted presence, therefore not a presence at all but an absence. Derrida's conclusion is not that the 'living present' is false, merely that it fails to possess living presentation. This is a form of judgement which tries to position itself beyond simple affirmation or negation.

Without further clarification this can seem paradoxical, even meaningless. However, Derrida's approach is better understood when the subtlety of his position is made clear. What the term 'living present' attempts to designate, Derrida argues, is experienced as something neither living nor present. The result is what 'could be called the immediate nonself-presence of the living present' (SP, p. 37). In spite of these difficulties, however, the living present' still does semiotic work. It is precisely because of its continuing function as a signifier that Derrida can still employ the term, long after he has demonstrated its inherent contradictions. Indeed, deconstruction takes such contradictions as the irreducible differential condition of all language.

This differential condition, *différance*, which deconstruction exploits, is not entirely negative, since *différance* must include the very difference between positive and negative. What deconstruction achieves through its negation of positivities is indeterminacy and uncertainty. But if negation itself is to be elevated to the level of a positivity – as it effectively is in negative theology – then negation itself must be negated or de-negated. In 'Sauf le nom', as has been shown, Derrida deconstructs negative theology in precisely this way, by arguing that the discourse of negative theology presupposes an excluded other: the de-negated positivity of intentional meaning. In 'How to Avoid Speaking: Denials', Derrida considers the *Durchstreichung* of Being from the point of view of negative theology. The crossing out of Being, although in one sense a negative gesture, is for Heidegger essentially positive: it combines denial with affirmation. Derrida elaborates more fully on this relationship between the negative and the positive in his subtle deconstruction (more an extrapolation, perhaps, than a deconstruction) of Heidegger's being-towards-death.

> Such a death [being-towards-death] is not given in the first instance as annihilation. It institutes responsibility as a *putting-oneself-to-death* or *offering-one's-death*, that is *one's life* in the ethical dimension of sacrifice. (GD, p. 48)

Thus *life*, death conceived as a gift, as a sacrifice, unsettles what Heidegger sees as the certain possibility of one's own death. Against the assertion of an absolute negation or death, deconstruction poses the logic of sacrifice, that is to say, all death is a giving. In a sense then, death *is* life. The logic of sacrifice contains the possibility of the positive within, beyond or through the negative. Derrida sees this logic illustrated in the story of Isaac and Abraham

> It is finally in renouncing life, the life of his [Abraham's] son that one has every reason to think is as precious as his own, that Abraham gains or wins. He risks

winning; more precisely, having renounced winning, expecting neither response nor recompense, expecting nothing that can be *given back* to him, nothing that will *come back* to him ... he sees that God gives back to him, in the instant of absolute renunciation, the very thing that he had already, in the same instant, decided to sacrifice. It is given back to him because he renounced calculation. Demystifiers of this superior or sovereign calculation that consists in no more calculating might say that he played his cards well. Through the law of the father economy reappropriates the *an*economy of the gift as a gift of life or, what amounts to the same thing, a gift of death. (GD, p. 97)

If negative theology can never be properly negative and must always contain the trace of a positive theology, then much the same ought to apply to Derrida's view of the death of God, which is perhaps not a proper death at all, but a gesture of sacrifice in which something still lives on.

Between Nietzsche's Death of God and Hegel's

Thomas J.J. Altizer and Mark C. Taylor among others see Derrida as a 'death-of-God' theologian who inherits the mantle of Nietzsche, the author of a 'hermeneutic of the death of God', or 'the death of God put into writing'. But there is a problem with this view since Derrida flatly denies collusion with the death of God. 'I say limit and not death, for I do not believe,' writes Derrida, 'in what is so easily called the death of philosophy (nor, moreover, in the simple death of whatever – the book, man or god, especially since, as we all know, what is dead wields a very specific power)' (P, p. 6).[14] There are a number of reasons for Derrida's reaction. First, he sees logocentrism operating not just in the concept of a living God but in the either/or between there definitely being a God and there definitely not being one (OG, p. 68). To replace the life of God with the death of God goes some way towards disturbing the binarism, but does not go to the root of the problem. In an early essay on Antonin Artaud, Derrida shows how even the most virulent and sacrilegious anti-theology can preserve a classic metaphysics, noting that Artaud's 'death of God will ensure our salvation because the death of God alone can reawaken the Divine' (WD, p. 184). Second, Derrida is also concerned that if we think that the death of God has ended metaphysics, then the 'dead god' is in fact 'more dangerous than ever' (D, p. 84) since the problem of the logocentric binarism not only remains unchallenged but has been obscured. Consequently, Derrida sees 'theological prejudices' alive in the Western tradition, 'even when it professes to be atheist' (OG, p. 9, n. 3). The positive function, for Derrida, of the death of God is to problematize logocentrism and therefore undermine its power. Third, Derrida understands deconstruction to be a positive activity with a positive outcome. In this respect he insists on the difference between what he calls 'Nietzschean demolition' (Psy, p. 388) – which attempts simply to flatten metaphysical concepts – and Heideggerian 'destruction' (*Destruktion*) which 'stake[s] out the positive possibilities' (BT, p. 44) of the traditions which it confronts. Therefore, in the Derridean 'deconstructive' understanding of the death of God we might expect to find something more than nihilism, something positive.

The key point is that Derrida does not believe in the *simple* death of God. Of course this begs the question of a more complicated 'death of God'. To discover what this more complicated 'death' might be, and to begin to open up the ground for a more positive determination of Derrida's own theological position, it is necessary to take a detour through Nietzsche and Hegel. By sketching out the character of the Nietzschean and Hegelian deaths of God, a clearer description of Derrida's own position becomes possible.

The death of God is a phrase that has become linked most particularly with Nietzsche, and which tends to be interpreted as proof of his nihilism, his atheism, his contempt for Christendom and the proclamation of radical humanism. But some of these assumptions can be misleading. For an accurate understanding of Nietzsche and in turn Derrida, we need to situate Nietzsche's talk about the death of God within the more general pursuits of his philosophy. In his earliest writing Nietzsche identifies a problem around which much of his later writing will revolve: the problem of a horizon, that is, some necessary cosmic frame of reference for the contingent flux of human life. Nietzsche's death of God is the disappearance of the Christian–Platonic horizon which had hitherto encircled Western culture. Nietzsche's philosophy can be read as the attempt to replace this lost theological horizon without repeating the theological errors of the past.

In *The Birth of Tragedy* Nietzsche says that 'only a horizon ringed around with myths can unify a culture'.[15] He repeats this idea in the second of the *Untimely Meditations*, where he asserts the 'universal law' that 'a living thing can be healthy, strong, and fruitful only when bounded by a horizon'.[16] Nietzsche speaks of the struggling chaos of the West, as its guiding myths and beliefs are subject to what he calls 'the concept-quake' of Enlightenment science. In destroying naïve theology, science robs humanity of any sense of the eternal. Nietzsche stresses the need for us to structure the chaos by a supra-historical aesthetic vision of the eternal which will give shape to the fluid, contingent world of historical events. The question for the later Nietzsche is what sort of horizon is both possible and desirable. By a horizon, Nietzsche means the formal aesthetic structures, the arts he calls 'Apollonian', which are needed to balance and express the chaotic play of life forces which he labels 'Dionysian'.[17]

It is against the backdrop of a vanishing horizon that we should read Nietzsche's parable of the madman in *The Gay Science*.[18] A madman appears in the marketplace and declares that God is dead. The bystanders mock him and the madman leaves, realizing that he has come too early for his prophecy to be understood. In the middle of his speech the madman asks: 'Who gave us the sponge to wipe away the entire horizon?' The death of God leaves the world without a frame, limit or any point of reference and poses the question of a new post-theological horizon.

Although, ultimately, the death of God means freedom for those who have the courage to grasp it as an opportunity, Nietzsche presents God's death as an event full of terror, 'a gruesome shadow'.[19] Even the fearless Zarathustra at first only dares to speak about the death of God *silently* to himself 'in his own heart'.[20] The event is all the more chilling because the madman's audience is blind to the colossal significance of what has occurred. A detail that is often ignored is that the madman is speaking not to believers (who are presumably only too aware of the significance of God's death) but to those who consider themselves *atheists*. It is the mocking non-believers – like Schleiermacher's cultured despisers, perhaps – who do not realize that the death of God means the emptying of the horizon and moral oblivion.

Nietzsche articulates the problem of a horizon in another image also from *The Gay Science*: Columbus's ship *The Genoese*. Nietzsche pictures humanity as a ship which has passed out of sight of land, and so the material horizon disappears as we enter the 'awesome' 'horizon of the infinite'.[21]

> Without plan, into the vast
> open sea I head my ship.
> All is shining, new and newer,
> upon space and time sleeps noon;
> Only your eye – monstrously,
> Stares at me, infinity! [22]

When Nietzsche returns to the subject of the death of God in an additional section of *The Gay Science*, he brings together the metaphors of God's death, the empty horizon and the boat on the open seas:

> We ... 'free spirits' feel, when we hear the news that 'the old god is dead', as if a new dawn shone on us; our heart overflows with gratitude, amazement, premonitions, expectation. At long last the horizon appears free to us again ... at long last our ships may venture out again ... to face any danger; all the daring of the lover of knowledge is permitted again; perhaps there has never yet been such an 'open sea'. [23]

If the madman is the prophet of the empty horizon, Zarathustra is the prophet of Nietzsche's new horizon. In an arresting image, Zarathustra imagines himself looking up from the tombs of gods, through the shattered roof of a desecrated church into the open, horizonless heaven. 'O, how should I not lust for eternity and the wedding ring of rings – the Ring of Recurrence.'[24] Eternal return – 'the Ring of Recurrence' – is Nietzsche's perverse solution to the problem of a horizon.[25] Eternal recurrence replaces God with a lord of misrule, structuring time with chaotic and meaningless repetition. Eternally recurring history is not going anywhere, but simply round in circles. The image of the circle is no coincidence: from Plato on, the circle is taken as an image of metaphysical and cosmological perfection. Eternal recurrence fulfils by sacrilege the Platonic dream of circular perfection. Nietzsche deliberately plays upon the metaphysical/theological significance of the circle, describing the circles of recurrence as 'holy boundaries'.[26]

There is not to space here to explore in detail the significance of eternal return. It suffices for this discussion to situate the death of God in relation to this wider Nietzschean scheme which passes from a horizon still cluttered with Christian–Platonism, to its antithesis, an empty horizon wiped away by God's death, to a synthesis in the horizon which is drawn again by the ring of eternal recurrence.

In the final paragraph of *The Will to Power*, Nietzsche offers his most vivid description of this new eternal horizon.

> Do you know what 'the world' is to me? ... This world: a monster of energy, without beginning, without end ... enclosed by 'nothingness' as by a boundary; not something blurry or wasted ... but set in a definite space as a definite force ... as a play of forces ... at the same time one and many ... eternally changing, eternally flooding back, with tremendous years of recurrence, with an ebb and flood of its forms ... the play of contradictions ... blessing itself as that which must return eternally ... this, my Dionysian world of the eternally self-creating, the eternally self-destroying. [27]

This definition of eternal return prefigures, in the most vivid way, the concept which Derrida places at the centre of deconstruction: *différance*. Derrida is only too aware of this. In the early essay 'Différance' he defines *différance* as 'the name we might give to the active, moving discord of different forces, and of differences of forces, that Nietzsche sets up against the entire system of metaphysical grammar' (M, p. 18). This is an interesting correlation, made all the more intriguing by a remark which Derrida lets slip into a conversation about Nietzsche which is published in *The Ear of the Other*. 'It may be,' Derrida says, 'that God and the eternal return – when both thought without facileness – are not as opposed as they might appear to be' (EO, p. 83). What Derrida hints at here is what Nietzsche himself says directly in *The Will to Power*: that the eternal return 'replaces metaphysics'. What is intriguing is whether Derrida's *différance* can also be seen to 'replace metaphysics'. Of course Derrida staunchly denies that there is any theological or metaphysical content whatsoever in *différance* and he makes much the same defence on Nietzsche's behalf:

> The point is that eternal return is not a new metaphysics ... The eternal return always involves differences of forces that perhaps cannot be thought in terms ... of ... any of the great metaphysical structures ... I would suggest that here perhaps may be found not the answer but the enigma. (EO, pp. 45–6. See also WD, p. 296)

But the problem with this position is that although *différance* and eternal return may not be theological, they do occupy the vanishing space or horizon of theology. Indeed, according to the logic of deconstruction itself, *différance* must be located in the empty horizon, since – and we have seen that Derrida is insistent about this too – deconstruction operates necessarily *within* those structures it deconstructs.

Leaving Nietzsche here, it is possible to follow a second path from Hegel back to Derrida. Heidegger points out in an essay on Nietzsche's death of God that it was not in fact Nietzsche, but Hegel, who first used the term 'the death of God', referring to 'the feeling on which rests the religion of the modern period – the feeling God himself is dead'.[28]

Unlike Nietzsche, for whom 'the death of God' is a metaphor for the condition of nihilism, Hegel sees God's death as a stage in the traditional Christian scheme: an unfolding revelation of the trinitarian God. For Hegel the dead God is pictured as the 'dead divine Man',[29] who is at once Christ in particular and universal humanity in general. The death of God is required to prove that God is truly infinite and absolute. As the truly infinite absolute, God must leave nothing outside himself, not even his own death. So God as a finite picture must die in order that God as an infinite idea may live.[30] In order that totality (that is, God) can be a true totality, it must be transformed by its other – in other words, its negation, what Hegel at the end of *The Phenomenology of Spirit* calls 'the Calvary of absolute Spirit'. The Hegelian totality is thus a paradox – it must supersede itself in order to become itself. The identity of totality must be negated in order to realize the totality of totality. Thus at the moment of its final realization, totality or God cancels itself out.

It is not just the death of God but death itself or negation which is essential to the change and development of the Hegelian dialectic. In fact death, as Hegel puts it, is change. The reality of death must be faced directly and courageously, as Hegel describes in the preface to *The Phenomenology of Spirit*: 'The life of the Spirit is not the life that shrinks from death and keeps itself untouched by its devastation, but rather the life that endures it and maintains itself in it.'[31] But the Hegelian view of history demands that change should end and therefore that change itself must change, death must be superseded, negation must be negated. The death of God is this negation of negation superseding death itself and ensuring the conclusion of *Geist*'s development. Without the death of God, *Geist* would remain eternally divided between the finite and the infinite. Therefore the death of God stands at the threshold of the closure of history.[32] Without death, change is not possible. Yet without the supersession of death, change is interminable and unbounded. But since the death of God is the fulfilment of *Geist*, it is in fact not merely negative but also affirmative. In Hegel a minus times a minus equals a plus. Or as Derrida puts it: 'the absolute spirit records a profit in any case, death included' (G, p. 141).

Although Hegel's death of God 'records a profit', we should not underestimate its negativity. Hegel asks us to look beyond what he calls 'the historic Good Friday' whose negation has been ameliorated by the passage of time. We should focus, Hegel says, upon the more radical 'speculative Good

Friday'. For Hegel, the Good Friday event, the death of God, must be thought not as a literal, finite event but a speculative, infinite event: 'restored in the whole truth and harshness of its Godlessness'. The positive freedom which results, says Hegel, 'can and must rise solely from this harshness' (G, p. 96). The temptation is to see Hegel's death of God as less radical than Nietzsche's. Hegel's God seems to make a miraculous if paradoxical recovery, whereas Nietzsche's God is dead and decaying. But Hegel's negation of God is in fact quite as total as Nietzsche's, although this often is not recognized. Indeed Kojève argues that Hegel is an 'atheist' who merely uses 'the categories of Christian thought' to write a finite, anthropological philosophy.[33] Suspicions of Hegel's atheism go back a long way. Hegel was dogged in his own lifetime by charges of atheism both from reactionary Protestants and from new-Left Hegelians like Feuerbach. Their accusation – delivered either as an insult or a compliment – was that Hegel had overcome theology with philosophy.

Derrida takes some important cues for his own thinking from his reading of Hegel. 'The immense revolution [of Hegel's thought],' writes Derrida, 'consisted – it is almost tempting to say consisted *simply* – in taking the negative seriously' (WD, p. 259). The dialectical process of negating in order to move on – which Hegel calls *Aufhebung* – is the motor of Hegelian history. The *Aufhebung* is not anything, it does not exist as anything, it is – in Kantian terms – a purely regulative idea, not an idea of a thing, but the idea of a kind of difference, a way of relating one thing to another in a process. The *Aufhebung*, Derrida says, realizes itself by 'denying itself', giving Hegel's system 'a very twisted form so difficult to grasp' (G, p. 121). Derrida's own *différance* clearly has much in common with *Aufhebung*, containing both spatial and temporal differentiation, so that meaning is both relative spatially and deferred temporally. What is interesting here is the teleology implicit in *différance*: by putting off closure, *différance* looks forward, anticipates, like *Aufhebung*. Derrida's *différance* can be seen as a radicalized version of *Aufhebung*, in fact Derrida speaks of the 'profound affinity' between *différance* and 'Hegelian discourse' from which *différance* is 'unable to break' (M, p. 14). But whereas the *Aufhebung* remains in the service of the Hegelian Absolute, Derrida insists that *différance* will not be included in any formal, restricted system. *Différance* will be a Hegelianism without reserve. 'I shall,' writes Derrida, 'be ... relaunching in every sense the reading of the Hegelian *Aufhebung*, eventually beyond what Hegel ... understood himself to say or intend to mean' (M, p. xi).

Although Derrida accepts Hegel's death of God as an exemplary form of negation, he will not accept the process of closure to which Hegel's Good Friday belongs. Derrida sums up this ambivalence in a memorable comment at the beginning of *Of Grammatology*: 'Hegel is ... the thinker of irreducible difference ... the last philosopher of the book and the first thinker of writing' (OG, p. 26). What Derrida means is that Hegel's philosophy is a contradiction. On the one hand Hegel attempts to bring to fruition the Western dream of a total, metaphysical system, completely self-reflexive, without any 'other', remainder, or supplement to threaten its stability or totality. On the other hand (from a certain point of view at least), Hegel's vision of totality consists of what Hegel calls the 'indeterminate immediate', a patchwork of unreconciled differences and contradictions, in which death is included. It is, then, the deconstruction of Hegel's system in so far as it is a 'closed book' that forms the basis of Derrida's critique. This takes place in a number of texts, so a couple of examples may be singled out by way of illustration: Derrida's preface to *Dissemination* and the column on Hegel in *Glas*.

Deconstructing Hegel is certainly Derrida's most demanding challenge, because Hegel had in a way already thought *différance* in the *Aufhebung*. In the Hegel column in *Glas*, Derrida searches for a way of resisting the apparently irresistible inclusivity of Hegelian dialectic. Since the dialectic feeds on negativity, to oppose the dialectic simply nourishes its evolving totality. Since the dialectic, the *Aufhebung*, does not have a position to defend, it cannot be opposed. All criticism is grist to the mill. So Derrida's approach is different, not resisting Hegel's dialectic, but working within it, seeing how it can be extended to a point at which it begins to unravel itself. At the end of *Glas*, Derrida asks whether, outside the final circle of Hegelian infinity, anything remains.[34] Is there, to borrow a phrase from another text, any 'absolute exterior which no longer permits itself to be internalized' (M, p. 285, n. 12)? Derrida observes that *time* remains, or continues beyond Hegel's view of totality. He sees two points in time which are outside the Hegelian Absolute: first, the point when the realized Absolute is described in a text – such as in Hegel's philosophy; and second, the point before dialectics gets started.

First, Derrida argues that the Hegelian system begins to open up at the point of its signification because the reflection or representation of the Absolute cannot be incorporated into the Absolute itself (G, p. 229). In order for the Hegelian totality to be realized self-consciously it must be represented to itself in language. Thus something remains outside the Absolute: its own reflection. The minute we say: '*there* is the Absolute', we have presupposed a viewpoint beyond it. So Hegel's attempt to complete the totalization of Spirit is deconstructed, because the language of his description must always stand beyond the total it describes, thereby falsifying the totality. The name of God, argues Derrida putting it theologically, will not be inscribed within God. Perfect self-reflection is not possible – something gets added in the process. The Absolute *must* be represented: if the Hegelian Absolute were to realize itself in silence, as a surd, no one would know about it.

An additional problem for Derrida – and he repeatedly complains about Hegel's craftiness – is that Hegel has already considered this dilemma. In the famous preface to *The Phenomenology of Spirit*, Hegel points out the paradox of prefacing a work of philosophy. He argues that texts of philosophy ought to be self-explanatory. Surely a properly written philosophical text should speak for itself without any preparatory remarks. To preface a text is to admit its inadequacy. Furthermore, a preface disturbs the organic unity of a philosophical work, indicating that its understanding lies to some extent outside it. Hegel says, in a surprising metaphor, that a preface – in striving to guarantee a total expression of the truth – kills the text it precedes, by undermining its sufficiency. In *Dissemination*, Derrida seizes upon the paradox of 'the preface that Hegel *must* write to denounce a preface' (D, p. 11) and observes that the preface – which purports to be a *pro*legomenon to the main text – is more truthfully a *post*face, written after the event. This is the double bind that, Derrida believes, confounds Hegel's philosophy in general. Hegel wants to close off his philosophy as a final, total statement. Yet to close it off, he must add to it, explain it, defend it against its critics, set it in the context of other texts. The Preface to *The Phenomenology* is taken by Derrida as a symbol of Hegel's totalizing desire to sum everything up, to tidy up all the loose ends. The trouble is that one good preface demands another, and so the preface itself becomes yet another loose end that needs tying up.

Second, Derrida points to a time *before* dialectics when something must be given – purely and non-dialectically – in order for dialectics to have something to get started on. The source of dialectics is for Hegel 'the self-surpassing origin' (*der sich aufhebende Ursprung*). But Derrida argues that something must be logically prior to dialectics: 'Before everything, before every determinate being, there is, there was, there will have been the irruptive event of the gift' (G, p. 242).

This second 'deconstruction' of Hegel, although significant in a consideration of Derrida's writing, is not particularly original. Heidegger, at the end of *Being and Time*, had already identified *Geist*'s location within time as a weakness in Hegel's philosophy. What is novel in Derrida's approach is the emphasis on language. It is language which makes total systems impossible. What Hegel dreams of – and this is for Derrida the logocentric dream of Western metaphysics – is a perfectly self-reflexive state which only has an inside, a sort of black hole from which nothing escapes – not even its own picture and name. But Derrida argues that reflection and language always break open this closed circle:

> For what is reflected is split in itself and not only as an addition to itself of its image. The reflection, the image, the double, splits what it doubles. The origin of the speculation becomes a difference. What can look at itself is not one; and the law of addition of the origin to its representation, of the thing to its image, is that one plus one makes at least three. (OG, p. 36)

Something extra is always thrown up in any representation.

So how do Hegel and Nietzsche's deaths of God stand in relation to one another? Interestingly, Heidegger makes the point that there is 'an essential connection' between Nietzsche's death of God and Hegel's (QT, p. 59). Derrida too, is aware of an uncanny affinity between these apparently incommensurable philosophers.

All of Nietzsche's affirmations can be interpreted as anti-Hegelian affirmations . . . As is always the case when one has a great adversary – and Hegel is Nietzsche's great adversary . . . – there will always be moments when the adversaries greatly resemble each other. It would be easy to show that there is a dialectic, a Hegelianism in Nietzsche. (EO, p. 59)

This resemblance is found in the play of forces which makes up not only eternal return and the *Aufhebung*, but also creates Derrida's *différance*. As far as Derrida is concerned, Hegel's shortcoming is that he tries to close off the play of the *Aufhebung*. Hegel's play is a serious adult game, working towards a serious goal. The play of Hegelian dialectic is always *knowing*, everything is always being gathered up into the mind. Nietzsche's play in eternal return is the anarchic play of a child. Hegel, Derrida seems to say, should be more like Nietzsche and release the *Aufhebung* from the constraints of a directional history. 'To be indifferent to the comedy of the *Aufhebung*, as was Hegel,' writes Derrida, 'is to blind oneself to the experience of the sacred, to the heedless sacrifice of presence and meaning' (WD, p. 257).

As for the problem of a horizon – although he never conceives it in these terms – Derrida finds an answer *between* his readings of Hegel and Nietzsche. We could say that Nietzsche and Hegel mutually correct what Derrida sees as their respective shortcomings. On the one hand Nietzsche opens up the enclosed Hegelian infinity to the wider, unrestricted play of eternal return. On the other hand Hegel's *Aufhebung* opens up the closed, dead-and-buried, good-riddance-to-bad-rubbish finality of Nietzsche's 'death of God', illuminating the possibility that the horizon after God's death is not entirely empty, but carries the remains of God, the very least of which is a God-shaped hole. Why must there be a choice, asked Derrida in the late 1980s, 'between a "divine" space and a "Nietzschean" space?' (Psy, p. 642). Derrida's implicit position is that God is both dead and alive: dead in the sense that logocentrism no longer grips Western philosophy with a transparent self-evidence, but alive in the sense that our human horizon is now a problem, undetermined, fluid, infinite, paradoxical, empty. Derrida sees this horizon overrun with language, or more specifically with *writing*, arche-writing, a dimension of *différance* and undecidable meaning.[35] But lest it be thought that this is the end of metaphysics, Derrida reminds us that *différance*, located as it is in the shadow of the death of God, 'remains a metaphysical name' (M, p. 26).

When Derrida talks of the horizon after the death of God, he has to employ characteristically paradoxical language. If a horizon is what is created by the presence of a determinate object, then there is, strictly speaking, no horizon after God's death. The horizon is, as Nietzsche puts it, 'wiped away'. Thus Derrida writes in 'Violence and Metaphysics' about 'the irreducibly common horizon of Death and the Other. The horizon of finitude or the finitude of the horizon' (WD, p. 115). But since Derrida does not believe in the 'simple death' of anything, is there after the death of God any remains of a horizon? It is not easy to determine with any clarity what sort of hazy, ruined boundaries might begin to mark the limits of Derrida's indeterminate realm of *différance*. In 'Living On: Border Lines', Derrida makes some remarks that hint at the problem, as he describes the limits of textual interpretation:

> all those boundaries that form the running border of what we used to call a text, of what we once thought this word could possibly identify: knowledge of the supposed close and opening of a work, the unity of a corpus, the title, the margins, the signatures, the referential zone beyond the frame, etc. What has happened, supposing that it has happened, is a sort of overflow that damages all these sharp-edged boundaries. (Par, p. 127)

After *their* respective deaths of God, both Hegel and Nietzsche leave us not only with images of the circle, but with competing versions of the eternal recurrence of the same. Hegel fills the horizon with the meaningful circle of identity, his recurrence is the permanent return of the Absolute to itself, the completion of a progressive metaphysical history. Nietzsche's circle is the meaningless circle of difference – everything reappears eventually, but without reason. Yet *both* circles form the basis of an affirmation of life. Nietzsche calls Zarathustra's wedding song about eternal recurrence 'The Song of Yes and Amen'. For Hegel, life finds an ideal accommodation with itself in the reflexive circle of *Geist*'s self-consciousness. In his own way Derrida also reaches a point of affirmation, an affirmation of the impossible God. God *survives* his own death in the form of his impossibility.

God: the Impossible Sacred

Does Derrida's concept of God's impossibility do any useful theological work? Does his thinking of divine impossibility provide any resources for thinking the sacred in late modernity? Or is this talk of impossibility and theology just an intellectual game designed to charm a circle of insiders? Such a cynical estimation of Derrida's theology is contradicted by his sustained commitment to theological thinking, 'the constancy of God in [his] life' (Cir, p. 155), which we can see expressed across a range of texts from the very start of his career. The question of divinity appears again and again in his writing both as a philosophical problem and as a personal issue.

One way to reach a positive evaluation of Derrida's argument for God's impossibility is to consider it as the inverse, or deconstruction, of the ontological argument. Derrida effectively argues for the *necessity* of God's impossibility based upon a definition of the sacred as that which refuses all definitive predicates. The divine 'does lend itself to a series of names, but calls for another syntax, and exceeds even the order and structure of predicative discourse. It "is" not and does not say what "is"' (H, p. 74). God is, as Derrida puts it, always *otherwise*, 'tout autre est tout autre'. The application of any predicate, even existence, would 'restrict' the divine. A true conception of God must transcend all predicates, even to the extent of becoming 'impossible'. For Derrida, the sacred can only be 'preserved' through its impossibility, since the conception of a possible God would always be 'restricted' theology, contingent upon prior conditions of linguistic description.

To say that Derrida implicitly 'deconstructs' the logic of the ontological argument is not the same thing as saying that he attempts to 'disprove' it. In fact Derrida's deconstruction would be better thought of as a kind of *proof*, the demonstration of the *possibility* of God's impossibility. We have seen how in considering Husserl and Heidegger Derrida argues (with Heidegger and against Husserl) that 'my death' is *necessarily* non-phenomenal because it cannot *by definition* be experienced as *my* death. Similarly he argues that it is not possible to think the identity of God without contradiction and an overspill of meaning. These are not sceptical arguments – unless we understand scepticism in its original sense as *skepsis*, the attempt to see and understand – but arguments designed to uncover the truth. Deconstruction is not destructive, but is – like the Husserlian *epochē* and Heideggerian *Destruktion* – an attempt to take ideas apart so that the true state of affairs can be seen more clearly. What we *see* in the case of theology is the impossibility of God.

Derrida's conclusion is, for example, quite unlike that of Georges Bataille – another thinker of 'the impossible' – who reaches the atheistic conclusion that 'instead of God there is only the impossible – not God'.[36] For Bataille the overcoming of God is necessary in order to reach 'the impossible', and having reached this point, God is ruled out. The awareness of impossibility is a moment of vital liberation, opening 'consciousness to all that it is possible for it to think'.[37] Derrida's criticism of Bataille (in 'From Restricted to General Economy') is that he does not see that the negation of God implies theological affirmation since 'negativity is always the underside and accomplice of positivity' (WD, p. 259). The realization of what Bataille calls 'the fascinating impossible'[38] is for him the joyous outcome of God's death. But for Derrida – who does not believe in 'the simple death of anything' – the impossibility of God is as much the overture as the closure of theology.

Unlike Anselm, Descartes and the other classic exponents of the ontological argument, Derrida treats 'impossibility' as a meaningful predicate.[39] Kant, in his rejection of the ontological argument, stated that to predicate 'impossibility' of God could only lead to rational gridlock:

> I cannot form the slightest conception of a thing which, when annihilated in thought with all its predicates, leaves behind a contradiction; and contradiction is the only criterion of impossibility, in the sphere of pure *a priori* conceptions.[40]

To an extent one can imagine some agreement between Kant and Derrida on this point, because Kant argues for the necessity of an *idea* of impossibility

('possibility–impossibility' is one of Kant's 'pure conceptions of the understanding' or 'categories' which enable human thought to take place). So Kant at least *thinks* the possibility of a divine predicate of 'impossibility', even if he then steps back from it, declaring it to be a surd. But Derrida effects a more radical overturning of the ontological argument. By contrast with Kant – who tries to show the logical flaw in the proof – Derrida attacks the basic rational grammar of the argument: that God must not contradict himself. For Derrida the self-contradiction of God is not a problem, indeed it may be of the essence of divinity, designating the point where all our thinking of the truth must end: with contradictions, with an excess of meaning for which there is no final language.

Before Derrida, Sartre had used a bastard version of the ontological proof to establish the necessary existence of an objective world beyond the individual's perception of it.[41] Sartre does this by arguing that objects in the world have a trans-phenomenal being beyond their mere appearance to consciousness. Using an inversion of the logic of the classic 'ontological argument', Sartre tries to establish that the being of an object is guaranteed by its *non-being*: 'It is defined as a lack. It is that which escapes, that which by definition will never be given, that which offers itself only in fleeting and successive profiles [appearances].'[42] When we try to grasp the objective world in its *plenitude*, as a series of *presences*, we turn the objectivity of the world into a series of appearances or phenomena available only to the consciousness of the individual subject. In other words, when we look at a thing which is *there* what we really encounter is not the *being* of the thing, but our *perception* of it. So the being of a thing is not guaranteed by its presence, but by its absence, since the absent object cannot be reduced to a subjective perception. The objectivity of a thing is *protected* by its not being there. The similarities with Derrida's argument for God's impossibility are striking and it would be strange if Derrida had not been influenced by Sartre.[43] We see that both thinkers invoke the meaningfulness of apparently empty attributes: 'non-existence' and 'impossibility'. But what concrete meaning can we find in such concepts?

A little further on in *Being and Nothingness*, Sartre gives an everyday example of non-being (what he calls a 'negative fact' or *négatité*). Imagine I enter a busy café intending to encounter Pierre, the waiter, but he is not there. Before me is my perception of the presence of the café.

> It is certain that the café by itself with its patrons, its tables, its booths, its mirrors, its light, its smoky atmosphere, and the sounds of voices, rattling saucers, and footsteps which fill it – the café is a fullness of being.[44]

Similarly, Pierre (wherever he is) is also a 'plenitude of being'. But since I have come to look for Pierre, I look around and each object in the scene is (for me) defined negatively as 'not-Pierre'. Piece by piece the entire scene falls away and becomes a field of absence, indeed a *double nihilation* since both

Pierre and the café are absent. By this example, Sartre was trying to give some 'real' content to the predicate 'non-being'.

For Derrida the idea of impossibility does not simply concern negation but a point of uncertainty between negation and position, life and death. Derrida never offers an explanatory instance of impossibility in quite the way Sartre does. But he does try to illustrate one kind of impossibility in *The Post Card*. *The Post Card* is written as a pastiche of an epistolary novel in order to show by example 'the impossible message' that is at the heart of every effort at communication. Derrida argues that in every communicative act meanings always get lost and distorted. When we receive a communication, the 'decision' about the final meaning of the message is impossible to make. We never can say *just* what we want to say, not even in soliloquy. So communication happens, but perfect communication is always impossible. Moreover, we experience this impossibility not as an absence, but as a fundamental undecidability or uncertainty of meaning. 'Impossibility' is not, therefore, simply a concept, but a state of affairs that induces very real human feelings of frustration, longing, ambivalence, humour, anxiety.

What is particularly interesting in Sartre's example is the way in which *both* the real absence of Pierre *and my expectation* of seeing him generate the experience of nihilation. The *desire* to see Pierre is crucial. For Derrida, too, the experience of the divine impossibility is bound up with feelings of desire and love. The reality of God's impossibility is not a free-standing 'fact' that I merely take note of as a passive observer. An awareness of God's impossibility is caught up with my concern *for* God. The experience of impossibility surfaces in one's search for the truth, out of one's love for the truth. We do not have to read far in Derrida's writing to find him speaking of love of the truth and of desire as a crucial dynamic in philosophy. The 'Envois' section of *The Post Card* is the most extended example, but the 'devotional' tone in Derrida's philosophy is very evident also in *Memoirs for the Blind* and 'Circumfession'.

In the decades following *The Post Card* we can see a development in Derrida's 'devotional' response to divine impossibility. In the 1970s – in texts such as *Glas* – Derrida writes about a metaphysical 'mourning' that sets in after the realization of God's impossibility. In *Glas*, Derrida is no doubt influenced by Hegel's comments about a moment of mourning that must follow the 'speculative' death of God. The dead God leaves not just a conceptual problem, but an emotional legacy of loss. In his earlier writing, Derrida's theological mood is one of brooding grief, melancholic reflections in the twilight of the gods. The impossibility of God appears to close off, for Derrida, the possibility of any absolute affirmation or beatitude. But this mood noticeably shifts over the years. Any grief conceals positive and joyous feelings of attachment, if not love, for the lost object. And so we see that in later texts – 'Circumfession' for example – Derrida writes more positively about the love of God, adopting in his own way Augustine's question 'what do I love, when I love God?', which he translates as 'what do I love, whom do

I love, that I love above all?' (Cir, p. 122). Later he cites God (and death) as the most 'impossible' but 'faithful' objects of love.

God's impossibility acts therefore not to deaden religious feeling or to close down theological discussion but to draw it out. The desertification of the divine works as a vacuum to draw out a messianic longing for the coming of God, for the arrival of truth and the institution of justice. It is an additional feature of God's impossibility that there will be no messianic arrival, that the *parousia* is infinitely and structurally delayed (deferred). The religion of God's impossibility, which John Caputo has described at length in *The Prayers and Tears of Jacques Derrida*, is stuck in an unresolved state of longing, an eternal Advent with no possibility of Christmas. This religion of God's impossibility, moreover, takes the form of a bleak fideism, where faith has become entirely performative, an act of abstract hope whose object remains 'undecided'.

'Faith' has been a significant theme in Derrida's writing since *The Post Card* in the 1970s, but is articulated most clearly in his essay 'Faith and Knowledge' (1996). Derrida uses the idea of faith to bridge the gap between his insistence that deconstruction is committed to disclosing the 'truth' and his assertion that the truth cannot be 'decided'. Derrida's commitment to truth takes the form of faith, not a specifically religious mode of faith, but a general faculty of faith in communication with the other and testimony in general. For Derrida every act of communication takes place not in the security of *knowing* that communication will work, but in *faith* that it will. So Derrida speaks of 'the appeal of faith that inhabits every act of language and every address to the other' (FK, p. 18). The messages in *The Post Card* are offered to the addressee (and to the reader) in faith. However scrupulous we are in speaking or writing, argues Derrida, the efficacy of communication can never be assured. Every act of communication is an act of faith, and the best we do is to act in *good* faith. 'Good faith,' says Derrida, is 'the condition of testimony' (FK, p. 59).[45]

It is reasonable to question whether there is any significance to an act of faith that is unfocused and non-specific. Recalling Husserl's critique of empty consciousness, we may ask whether faith, like consciousness, should not be intentional, that is to say faith *in* something. The point, surely, is that out of uncertainty faith makes a commitment to one thing as opposed to all others: it is a declaration of partiality. In making our commitment to the object of faith we surely must to some extent *decide* what it is. If we say that the object of faith remains *undecided*, does this not reduce faith to an empty attitude, a posture or performance that has no real content? Would this not be a version of the religious nihilism that Nietzsche so despised, where the 'last men' continue to practise Christianity even though God has ceased to hold any meaning for them?

This criticism would only apply if Derrida were to equate 'undecidability' with emptiness, which he does not. When Derrida says that truth cannot be decided, he does not mean that no decisions can be taken with regard to truth. On the contrary, the truth *must* always be decided.[46] But the undecidability of truth means that the question of truth never gets closed off, that our decisions with respect to the truth are never final. The truth has not been decided in advance in such a way that we merely have to stand in thrall to it. The truth (the God) in which Derrida has faith is clear enough from his writing: against the traditions of logocentrism his truth is perspectival and plural: 'God sees from your side and from mine at once, as absolute third; and so *there* where he is not there, he is there; *there* where he is not there, is his place' (TS, p. 71). The question of truth constantly calls for decisions, but these decisions – precisely because of their partiality – can never master the truth. It is in this sense that both truth and God remain undecided.

Having said this, Derrida's faith in God is structurally restricted to some extent by the anti-metaphysical trajectory of deconstruction. The thinking of the impossible God emerges out of Derrida's critique of the metaphysics of presence and heads away from metaphysical conceptions of God towards a non-metaphysical theology. The possible forms of the impossible God do not include the existence of God as a 'real presence', or an agent able to act in human affairs. The simple assertion of God's reality is excluded by the 'logic' of his impossibility, indeed the argument for God's impossibility is a way of protecting God from the restrictions of realist classification.

Christianity and the Impossible God

The full extent to which this non-real, impossible God provides any other resources for a Christian (or any other) theology will have to be the subject for another book. However, we may at least indicate two areas of possibility: deconstruction as idoloclasm, and deconstruction and divine paradox. Christian theology has, since the earliest times, pushed language and meaning to their limits in the search for an adequate expression of divinity. The repetition of dogmatic credal formulas is only one aspect of Christian testimony. Christian theology also has a history of inventiveness – at times a ruthless inventiveness – in the quest for a language of witness to God. We do not have to look far – even in the New Testament – to find the Christian God spoken of as self-emptying, paradoxical, beyond human calculus, tautologous, secret/hidden and invisible. Given this context, it would be surprising if there were no points of dialogue between Derrida's impossible divinity and the Christian God.

Deconstruction as Idoloclasm

We have seen that deconstruction takes place in the name of truth, but of truth beyond the restrictions of logocentrism – a truth that allows for the non-systematic, the playful, the contradictory, the supplementary, the non-rational, the non-real, the undecidable and what is hidden or secret. We could say – although Derrida doesn't put it this way – that deconstruction is a way of thinking that seeks to *protect* the truth against restricted description. In this respect deconstruction is allied to Adorno's 'negative dialectic', which attacks all truth-claims – even its own. A more profound alliance is to be found outside philosophy: theological alliance here between Derrida and the idoloclastic arguments of the Old Testament prophets, particularly Deutero-Isaiah where the 'living God' exceeds all restricted representation. The prophetic task is to 'deconstruct' the idols: 'To whom can you compare God? What image can you contrive of him?' (Isaiah 40:18). This 'deconstruction' leaves space for the living God to enjoy freedom of self-representation, liberated from the clutter of misleading or pernicious depictions of the divine.

Jean-Luc Marion (*God without Being*) uses a 'deconstructive' critique of idolatry as the starting-point for a theology of Christ as the 'icon of the invisible God' (1 Corinthinans 1:15). The idol stands for the entire order of restricted theology, that is, any attempt to reduce the divine to an *image*, something *visible*. Only the *invisibility* (*aoratos*) of God can protect the divine against the imaginations of idolatry. Marion contrasts the idol (which subjects 'the divine to the measure of a human gaze') (*God without Being*, p. 14), with the icon (which *preserves* the invisibility of the invisible *as such*). Invisibility is not the same thing as 'not-visible' or 'not-yet-visible'; it is rather the dimension of the non-visible. Whereas the 'not-visible' and the 'not-yet-visible' are really just versions of the visible (the visible blocked by obstacles of place and time), the invisible (or non-visible) is the *other* of visibility. The idol and the icon belong to two separate orders of phenomenology: the idol seeks to show by making visible; the icon seeks to show the invisible *as* invisible.

> Thus the icon shows, strictly speaking, nothing ... The icon summons the gaze to surpass itself by never freezing upon the visible ... The gaze can never rest or settle if it looks on an icon ... the icon makes visible only by giving rise to an infinite gaze.[47]

To make graphic the distinction between idol and icon, Marion writes the word God in two ways: first, as 'God' (within speech marks) – God made visible as an idol; second, as God (superimposed with the cross of St Andrew) – God disclosed iconically as invisible.

In a similar vein, Kevin Vanhoozer credits deconstruction with the virtue of 'checking interpretive pride' by showing that language sets limits to interpretive competence.[48] Deconstruction shows that final knowledge and perfect communication are not possible and that it is arrogant to claim that we have achieved finality in theological interpretation. Although deconstruction serves a useful theological function in this respect, Vanhoozer criticizes Derrida for failing to provide any basis for positive theological interpretation, leaving us isolated in theological scepticism. In the end, for all his talk of the 'other', Derrida fails, in Vanhoozer's estimation, to respond properly to the otherness of the author and his agency.[49]

Vanhoozer's criticism chimes with that of Habermas (see p. 11 above), who disparages the failure of deconstruction to discriminate between interpretations, letting 'the refuse heap of interpretations, which it wants to clear away to get at the buried foundations, mount even higher'.[50] A vigilance against idolatrous interpretation is all very well, Habermas argues, but at what point does it *positively* reveal its commitment to *the truth against which* the pile of discarded graven images has been found lacking? Without such a commitment, Habermas judges deconstruction to be an empty mysticism that has effectively abandoned any serious obligation to truth and (as Habermas puts it) to philosophical 'problem solving'. In Habermas's estimation deconstruction is 'a negative extremism', a kind of philosophical anarchism that takes place in the name of truth, but never ventures to say what this truth is. This criticism carries a certain weight: deconstruction is quite clearly open to such a critique and in the foregoing discussion of the negative procedures of deconstruction (pp. 130–134) the paradoxes inherent in a thoroughgoing idoloclastic critique have been explored.

However, as we have now elaborated at some length, Derrida does move *through* negation positively to assert 'the impossible' and the 'impossible God'. God's impossibility is a necessary feature of his 'wholly otherness', beyond all representation and projection. Our *distance* from the other, our *refusal to define* the other in this or that image, *preserves* God's status as wholly other. Thinking of God in this way implies a humility before God, closing off all claims to 'have God on one's side' and confounding all pretensions to divine knowledge. We have seen in *The Gift of Death* (pp. 107–110) how for Derrida the 'otherness of the other' opens the space of human ethics. Similarly, the otherness of God opens the space for theology.

So God's impossibility takes us beyond the merely negative function of idoloclasm. This is because deconstruction harbours a range of positive values. In protecting the divine from theological *hubris*, deconstruction also protects against 'violence' in the name of God. Faith in God's impossibility, his messianic failure, is a defence against totalitarianism and fundamentalism. There can be no dogma of the impossible God, because the impossible, undecided God subverts all absolutist claims. The impossible God can never be used to justify tyranny, oppression or racism. Furthermore, the impossible God implies – but without the coercion of divine law – the necessity of an ethic of love, hospitality, freedom, forgiveness and openness. These ethical themes – which were central to Derrida's writings in the 1990s – are hardly strange to Christianity, which values humility, turning the other cheek, respect for the other and love of one's enemies. But Christianity does not share Derrida's anxiety about making positive theological statements. Once the idols have been smashed, Christian theology is happy to develop positive theological discourses. Derrida is so fearful of reinstating idols that he constantly infuses his ethics and theology with self-deconstructing critique:

friendship always involves alienation, hospitality always involves hostility, forgiveness always involves relations of power, and so on. Derrida's miscalculation perhaps is that deconstruction can also become an idol, whose graven image restricts the divine to self-denying ordinances.

Deconstruction and Paradox

In ordinary language the word paradox is now simply another way of speaking of logical contradiction, absurdity or stumbling blocks in our thinking. However, in its original Greek sense, paradox meant something rather different: *paradoxa* were those things that went against expectations, which were incredible, marvellous and admirable. The *paradoxalogia* were tales of wonder, and St Luke uses the term to describe the works of Jesus: 'amazement seized them all, and they glorified God and were filled with awe saying, "we have seen strange things (*paradoxa*) today"' (Luke 5:26).

At the heart of Christian theology there is a paradox of this kind which is not a problem for Christians but a source of wonder and marvel: the paradox of the Incarnation, the God-man, one person with two natures. The human/ divine contradiction of the Incarnation is not supposed to be 'explained away' by Christian theology, but celebrated. The very *tension* between the divinity and humanity of Christ is the essence of its glory, and attempts to eliminate the paradox – by a Docetic reduction of Christ to divinity, or an Arian reduction of Christ to humanity – have been dismissed as heresy. In short, the apparent *impossibility* of the Incarnation is built into orthodox Christian theology. This orthodoxy took its clearest (or at least most acceptable) form in the Chalcedonian Definition, which Dietrich Bonhoeffer has described in the following terms:

> What did the formula of Chalcedon say? It stated the a priori impossibility and impermissibility of taking the divinity and humanity in Jesus Christ side by side or together as a relationship of objectifiable entities. Simple negotiations remain. No positive pattern of thought is left to explain what happens in the God-man Jesus Christ. Thus the mystery is left as a mystery and must be left as a mystery and must be understood as such. Access is reserved solely for faith. All thought forms are cut short.[51]

However, the 'impossibility' of the two natures of Christ was subsumed under the doctrine of God's simplicity which asserted (alongside the incommensurability of divinity and humanity) the single substance of God: 'without confusion, without change, without division, without separation'. This apparent solution in fact only set up a further 'impossible' relationship between an absolute divine incommensurability and an absolute divine unity.

One orthodox response to this paradox is, as Bonhoeffer says, to declare the incarnation a mystery. The appeal to mystery, however, can be a form of laziness, absolving theology from the responsibility to explain and Derrida eschews it. Rather than throwing up his hands and saying 'It's a mystery!', Derrida makes repeated attempts to explain 'impossibility', in particular in relation to the phenomenon of 'my death'. It is this discussion of the impossible which is perhaps of use to Christian theology.

Another response to the Chalcedonian paradox was contained in Karl Barth's 'dialectical theology', which saw Christ's 'impossible possibility' as the product of the gap between human history and divine reality. But as Paul Tillich points out, Barth only understands the divine to be impossible from the human perspective.[52] God's 'impossibility' therefore really only points to the poverty of human theology and not the divine nature itself. Tillich's contention is that Barth's celebration of theological paradoxes is in fact a non-paradoxical affirmation of the saying that 'all things are possible with God' (Mark 10:27). Bonhoeffer, by contrast, sees impossibility as the essence of God. For Bonhoeffer the point of Christological impossibility is to generate radical human self-questioning. The Anglican theologian Rowan Williams has said something in a similar spirit: that theological paradoxes function to *sustain* theology:

> We utter paradoxes not to mystify or avoid problems, but precisely to stop ourselves making things easy by pretending that some awkward or odd feature of our perception isn't really there. We speak in paradoxes because we have to speak in a way that keeps a question alive.[53]

Generally, however, ecclesiastical theologians have been reluctant to think positively about the category of 'impossibility' itself and shy away from asking whether the attribution of 'impossibility' actually says something about God. It is here, perhaps, that deconstruction has a role to play, since it is clearly not *irrelevant* for Christian theology to consider the status of 'impossibility' with respect to God.

One of the challenges that Derrida faces whenever he tackles the theme of impossibility is how to *represent* the impossible. What name should he give the impossible God? How is he to imagine or describe God? How should he write the word God so that the divine impossibility is explicit? In various texts and at various times Derrida offers a series of possible figures or motifs which may begin to provide a title or crest for the impossible state between life and death, the life of God and his death. Some of the motifs are more or less to be expected, such as that of the phoenix (EO, p. 26 / C, p. 37), the tomb, or, in *Margins* and *Glas*, the image of the pyramid, which is for Hegel a metonym for the signifier and is 'the monument-of-life-in-death, the monument-of-death-in-life, the sepulchre of a soul or of an embalmed proper body' (M, p. 83 / G, p. 240). In *Glas*, too, Derrida cites the image of the sacrificial elements at the Last Supper as another death/life emblem (G, pp. 71–2). In *Dissemination*, Derrida introduces the equivocal *pharmakon*, the emblem of writing, the death-dealing/life-giving drug that opens up the 'play' of philosophy's discourse. Elsewhere in the same volume, the Egyptian 'god of resurrection' is concerned with 'death as repetition of life, and life as a rehearsal for death, in the awakening of life in the recommencement of death (D, p. 93). In '+ R' in *The Truth in Painting*, Derrida offers the image of 'the fish between life and death, still hanging on the hook' (TP, p. 159). [54] In *Cinders* the cinders themselves are 'the best paradigm of the trace', which is beyond the life/death distinction (C, p. 43). In a range of imagery about 'ghosts', Derrida opens up a middle realm between life and death, the world of the *diamonion*, the 'undead' or the 'living dead', an abstract 'function' or 'phantom', as Derrida puts it, 'moving between life and death' (D, p. 325). Most recently, in *Specters of Marx*, Derrida calls this dimension an 'element neither living nor dead ... *hauntology*. We will take this category to be irreducible, and first of all to everything it makes possible: ontology, theology, positive or negative onto-theology' (SM, p. 51). In *Given Time* and *The Gift of Death* Derrida's notion of 'the gift' stands beyond the order of pure life or death (GT, p. 102).

However, the most prolific image used by Derrida is a potentially religious one, that of the cross: the sign of the chiasmus, chi or *X* as a way of indicating the indeterminacy of 'life–death': '*X* is the name of the sculptor, of he who, *par excellence*, freezes life-death' (Par, p. 209). It is to this motif that we now turn by way of a conclusion to this book.

Notes

1   M.C. Taylor, 'nO nOt nO', in H. Coward and T. Foshay, eds, *Derrida and Negative Theology* (State University of New York Press, Albany, 1992), p. 194.
2   *The Prayers and Tears of Jacques Derrida* (Indiana University Press, Bloomington, 1997), pp. 1–61.
3   K. Hart, *The Trespass of the Sign: Deconstruction, Theology and Philosophy* (Cambridge University Press, Cambridge, 1989), p. 269.
4   Ibid., p. 95.
5   D. Cupitt, *Creation out of Nothing* (SCM Press, London, 1990), p. 12.
6   R. Gasché, *The Tain of the Mirror: Derrida and the Philosophy of Reflection* (Harvard University Press, Cambridge, 1986), pp. 275f.
7   See particularly 'The Conflict of Faculties', in M. Riffaterre, ed, *Languages of Knowledge and of Inquiry* (Columbia University Press, New York, 1982).
8   See also ON, p. 20 where Derrida says that the equation of deconstruction with critique is a 'dogmatic naïvety'.
9   See, for example, M, pp. 6 and 282; WD, pp. 146, 271 and 297; Psy, pp. 390 and 540; D, p. 5; ON, pp. 67–9.
10 Derrida has not written extensively on Kant. His main contributions in this area are the essays 'Parergon', 'Of an Apocalyptic Tone' and 'Faith and Knowledge'.
11 Derrida's deconstruction of apophatic discourse revives the historical and rhetorical meaning of apophasis as *irony*. As J. Smith defines it in his *Mystery of Rhetoric* (1657), 'Apophasis ... a kind of an Irony, whereby we deny that which we especially say or doe.'
13 The abandonment Derrida refers to takes a number of forms – whether it is 'the specific kind of forgetting' which is 'essential for the temporality of *Dasein*'; or the 'forsakenness' (*Verlassenheit*) with which *Dasein* is 'abandoned' (*Überlassen*) to itself and thereby able to recognize itself; or the 'thrownness into death' which 'unveils the nullity by which *Dasein*, in its very *basis*, is defined' (BT, pp. 405, 322 and 356).

13 A comment by Derrida in an interview with R. Kearney in R. Kearney, ed., *Dialogues with Contemporary Continental Thinkers* (Manchester University Press, Manchester, 1984), p. 123.

14 In fact Derrida is very *interested* in the 'death of God' in a very specific sense which he sets out in his essay on Artaud in *Writing and Difference*. See particularly WD, pp. 184 and 326, n. 29.

15 F. Nietzsche, *The Birth of Tragedy*, tr. S. Whiteside (Penguin, London, 1993), §23, p. 109.

16 F. Nietzsche, *Untimely Meditations*, tr. R.J. Hollingdale (Cambridge University Press, Cambridge, 1983), §1, p. 63.

17 Nietzsche connects the balance of the Apollonian and Dionysian with eternal return in *The Will to Power*, tr. W. Kauffman and R. Hollingdale (Vintage, New York, 1968), §1050, p. 539.

18 In the sections before the parable of the madman, Nietzsche says that a 'horizon' is essential to human health (*The Gay Science*, tr. W. Kauffman, Vintage, New York, 1974, §120, p. 177).

19 Nietzsche, *The Gay Science*, §108, p. 167.

20 F. Nietzsche, *Thus Spoke Zarathustra*, tr. R. Hollingdale (Penguin, London, 1969), 'Zarathustra's Prologue', §3, p. 41.

21 Nietzsche, *The Gay Science*, §124, p. 180; see also §283, p. 228, 'Send your ships into uncharted seas'; §289, pp. 231f. and §291, p. 233.

22 Ibid., p. 371.

23 Ibid., p. 280.

24 Nietzsche, *Thus Spoke Zarathustra*, p. 244.

25 'To the paralyzing sense of general disintegration and incompleteness, I opposed the eternal recurrence' (Nietzsche, *The Will to Power*, §417, p. 224); and later: 'In place of "metaphysics" and religion, the theory of eternal recurrence' (§462, p. 255).

26 Nietzsche, *Thus Spoke Zarathustra*, 'The Old and New Law-Tables', §19, p. 225.

27 Nietzsche, *The Will to Power*, § 1067, pp. 549f.

28 Hegel refers to Luther's hymn '*O Traurigkeit, O Herzeleid*', which says 'God himself is dead'. *Lectures on the Philosophy of Religion* (1827), tr. R.F. Brown et al. (University of California Press, Berkeley, 1988), p. 468.

29 G. Hegel, *Phenomenology of Spirit*, tr. A.V. Miller (Oxford University Press, Oxford, 1977), §781, p. 473.

30 Ibid., pp. 475f.

31 Ibid., §32, p. 19.

32 Ibid., §802f., p. 488: 'Until Spirit has completed itself *in itself*, until it has completed itself as world-Spirit, it cannot reach its consummation as *self-conscious* Spirit ... The movement of carrying forward the form of its self-knowledge is the labour which it accomplishes as actual History.'

33 A. Kojève, *Introduction to the Reading of Hegel*, tr. J.H. Nichols (Basic Books, New York, 1960), p. 259.

34 It may be objected that Hegel's system is not so much circular as triangular or trinitarian. It is significant that in *Glas* Derrida sees the triangle as essentially circular in nature, a figure which is all-inclusive and returns to itself. Thus he refers to Hegel's system as 'a triangulo-circular structure' (G, p. 227).

35 See the beginning of *Of Grammatology*: 'In spite of itself ... a historico-metaphysical epoch must finally determine as language the totality of its problematic horizon' (OG, p. 6).

36 G. Bataille, *On Nietzsche* (Athlone, London, 1992), p. 115.

37 G. Bataille, *Theory of Religion* (Zone, New York 1992), p. 10.

38 Bataille, *On Nietzsche*, p. 106.

39 Spinoza is perhaps the least remote from Derrida in his controversial insistence upon an infinite number of divine attributes. This implies that God possesses an attribute of impossibility in the sense that his nature is impossible finally to determine.

40 Kant, *Critique of Pure Reason*, II, II, III, V.
41 Jean-Paul Sartre, *Being and Nothingness* tr. H. Barnes (Routledge, London, 1989), pp. xxxvi–xxxviii.
42 Ibid., p. xxxvii.
43 Christina Howells has argued that Derrida is extensively indebted to Sartre, although Derrida has not always appeared ready to acknowledge this debt. Christina Howells, *Derrida: Deconstruction from Phenomenology to Ethics* (Polity, London, 1998).
44 Sartre, *Being and Nothingness*, p. 9.
45 See GD, pp. 79f. and PF, pp. 14–16.
46 See PF, p. 19. 'The possibilization of the impossible possible must remain at one and the same time as undecidable – and therefore as decisive – as the future itself.'
47 J-L. Marion, *God Without Being* (University of Chicago Press, Chicago, 1991), p. 18.
48 K. Vanhoozer, *Is there a Meaning in this Text?* (Apollos, Leicester, 1998), p. 464.
49 From a secular quarter, Mark Bevir has offered a similar critique of Derrida's scepticism. Bevir argues that we can secure philosophy on the intention of human agents, since at any given moment there is only one intention to any given action: *The Logic of the History of Ideas* (Cambridge University Press, Cambridge, 1999).
50 J. Habermas, *The Philosophical Discourse of Modernity* (Polity, Oxford, 1997), p. 183.
51 Dietrich Bonhoeffer, *Christology* (Collins, London, 1966), p. 91.
52 Paul Tillich, 'What is Wrong With Dialectic Theology?', *The Journal of Theology* (1935), pp. 127–45.
53 Rowan Williams, *Open to Judgement* (Darton, Longman and Todd, London, 1994), p. 119.
54 In 'Survivre' Derrida links this image directly with the figure of the chi (Par, p. 209). For a variation on this image, see also WD, p. 298.

Chapter 6

God, this Subject, Entity, or *X*

the stumbling block (skandalon) of the Cross . . .
Galatians 5:11

The cross is nearer in chiasmus
Than in the theme 'cross'.
Paul Celan

Each X, each name, and each name of God
can become the example of other substitutable Xs.
(ON, p. 76)

This X of ours is not precisely this experience, but akin to this one and the
opposite of that other. Cannot you realise for yourself what it is? In other words
our X cannot, strictly speaking, be taught, it can only be evoked, awakened in
the mind; as everything that comes 'of the spirit' must be awakened.
(Rudolf Otto, *The Idea of Holy*)

God himself is, and appears as what he is,
within difference, that is to say as difference
and within dissimulation.
(WD, p. 74)

God, this subject, entity, or X . . .
(GD, p.108)

Let us briefly review the journey taken so far by this book. The introductory chapter attempted to establish the necessity of a theme in Derrida: a theme of death. Despite Derrida's efforts to escape conventional thematics, the theme of death appears as (among other things) the by-product of his resistance to this thematization. If one keeps asserting that there is no theme – only aporia, *différance*, blank – this sooner or later becomes one's theme. This first chapter also elaborated the theme of death as a field or *resemblement* of related metaphors: absence, negation, aporia, and so on.

The chosen path of investigation has been Derrida's writing on Husserl and Heidegger. This is because a key issue at stake is the question of phenomenality or revelation – how anything ever shows itself as an object of human cognition. For Derrida, the assumption of a perfect phenomenality is the kernel of Western metaphysics, what Levinas calls a metaphysics of 'light' in which metaphors of vision predominate. The possibility of phenomenality is also a precondition for religious revelation. Death challenges the security of any absolute phenomenality by pointing to the aporia underlying all life and consciousness. Death, the presumed end of consciousness, is – as Levinas and Heidegger have both famously pointed out – the non-phenomenal moment *par excellence*. But a paradox arises. The non-phenomenal moment – if it is to be spoken of at all – must make itself phenomenal, just as anti-thematics must become thematic. So the theme of death incorporates a necessary gesture of self-negation.

The second chapter tackled Derrida's major writing on Husserl to see how the theology of the theme of death comes into focus out of the deconstruction of Husserl's transcendental phenomenology. Derrida's purpose is to show that consciousness does not constitute a moment of self-certainty but a moment of temporal and interpersonal uncertainty. It is not life or 'living presence' that constitutes the foundational experience of the transcendental ego but an experience of death, loss and absence: the step of time which constantly robs the ego of its living moments, and the faces of other isolated egos with whom I can find no living connection.

Chapters 3 and 4 attempted to show how Derrida both inherits and deconstructs Heidegger's philosophy. Heidegger is shown to have reconfigured the question of phenomenality as the question of being, driving a path through mere conscious phenomenality to a phenomenality that can only be thought and felt through the business of existence. Derrida in his turn still finds Heidegger frustratingly metaphysical and seeks to step behind Being to uncover a primal difference, *différance*, which is irreducible and behind which there are no earlier differences or identities. This *différance* does not appear as such, rather it constitutes the undecidability of what does appear for us – including the undecidability of life itself. Thus life is always life-death, life intersected with its own erasure.

The fifth chapter tried to determine more precisely the nature of Derrida's theology, positioning it in relation to negative theology and the so-called 'death of God'. Both negative theology and the death of God are forms of theological non-phenomenality: in the first, God appears by not appearing; in the second, God disappears. In both cases, Derrida argues against the possibility of pure negation or absolute theological non-phenomenality, claiming that negative theology harbours a presupposed super-theology and that the death of God is never fully accomplished because it leaves behind a theological remainder, at the very least an evacuated theological space. So the theme of death does not necessarily demonstrate the end of theology, but cross-hatches a possible theological site between negative and positive theology and between the death and the life of God: the space of an impossible God who inspires religious faith, love and an ethic of radical openness to 'the other'.

The final task of this study is to attempt to show how Derrida indicates or signifies this impossibility. By what image or inscription does Derrida indicate the point where phenomenality becomes an impossible possibility, or the zone in which God becomes both a possibility and an impossibility?

Earlier chapters have claimed a special significance for the image of the chi, *X* or chiasmus – a saltire cross. This concluding chapter will attempt to examine the significance of this motif in Derrida's text.[1]

Although Derrida never thematizes the chiasmus as such, the chi figure is announced formally in *Dissemination* as a 'quick, thematic diagram of dissemination' (D, p. 44). Later, in *Positions*, Derrida begins to explain its significance:

> The form of the chiasm, of the X, interests me a great deal, not as the symbol of the unknown, but because there is in it ... a kind of fork (the series *crossroads*, *quadrifurcum*, *grid*, *trellis*, *key*, etc) that is, moreover, unequal, one of the points extending its range further than the other: this is the figure of the double gesture, the intersection. (P, p. 70)

This 'fork' shows the disseminal property of language, which constantly breaks up the possibility of gathering meaning into a self-contained moment of presence. The chiasmus indicates that everything is secondary, disaggregated, spilling out of the encircling, or encyclopaedic, arms of even the most ambitious gathering. 'Dissemination interrupts the circulation that transforms into an origin what is actually an after-effect of meaning' (D, p. 21). The chiasmus is an attempt at the pure grapheme, a silent writing devoid of meaning, the 'exemplary supplement'.

It is significant that the chiasmus is a staunchly ungathered, non-circular figure, because the key to understanding the chiasmus in Derrida's writing is the way in which he deploys it as the 'other' of the circle. In *Parages* Derrida argues that the 'closure of metaphysics, above all, is not a circle surrounding a homogeneous field ... The limit has the form of always different faults, of fissures whose mark or scar is borne by all the texts of philosophy' (P, pp. 56–7). In 'The Double Session' Derrida also makes reference to a sketching of the closure of metaphysics 'not as a border enclosing some homogeneous space but according to a noncircular, entirely *other* figure' (italics added). This 'other figure' appears

> whenever any writing both marks and goes back over its mark with an undecidable stroke. This double mark escapes the pertinence or authority of truth: it does not overturn it but rather inscribes it within its play as one of its functions or parts. This displacement does not take place, has not taken place once, as an *event*. It does not occupy a simple place. It does not take place in writing. This dis-location (is what) writes/is written. (D, p. 194)

In *Glas*, most notably, Derrida tries to deconstruct what he sees as the circular structure of Hegelian thought.[2] Hegel manages to *include* the cross and crucifixion within the logic of *Geist*'s circular return to itself. Derrida describes this as the 'simultaneous effects of chiasm(us) and circle, of encircled chiasm(us)' (G, p. 189) – in other words difference, division, diremption are internal to the circular unity of Hegel's totality. Derrida identifies this unity as 'life': 'a relation of living to living, emanation lets itself be worked (over) by discontinuity, division, negativity. Life and division go together, and with them sight, since the dehiscence of the living being is just what opens it to the light and thus to the truth' (G, p. 77). By contrast, the chiasmus is deathly. Derrida contrasts 'the curve, roundness, the curvilinear which can be produced only by the living spirit' with the 'cold, formal, and death-dealing ... angular forms' which try to cut across what he sees as the 'living' circular form of Hegel's philosophy (ibid., p. 249). Perhaps Derrida's deconstruction of Hegel could be described, poetically, as the attempt to superimpose the chiasmus on the circle.

However, it is not Hegel's circle in particular that the chiasmus crosses through, but the circle *per se*, in so far as it stands for the theological horizon of Western metaphysics since Plato.[3] In 'White Mythology', Derrida argues that the 'dream' of Western philosophy finds its badge in the image of the circle as Plato's sun, which is

> a specular circle, a return to itself without loss of meaning, without irreversible expenditure. This return to itself – this interiorization – of the sun has marked not only Platonic, Aristotelian, Cartesian, and other kinds of discourse, not only the science of logic as the circle of circles, but also by the same token the man of metaphysics. (M, p. 269)

Derrida elsewhere says that philosophy's self-representation in the form of circular or linear closure is 'the theme I have emphasized most' (Psy, p. 72). It is this circle, Derrida argues, which breaks at the point of its self-representation or reflection. At this point the interminable labyrinth of language opens up never to be closed, 'traverses its own field, endlessly displaces its closure, breaks its line, opens its circle' (M, p. 271). It would not be difficult to show how throughout his writing Derrida consistently opposes the closed, self-sufficiency of the circle with the crossed figure of the chi.[4] Indeed, since the circle represents metaphysics, it would also not be hard to argue that the chi functions as an image of deconstruction itself.

In '+R', Derrida teasingly points out that there is, in Plato, a more primordial figure than that of the circle. He cites the passage about creation in the *Timaeus*:

> Having thus obtained the systasis, he split it in two from one end to the other with a lengthwise slit; he fixed these two bands across one another at the centre, in the form of an X; then he plied them to make a circle of each one and joined up all the ends opposite the crossing point ... He adjudged the movement of the outside circle to the nature of the Same, and that of the inside circle to the nature of the Other. (TP, p. 166)

This chi, which grants the structure of the circle is also, for Derrida, the emblem of the Platonic *khora*:

With *khora* itself/herself, if one could at all speak thus about this X (x or khi) which must not have any proper determination, sensible or intelligible, material or formal, and therefore must not have any identity of its/her own, must not be identical with herself/itself. (ON, p. 99)

Khora is atopical, a dis-place(ment), nowhere, the *mise en abyme*, the desert, 'an abyss without bottom or surface, an absolute impassability (neither life nor death)' (ibid., p. 7). But even with such an 'open' concept Derrida is cautious, forbidding the use of the definite article – 'the definite article presupposes the existence of a thing' (ibid., p. 96) – and asserting, along with Plato, that '*khora* is neither sensible nor intelligible'. Yet Derrida sees the *khora*, or desert, conceived as a dimension of play. The vacation, kenosis, desertion or *Gelassenheit* of the *khora* 'opens up the play of God (of God and with God, of God with self and with creation): it opens a passion to the enjoyment of God ... *desert* is the other name, if not the proper place of desire' (ibid., pp. 79–80). To grasp the notion of *khora*, one must let go of God. This is the gesture of *Gelassenheit*. But the letting go is also a grasping, or yearning for God (ibid., p. 84). The logic of this grasping-by-letting-go is gratuitous, belonging to the economy of sacrifice, the occasion of the gift. This is what Derrida elsewhere calls the duplicity of 'l'arrêt de mort', the death sentence which stops death. In *khora*, God crosses himself in a double gesture of sacrilege and consecration.[5]

Chi, 'the figure of the double gesture', remains structurally intersected, structurally self-contradicted, between negative and positive strokes, concealment and revelation, cancellation and affirmation. The attempt to 'practise impossibility', Derrida says, will combine 'bringing to light' with 'nullification' and 'the workings of a certain textual zero' (D, p. 296). Following Blanchot, Derrida summarizes this paradox of chi in the formula, 'X without X'.

Thus we see on the one hand in Derrida's text the negative application of chi: *X* is the signifier which has no signified, the signifier of the absent presence, of the double bind, of the erased 'I' or subject. *X* signals the blind spot, the non-phenomenon, and also blind faith. *X* marks an error, the failure to produce the true answer. *X* is what one writes when one does not know what word to write, or whose name to write. *X* is the unknown factor, the mark of an ownership or propriety which is unattributable. As the crossing-through of propriety, *X* is a sign of both the law of transgression and the transgression of law. *X* indicates a secret inscription/encryption, a secret name or location, a privacy that nevertheless makes its privacy public. *X* is that which cannot be determined but which must nevertheless be indicated. *X* is that which attempts to 'signify nothing': the sign of the phenomenon of non-phenomenality. *X* is also pre-eminently the crossing-through of death and erasure. *X* therefore, is a gesture of exemplary denial and as such, a possible sign of a negative theology:

> Every time I say: X is neither this nor that, neither the contrary of this nor that, neither the simple neutralization of this nor that with which it has nothing in common, being absolutely heterogeneous to or incommensurable with them, I would start to speak of God. (H, p. 76)

Yet for all this, *X* is also the very opposite of negation, the sign which shows the *presence* of something, where something *is*. This is the mark that says 'there is something secret' (ON, pp. 23–7). *X* is a signature, a vote in favour, a kiss. *X* signs *both* what is lost *and* the point where the lost thing may be found. *X* is the structure of *khora*, that which grants all differences, that which makes the gift of philosophy's beginning. *X* is the sign of messianic hope, the longing for a blessed and just future. Derrida speaks (in 'Ulysses Gramophone') of the chiasmatic opening of the circle as 'a joyful dispersion' giving rise to affirmation and laughter.

Somewhere in the undecidable cross(ing) or chiasmus of language is what replaces, or remains after, the horizon of theology has been erased. Derrida effectively proposes the installation of the chiasmus within the space of deconstructed metaphysics. Is it at this crossing point that we see 'Derrida's theology': one which moves between life and death, between the old life-of-God theology of the metaphysics of presence and its repressed other: the theology of the death of God? If so, this is not a new 'life-of-God' theology (in either its negative or positive guises) and not a thoroughgoing 'death-of-God' theology. Derrida's theology is at the crossing of the two. And, as Derrida points out, 'crossing is not a neutral word ... recalling the cross-shaped crossing through under which one leaves Being or God to suffer' (OS p. 6), what Derrida elsewhere refers to as 'la figure christique' (Par, p. 209). Such a theology would mean that 'God is or appears, *is named*, within the difference between All and Nothing, Life and Death. Within Difference, and at bottom as Difference itself' (WD, p. 116).

Thus, in a very particular way we may say, and in the Derridean sense of the term, that God *survives* deconstruction. Derrida describes this 'survival' in 'Living On: Border Lines' as something other than 'living' in the sense of a stable or determinable state, namely progression, process, modulation, seriature, deferral, transfiguration, dissimulation. Survival is

> *arrêt de mort* that cannot be decided, neither life nor death, but rather LIVING ON, the very progression that belongs, without belonging, to the progression of life and death. Living on is not the opposite of living, just as it is not identical with living. The relationship is different, different from being identical, from the difference of distinctions – undecided, or, in a very rigourous sense, 'vague', *vagus*, evasive. (LO, p. 135)

God's survival, then, and the survival of theology depend upon the difference, or the process of the difference, between the life and the death of God. This is not theology *as such*, or the theo-phenomenological 'as such'. 'Theology not-as-such' is perhaps the clearest formula available.

Yet the determination of Derrida's 'theology' in this way instantly calls for a series of self-denying amendments and qualifications in order to block any drift towards a subtle coalescence of difference, or the non-phenomenal, into a determinate theological identity. What has just been designated as Derrida's 'theology' is, from another perspective, not theology at all, but the impossibility of theology. Or put otherwise, Derrida's theology is *only* theology *in so far as* it traverses a zone *formerly constituted* as theological. In this case the chi marks out a theology or even an atheology which cannot be calculated and which does not institute a determinate discourse. So the chi is not meant as an icon of any kind (as it arguably becomes in Jean-Luc Marion's God), but as a transcendence of the icon: a self-erasing intersection. Each of the twofold strokes of the chi cancels the iconography of the other – as Derrida puts it in *Glas* when he describes the chiasmatic structure of the book:

Two unequal columns, they say distyle, each of which – envelop(e)(s) or sheath(es), incalculably reverses, turns inside out, replaces, remarks, overlaps the other.

The incalculable of what remains calculates itself, elaborates all the *coups* [strokes, blows, etc.], twists or scaffolds them into silence, you would wear yourself out even faster by calculating them. Each little square is delimited, each column rises with an impassive self-sufficiency, and yet the element of contagion, the infinite circulation of general equivalence relates each sentence, each stump of writing . . . to each other, within each column and from one column to the other of what remained infinitely incalculable.

Almost. (G, p. 1)

The chiasmus of *Glas* remains in twisted circulation, always *otherwise* and never reduced to an *essence* or *foundation* of chi.

It would have to be said too that, for all its Christian resonance, the chi does not constitute a properly Christological figure, since the Derridean chi is a constant re-marking, or criss-crossing which deletes the cross. At best the chi would be a transfigured Christogram of the sort hinted at in the final lines of *Glas*, when Derrida speaks of a 'time to perfect the resemblance between Dionysus and Christ' (G, p. 262). So the chi might be Christological (or perhaps it would be better to say christogrammatological) on the condition of Christology thinking itself heterologically through its alternatives.

Perhaps this is possible and desirable – indeed Derrida notes in *Of Spirit* that 'certain Christian theologians' would readily argue for a Christological heterology (OS, pp. 109ff.) – but reflections of this kind would have to begin where Derrida's text leaves off. For his part Derrida illuminates the *possibility* of the impossible God. As for the Christian implications of the impossible God – theological, ecclesiastical, doctrinal, liturgical, spiritual – these are not elaborated in Derrida's writing.

Notes

1   The presence of the chi image in Derrida's text has already been noted, Derrida himself refers to Hans Miller's essay on this subject, 'Ariadne's Thread', *Critical Enquiry* (1976), p. 75. It is likely that Derrida was influenced by Merleau-Ponty's use of the image of the chiasmus to indicate the indeterminate space between subject and object: 'the joints where the multiple entries of the world cross' (M. Merleau-Ponty, *The Visible and the Invisible*, Northwestern University Press, Evanston, 1968, p. 260). Like Derrida, Merleau-Ponty deploys the chiasmus against the transcendental phenomenology of Husserl (for a sustained analysis of the *chiasm* in Merleau-Ponty see Petra Herkert, *Das Chiasma, zur Problematik von Sprache Bewußtsein und Unbewußtem bei Maurice Merleau-Ponty* (Königshausen und Neumann, Würzburg, 1987). M.C. Taylor notes the use of the chi figure as an emblem for *Glas* as a whole and a reinscription of the 'a' in *différance* (*Altarity*, University of Chicago Press, Chicago 1987, pp. 275f.). Gasché briefly identifies the *X* as an emblem of what he terms 'infrastructure' (R. Gasché, *The Tain of the Mirror: Derrida and the Philosophy of Reflection*, Harvard University Press, Cambridge, 1986, pp. 166f. and 172). Simon Critchley (*The Ethics of Deconstruction*, Blackwell, Oxford, 1992 and 'The Chiasmus: Levinas, Derrida and the Ethical Demand for Deconstruction', *Textual Practice*, III, April 1989, pp. 91–106) also notes the chiasmus as an emblem of the 'double gesture' of deconstruction. Critchley takes his lead from Levinas, who comments: 'En soulignant l'importance primordiale des questions posées par Derrida, nous avons voulu dire le plaisir d'un contact au coeur d'un chiasme' (E. Levinas, 'Tout Autrement in Jacques Derrida', *L'ARC*, 54, 1973). G. Hartman (*Saving the Text*, Johns Hopkins University Press, Baltimore, 1981) identifies the chi as the figure which marks the disruption of a metaphysics of subjectivity. See also Geoffrey Bennington's essay 'X', in J. Branningan, R. Robbins and J. Wolfreys, eds, *Applying: To Derrida* (Macmillan, Basingstoke, 1996).

2   In '+ R' Derrida claims that the figure *X* is the 'general intersection' of *Glas* (TP, p. 166).

3   For Derrida's comments on the circle in this respect see for example, 'Différance', M, p. 12; or PC, p. 474.

4   In *The Archaeology of the Frivolous*, for example. Derrida contrasts Condillac's serious, purposeful circle of 'semantic identity' with the 'elliptical and frivolous blow' of his own text (AF, pp. 117–8). This blow is later described as producing a 'line of disintegration, which is not straight or continuous or regular ... philosophy deviates from itself and gives rise to the blows that will strike it nevertheless from the outside. On this condition alone, at once internal and external, is deconstruction possible' (ibid., p. 132). Desire (frivolity) and necessity (seriousness) inevitably cross one another in philosophical texts to produce a condition Derrida calls 'chiasmatic' (ibid., p. 134). For other references to the chi or *X* see: P, pp. 46, 56f. and 70; G, pp. 43, 189 and 192; OG, pp. 65–73; M, pp. 260–71; WD, p. 296; D, pp. 24–5, 35, 44, 348–9, 354–5 and 362; Par, pp. 36, 151, 209, 246 and 272; TP, p. 166; OS, pp. 51–4 and 112; Psy, pp. 63, 81 and 536–7; LG, p. 238; GT, pp. 6–9; S, pp. 54, 130; PC, pp. 92, 393 and 401; ON, pp. 12 and 97; RD, p. 85; Pol, p. 296; Dem, pp. 28, 89 and 92; TS, p. 58.

5   This double gesture echoes strongly the twin aspects of Heidegger's chiasmus over Being, what he calls 'the zone of the critical line': at once 'the locale of the essence of complete nihilism' and the place where 'the essence of metaphysics unfolds its utmost possibilities' (QB, p. 87). This is a place which overcomes the metaphysics of both 'the living and the dead God' (ibid., p. 71).

Bibliography

Texts by Jacques Derrida

Adieu à Emmanuel Levinas, Editions Galilée, Paris, 1997. [Tr. Pascale-Anne Brault and Michael Nass, *Adieu to Emmanuel Levinas*, Stanford University Press, Stanford, 1999.]

Altérités, Osiris, Paris, 1986. [Written with Pierre-Jean Labarrière, Francis Guibal and Stanislas Breton.]

'Apories: Mourir – s'attendre aux limites de la vérité', in *Le Passage des frontières: Autour du travail de Jacques Derrida*, Editions Galilée, Paris, 1993. [Tr. Thomas Dutoit, *Aporias*, Stanford University Press, Stanford, 1993.]

'*As if* I were Dead', interview in John Brannigan, Ruth Robbins and Julian Wolfreys, eds, *Applying: To Derrida*, Macmillan, London, 1996.

L'archéologie du frivole: Lire Condillac, Denoël/Gonthier, Paris, 1976. [Tr. John P. Leavey Jr, *The Archaeology of the Frivolous: Reading Condillac*, University of Nebraska Press, Lincoln, 1987.]

L'autre cap, Editions de Minuit, Paris 1991. [Tr. Pascale-Anne Brault and Michael Nass, *The Other Heading: Reflections on Today's Europe*, Indiana University Press, Bloomington, 1992.]

'Avances', an introduction to Serge Margel, *Le Tombeau du Dieu Artisan*, Editions de Minuit, Paris, 1995.

'Before the Law' in Derek Attridge, ed., *Acts of Literature*, Routledge, London, 1992.

La Carte Postale: de Socrate à Freud et au-delà, Aubier-Flammarion, Paris, 1980. [Tr. Alan Bass, *The Post Card: From Socrates to Freud and Beyond*, University of Chicago Press, Chicago, 1987.]

'Che cos'è la poesia?', *Poesia*, vol. 1, no. 11. [Tr. Peggy Kamuf, 'Che cos'è la poesia?', in *A Derrida Reader*, Columbia University Press, New York, 1991.]

'Circonfession: cinquante-neuf périodes et périphrases', in *Jacques Derrida,* (written with Geoffrey Bennington), Editions du Seuil, Paris, 1991. [Tr. Geoffrey Bennington, *Jacques Derrida*, University of Chicago Press, Chicago, 1993.]

De la grammatologie, Editions de Minuit, Paris, 1967. [Tr. Gayatri Spivak, *Of Grammatology*, Johns Hopkins University Press, Baltimore, 1976.]

De L'espirit: Heidegger et la question, Editions Galilée, Paris, 1987. [Tr.

Geoffrey Bennington and Rachel Bowlby, *Of Spirit: Heidegger and the Question*, University of Chicago Press, Chicago, 1989.]

Demeure: Maurice Blanchot, Editions Galilée, Paris, 1998. [Tr. Elizabeth Rottenberg, *Demeure: Fiction and Testimony*, Stanford University Press, Stanford, 2000.]

La dissemination, Editions du Seuil, Paris, 1972. [Tr. Barbara Johnson, *Dissemination*, Athlone Press, London, 1981.]

'Donner la mort', in *L'éthique du don, Jacques Derrida et la pensée du don*, Métailié-Transition, Paris, 1992. [Tr. David Wills, *The Gift of Death*, University of Chicago Press, Chicago, 1995.]

Donner le temps I, La fausse monaie, Editions Galilée, 1991. [Tr. Peggy Kamuf, *Given Time I: Counterfeit Money*, University of Chicago Press, Chicago, 1992.]

Du droit à la philosophie, Editions Galilée, Paris, 1990.

'D'un ton apocalyptique adopté naguère en philosophie', in Philippe Lacoue-Labarthe and Jean-Luc Nancy, eds, *Les fins de l'homme: à partir du travail de Jacques Derrida*, Editions Galilée, Paris, 1981. Also published as a volume: *D'un ton apocalyptique adopté naguère en philosophie*, Editions Galilée, Paris, 1983. [Tr. John P. Leavey Jr, 'Of an Apocalyptic Tone Recently Adopted in Philosophy', *The Oxford Literary Review*, vol. 6, no. 2, 1984.]

'Economimesis', in *Mimesis: Des articulations*, Syliane Agacinski et al., eds, Aubier-Flammarion, Paris, 1975. [Tr. Richard Klein, 'Economimesis', *Diacritics*, vol. 11, no. 2, 1981.]

L'écriture et la différence, Editions du Seuil, Paris, 1967. A collection of essays published from 1963 to 1967. [Tr. Alan Bass, *Writing and Difference*, Routledge and Kegan Paul, London, 1978.]

Edmund Husserl's 'L'origine de la géometrie', Presses Universitaires de France, Paris, 1962. [Tr. John P. Leavey Jr, *Edmund Husserl's Origin of Geometry: An Introduction*, University of Nebraska Press, Lincoln, 1989.]

Epérons: Les styles de Nietzsche, Aubier-Flammarion, 1978. [Tr. Barbara Harlow, *Spurs: Nietzsche's Styles*, University of Chicago Press, Chicago, 1979.]

Feu la Cendre, Editions des femmes, Paris, 1987. [Tr. Ned Nukacher, *Cinders,* University of Nebraska Press, Lincoln, 1991.]

'Foi et Savoir: Les deux sources de la "religion" au limites de la simple raison', in Jacques Derrida and Gianni Vattimo, eds, *La Religion*, Editions du Seuil, Paris, 1996. [Tr. Samuel Weber, 'Faith and Knowledge', in *Religion*, eds. Derrida and Vattimo, Polity, Oxford, 1998.]

Force de loi, Editions Galilée, Paris, 1994. [Tr. M. Quaintance, 'Force of Law', in G Anidjar, ed., *Acts of Religion*, Routledge, London, 2002.]

'Glas', in *Jacques Derrida: L'ARC,* no. 54, 1973.

Glas, Editions Galilée, Paris, 1974. [Tr. John P. Leavey Jr and Richard Rand, *Glas*, University of Nebraska Press, Lincoln, 1986.]

'I Have a Taste for the Secret', in Jacques Derrida and Maurizo Ferraris, *A Taste for the Secret,* Polity, Oxford, 2001.

Khora, Editions Galilée, Paris, 1993. [Tr. Ian McLeod, 'Khora', in Thomas Dutoit, ed., *On The Name*, Stanford University Press, Stanford, 1993.]

Limited Inc abc..., ed. Gerald Graff, Northwestern University Press, Evanston, 1988.

Mal d'Archive, Editions Galilée, Paris, 1995. [Tr. Eric Prenowitz, *Archive Fever*, University of Chicago Press, Chicago, 1996.]

Marges de la philosophie, Editions de Minuit, Paris, 1972. [Tr. Alan Bass, *Margins of Philosophy*, University of Chicago Press, Chicago, 1982.]

Mémoires d'aveugle: L'autoportrait et autre ruines, Editions de la réunion des musée nationaux, Paris 1990. [Tr. Pascale-Anne Brault and Michael Nass, *Memoirs of the Blind: The Self-Portrait and Other Ruins*, University of Chicago Press, Chicago, 1993.]

Mémoires pour Paul de Man, Editions Galilée, Paris, 1988. [Tr. Cecile Lindsay, Jonathan Culler, Eduardo Cadava, Kevin Newmark and Peggy Kamuf, *Mémoires for Paul de Man*, Columbia University Press, New York, 1989 (rev. edn).]

L'Oreille de l'autre: Otobiographies, transferts, traductions: Texts et débats avec Jacques Derrida, eds, C. Lévesque and Christie V. McDonald, VLB Editions, Montréal, 1982. [Tr. Peggy Kamuf and Avital Ronell in Christie V. McDonald, ed., *The Ear of the Other: Otobiography, Transference, Translation: Texts and Discussions with Jacques Derrida*, University of Nebraska Press, Lincoln, 1988.]

'La phénoménologie et la clôture de la métaphysique', *Epochés*, vol. 7, 1966.

Parages, Editions Galilée, Paris, 1986.

Passions, Editions Galilée, Paris, 1993. [Tr. David Wood, 'Passions: An Oblique Offering', in Thomas Dutoit, ed., *On The Name*, Stanford University Press, Stanford, 1993.] A first version was published in an English translation as 'Passions: An Oblique Offering, in David Wood, ed., *Derrida: A Critical Reader*, Blackwell, Oxford, 1992.

Points de suspension, Entretiens, Editions Galilée, Paris, 1992. [Tr. Peggy Kamuf et al., *Points ... Interviews, 1974–1994*, Stanford University Press, Stanford, 1995.]

Politiques de l'amitié, Editions Galilée, Paris, 1994. [Tr. George Collins, *The Politics of Friendship*, Verso, London, 1997.]

Positions, Editions de Minuit, Paris, 1972. A collection of interviews from 1967 to 1971. [Tr. Alan Bass, *Positions*, University of Chicago Press, Chicago, 1981.]

Le problème de la genèse dans la philosophie de Husserl, Presses Universitaires de France, Paris, 1990.

Psyché: Inventions de l'autre, Editions Galilée, Paris, 1987.

'Remarks on Deconstruction and Pragmatism', S. Critchley et al., eds, *Deconstruction and Pragmatism*, Routledge, London, 1996.

Sauf le nom, Editions Galilée, Paris, 1993. [Tr. John P. Leavey Jr, 'Sauf le nom (Post-Scriptum)', in Thomas Dutoit, ed., *On The Name*, Stanford University Press, Stanford, 1993.] An earlier version of this essay appeared a year earlier in English under the title 'Post-Scriptum: Aporias, Ways and Voices', in Toby Foshay and Harold Coward, eds, *Derrida and Negative Theology*, State University of New York Press, Albany, 1992.

Schibboleth, pour Paul Celan, Editions Galilée, Paris 1986. [Tr. Joshua Wilner, 'Shibboleth', in Geoffrey Hartman and Sanford Budick, eds, *Midrash and Literature*, Yale University Press, New Haven, 1986.]

Signéponge/Signsponge [bilingual edition] tr. Richard Rand, Columbia University Press, New York, 1984. Earlier versions of this essay appeared in translation in *Oxford Literary Review*, vol. 5, nos 1–2, 1982; and in Philippe Bonnefis and O. Oster, eds, *Ponge Inventeur et Classique*, Union Générale d'Editions, Paris, 1975.

Spectres de Marx, Editions Galilée, 1993. [Tr. Peggy Kamuf, *Specters of Marx: the State of the Debt, the Work of Mourning and the New International*, Routledge, New York, 1994.]

Ulysses Gramophone: Deux mots pour Joyce, Editions Galilée, Paris, 1987.

La vérité en peinture, Aubier-Flammarion, Paris, 1978. [Tr. G. Bennington and Ian McLeod, *The Truth in Painting*, University of Chicago Press, Chicago, 1987.]

'Un ver à soie: Points de vue piqués sur l'autre voile', in J. Derrida and H. Cixous, *Voiles*, Editions Galilée, Paris, 1998. [Tr. G. Bennington, 'A Silkworm of One's Own', in G. Anidjar, ed., *Acts of Religion*, Routledge, London, 2002.]

La voix et le phènomène: Introduction au problème du signe dans la phénoménologie de Husserl, Presses Universitaires de France, Paris, 1967. [Tr. David B. Allison, *Speech and Phenomena and other Essays on Husserl's Theory of Signs*, Northwestern University Press, Evanston, 1973.]

Texts by Other Authors

Adorno, T. W., *Negative Dialectics*, tr. E.B. Ashton, Routledge and Kegan Paul, London, 1973.

———, *The Jargon of Authenticity*, tr. K. Tarnowski and F. Will, Routledge and Kegan Paul, London, 1973.

Agamben, G., *Language and Death: the place of negativity*, tr. K. Pinkus and M. Hardt, University of Minnesota Press, Minneapolis, 1991.

Altizer, Thomas J.J., *The Descent into Hell: A Study of the Radical Reversal of the Christian Consciousness*, Seabury Press, New York, 1979.

———, *Genesis and Apocalypse*, Westminster/John Knox Press, Louisville, 1990.

———, *History as Apocalypse*, State University of New York Press, New York, 1985.

Altizer, Thomas J.J. et al., *Deconstruction and Theology*, Crossroad Publishing, New York, 1982.

Barthes, Roland, *Camera Lucida*, tr. Richard Howard, Fontana, London, 1984.

———, *S/Z*, tr. Richard Howard, Hill and Wang, New York, 1974.

Baudrillard, Jean, *L'Echange symbolique et la mort*, Gallimard, Paris, 1976.

———, *Fatal Strategies*, tr. P. Beitchman and W. Niesluchowski, Semiotext(e), New York, 1990.

———, *Selected Writings*, ed. M. Poster, Polity Press, 1989.

Bell, David, 'Solipsism and Subjectivity', *European Journal for Philosophy*, vol. 4, no. 2, 1996.

———, *Husserl*, Routledge, London, 1989.

Beardsworth, Richard, *Derrida and the Political*, Routledge, London, 1996.

Bernet, Rudolf, 'Derrida–Husserl–Freud', *The Southern Journal of Philosophy*, vol. 32, 1993. (A supplement edited by Leonard Lawlor, including papers on Husserl and Derrida from The Spindel Conference, 1993.)

———, 'Is the Present ever Present? Phenomenology and the Metaphysics of Presence', *Research in Phenomenology*, 12, 1982.

Bernet, Rudolf et al., *An Introduction to Husserlian Phenomenology*, Northwestern University Press, Evanston, 1993.

Berry, Phillipa and Wernick, Andrew, eds., *Shadow of Spirit: Postmodernism and Religion*, Routledge, London, 1992.

Bernstein, Richard, ed., *Habermas and Modernity*, Polity Press, Cambridge, 1985.

Bonhoeffer, Dietrich, *Christology*, Collins, London, 1966.

Breech, James, *Jesus and Postmodernism*, Fortress Press, Minneapolis, 1989.

Bubner, Rüdiger, *Modern German Philosophy*, Cambridge University Press, Cambridge, 1981.

Bucher, Gérard, 'The Metaphor of the Sacred, or the Allegory of Origin', in Anna Teresa Tynieniecka, ed., *From the Sacred to the Divine: Analecta Husserliana*, vol. 43, Kluwer, Dordrecht, 1993.

Buckley, Michael, *At the Origins of Modern Atheism*, Yale University Press, New Haven, 1987.

Cairns, Dorian, *Conversations with Husserl and Fink*, Martinus Nijhoff, The Hague, 1976.

Caputo, John, 'A Community Without Truth: Derrida and the Impossible Community', *Research in Phenomenology*, vol. 26, 1996.

———, *The Prayers and Tears of Jacques Derrida: Religion without Religion*, Indiana University Press, Bloomington, 1997.

Carr, David, *Interpreting Husserl. Critical and Comparative Studies*, Martinus Nijhoff, Dordrecht, 1987.

Claude Evans, J., *Strategies of Deconstruction, Derrida and the Myth of the Voice*, University of Minnesota Press, Minneapolis, 1991.

Critchley, Simon, *The Ethics of Deconsruction: Derrida and Levinas*, Blackwell, Oxford, 1992.

———, 'The Chiasmus: Levinas, Derrida and the Ethical Demand for Deconstruction', *Textual Practice*, no.1, 1989.

Critchley, Simon, ed., *Deconstruction and Pragmatism*, Routledge, London, 1996.

———, *Deconstructive Subjectivities*, State University of New York Press, New York, 1996.

Clarke, Maudmarie, *Nietzsche on Truth and Philosophy*, Cambridge University Press, Cambridge, 1990.

Culler, Jonathan, *On Deconstruction: Theory and Criticism after Structuralism*, Routledge and Kegan Paul, London, 1983.

Cumming, Robert, *Phenomenology and Deconstruction* (3 vols), University of Chicago Press, Chicago, 1991.

———, 'The Odd Couple: Heidegger and Derrida', *The Review of Metaphysics*, vol. 34, no. 3, 1978.

Cupitt, Don, 'Kant and the Negative Theology', in B. Hebblethwaithe and S. Sutherland, eds, *The Philosophical Frontiers of Christian Theology*, Cambridge University Press, Cambridge, 1982.

———, *Creation out of Nothing,* SCM Press, London, 1990.

Danto, Arthur, *Nietzsche as Philosopher*, Columbia University Press, New York, 1965.

Descartes, René, *Meditations on First Philosophy*, tr. John Cottingham, Cambridge University Press, Cambridge, 1986.

Descombes, Vincent, *Modern French Philosophy*, Cambridge University Press, Cambridge, 1980.

Dastur, Françoise, 'Finitude and Repetition in Husserl and Derrida', in *The Southern Journal of Philosophy*, vol. 32, 1993. (A supplement edited by Leonard Lawlor, including papers on Husserl and Derrida from The Spindel Conference, 1993.)

Detweiler, Robert, ed., *Derrida and Biblical Studies*, Scholars Press, Chicago, 1982.

Davies, Paul, 'Commentary: Being Faithful to Impossibility', *The Southern Journal of Philosophy*, vol. 32, 1993. (A supplement edited by Leonard Lawlor, including papers on Husserl and Derrida from The Spindel Conference, 1993.)

Dillon, M.C., ed., *Ecart and Différance: Merleau-Ponty and Derrida on Seeing and Writing*, Humanities Press, New Jersey, 1997.

Dreyfus H. and Hall H., eds., *Heidegger: A Critical Reader*, Blackwell, Oxford, 1992.

Dupré, Louis, *A Dubious Heritage: Studies in the Philosophy of Religion after Kant*, Paulist Press, New York, 1977.

———, 'Husserl's Thought on God and Faith', *Philosophy and Phenomenological Research*, vol. 29, no. 2, 1968–69.

Eagleton, Terry, *The Ideology of the Aesthetic*, Blackwell, Oxford, 1990.

Edie, James, *Edmund Husserl's Phenomenology: A Critical Commentary*, Indiana University Press, Bloomington, 1987.

Farber, Marvin, *The Aims of Phenomenology: The Motives, Methods and Impact of Husserl's Thought*, Harper and Row, New York, 1966.

————, *The Foundations of Phenomenology: Edmund Husserl and The Quest for a Rigorous Science of Philosophy*, State University of New York Press, Albany, 1968.

Farley E., *Ecclesial Man*, Fortress Press, Philadelphia, 1975.

Finlayson, Clarence, 'The Problem of God', *Philosophy and Phenomenological Research*, vol. 9, no. 3, 1948–49.

Foucault, Michel, *The Archaeology of Knowledge*, Tavistock Publications, London, 1972.

————, 'Nietzsche, Genealogy and History', in D. Bouchard, ed., *Language, Counter-memory, Practice: Selected Essays and Interviews by Michel Foucault*, Blackwell, Oxford, 1977.

————, *The Order of Things*, Tavistock Publications, London, 1970.

Fraser, Giles, *Redeeming Nietzsche*, Routledge, London, 2002.

Fynsk, Christopher, *Heidegger: Thought and History*, Cornell University Press, Ithaca, 1986.

Gadamer, Hans-Georg, *Heidegger's Ways*, State University of New York Press, 1994.

————, *Philosophical Hermeneutics*, tr. David Linge, University of California Press, 1976.

Gasché, Rodolphe, 'Infrastructures and Systematicity', in J. Sallis, ed., *Deconstruction and Philosophy: The Texts of Jacques Derrida*, University of Chicago Press, Chicago, 1987.

————, *Inventions of Difference: On Jacques Derrida*, Harvard University Press, Cambridge, 1994.

————, *The Tain of the Mirror: Derrida and the Philosophy of Reflection*, Harvard University Press, Cambridge, 1986.

Grene, Marjorie, 'Life, Death and Language: Some Thoughts on Wittgenstein and Derrida', *Partisan Review*, 43, 1976.

Guerrière, D., ed., *Phenomenology of the Truth Proper to Religion*, State University of New York Press, New York, 1990.

Guignon, Charles, ed., *The Cambridge Companion to Heidegger*, Cambridge University Press, Cambridge, 1993.

Habermas, Jürgen, *Legitimation Crisis*, Polity Press, Cambridge, 1988.

————, *The Philosophical Discourse of Modernity*, Polity Press, Cambridge, 1987.

Halliburton, David, *Poetic Thinking*, University of Chicago Press, Chicago, 1981.

Hart, James, 'The Study of Religion in Husserl's Writings', in M. Daniel and L. Embree, eds, *Phenomenology of the Cultural Disciplines*, Kluwer Academic Publishers, Dordrecht, 1994.

Hart, J.G. and Laycock, S., eds., *Essays in Phenomenological Theology*, State University of New York Press, New York, 1986.

Hart, Kevin, *The Trespass of The Sign: Deconstruction, Theology and Philosophy*, Cambridge University Press, Cambridge, 1989.

Hartman, G., *Saving the Text*, Johns Hopkins University Press, Baltimore, 1981.

Hartman G., ed., *Deconstruction and Criticism*, Routledge and Kegan Paul, London, 1979.

Hegel, G.W.F., *Early Theological Writings*, tr. T.M. Knox, University of Chicago Press, Chicago, 1948.

————, *Faith and Knowledge*, tr. H.S. Harris and W. Cerf, State University of New York Press, New York, 1977.

————, *Lectures on the Philosophy of Religion (1827)*, tr. R.F. Brown et al., University of California Press, Berkeley, 1988.

————, *Phenomenology of Spirit*, tr. A.V. Miller, Oxford University Press, Oxford, 1977.

————, *Lectures on the Philosophy of History*, tr. R. Brown et al., University of California Press, Berkeley, 1990.

Heidegger, Martin, *Basic Problems of Phenomenology*, tr. Albert Hofstadter, Indiana University Press, Bloomington, 1982.

————, *Basic Questions of Philosophy*, tr. Richard Rojcewicz and André Schuwer, Indiana University Press, Bloomington, 1994.

————, *Basic Concepts*, tr. Gary E. Aylesworth, Indiana University Press, Bloomington, 1993.

————, *Being and Time*, tr. Edward Robinson and John Macquarrie, Harper and Row, New York, 1982.

————, *Beiträge zur Philosophie (vom Ereignis)*, Gesamtausgabe Band 65, III. Abteilung: Unveröffentliche Abhandlungen, Vittorio Klostermann, Frankfurt, 1989.

————, 'Das mögliche Ganzsein des Daseins und das Sein zum Tode', in *Der Tod in der Moderne*, Anton Hain Meisenheim, Königstein, 1979.

————, *The Essence of Reasons*, Northwestern University Press, Evanston, 1969.

————, *Gelassenheit*, Neske, Tübingen, 1959.

————, *Hegel's Phenomenology of Spirit*, Indiana University Press, Bloomington, 1988.

————, *History of the Concept of Time*, tr. Theodore Kisiel, Indiana University Press, Bloomington, 1992.

————, *Identity and Difference*, tr. Joan Stambaugh, Harper and Row, New York, 1969.

————, *Introduction to Metaphysics*, tr. Ralph Manheim, Yale University Press, New Haven, 1987.

————, *Nietzsche I: The Will to Power as Art*, tr. David Farrell Krell, Harper and Row, New York, 1979.

————, *Nietzsche II: The Eternal Recurrence of the Same*, tr. David Farrell Krell, Harper and Row, New York, 1984.

————, *Nietzsche III: The Will to Power as Knowledge and Metaphysics*, tr. Joan Stambaugh, Harper and Row, New York, 1987.

————, *Nietzsche IV: Nihilism*, tr. Frank Capuzzi, Harper and Row, New York, 1982.

————, *On The Way To Language*, tr. Peter Hertz, Harper and Row, New York, 1971.

————, 'Only a God Can Save Us Now', in Günther Neske and Emil Kettering, eds, *Martin Heidegger and National Socialism: Questions and Answers*, Paragon House, New York, 1990.

————, *The Piety of Thinking*, tr. James G. Hart and John C. Maraldo, Indiana University Press, Bloomington, 1976.

————, *Poetry, Language, Thought*, tr. Albert Hofstadter, Harper and Row, New York, 1971.

————, *The Principle of Reason*, tr. Reginald Lilly, Indiana University Press, Bloomington, 1991.

————, *The Question Concerning Technology and Other Essays*, tr. William Lovitt, Harper and Row, New York, 1977.

————, *The Question of Being*, tr. William Kluback and Jean T. Wilde, Twayne, New York, 1958.

————, 'The Rectorate 1933/4: Facts and Thoughts', in Günther Neske and Emil Kettering, eds, *Martin Heidegger and National Socialism: Questions and Answers*, Paragon House, New York, 1990.

————, 'The Self Assertion of the German University', in Günther Neske and Emil Kettering, eds, *Martin Heidegger and National Socialism: Questions and Answers*, Paragon House, New York, 1990.

————, *What Is Called Thinking?*, tr. Fred D. Wieck and J. Glenn Gray, Harper and Row, New York, 1968.

————, *What Is Philosophy?*, tr. William Kluback and Jean T. Wilde, College and University Press, New Haven, 1958.

————, *What Is a Thing?*, tr. W.B. Barton and Vera Deutsch, Regnery, Chicago, 1969.

Held, K., *Lebendige Gegenwart*, Martinus Nijhoff, The Hague, 1966.

Henry, Michel et al., *Phénoménologie et Théologie*, Criterion, Paris, 1992.

Herkert, Petra, *Das Chiasma, zur Problematik von Sprache Bewußtsein und Unbewußtem bei Maurice Merleau-Ponty*, Königshausen und Neumann, Würzburg, 1987.

Housset, Emmanuel, 'Husserl et le Dieu d'Aristote', *Les Etudes Philosophiques*, 4, 1995.

Howells, Christina, *Derrida: Deconstruction from Phenomenology to Ethics*, Polity, Oxford, 1998.

Husserl, Edmund, *Cartesian Meditations*, tr. Dorian Cairns, Martinus Nijhoff, Dortrecht, 1960.

————, *The Crisis of the European Sciences and Transcendental Phenomenology*, tr. David Carr, Northwestern University Press, Evanston, 1970.

————, *Experience and Judgement*, tr. J. Churchill and Karl Ameriks, Northwestern University Press, Evanston, 1973.

————, *Ideas – General Introduction to Pure Phenomenology*, tr. W.R. Boyce Gibson, George Allen and Unwin, New York, 1931.

————, *Ideas Pertaining to a Pure Phenomenology and to a Phenomenological Philosophy (Second Book)*, tr. R. Rojcewicz and A. Schuwer, Kluwer Academic Publishers, Dordrecht, 1989.

————, *On the Phenomenology of the Consciousness of Internal Time (1893–1917)*, tr. J.B. Brough, Kluwer Academic Publishers, Dordrecht, 1991.

————, *Phenomenology and the Crisis of Philosophy*, tr. Quentin Lauer, Harper and Row, New York, 1965.

————, 'Der Ursprung der Geometrie als intentional-historishes Problem', *Revue internationale de philosophie*, vol. 1, no. 2, 1939.

————, Manuscripts from the *Nachlass*, Husserl Archive, Leuven:

A V 21	Ethnisches Leben. Theologie – Wissenschaft. [1924]
C 2 I	Rückgang zur urtümlichen Gegenwart. Ich und Ichprobleme, durchdacht von lebendigen Gegenwart aus. Ich als konkretes Thema der Selbstauslegung. [1932]
C2 II	Ich, das Ich meines Bewußtseinslebens als konkretes Thema . [1932]
C 2 III	'Ich' – durchdacht von der lebendige Gegenwart aus. [1932]
C 3 I	Urströmende Gegenwart: Weltzeitung durch Zeit-modalitäten. [1930]
C 3 II	Urströmende Gegenwart: Das Immanente Zeitfeld. [1930]
C 3 III	Reduktion auf die lebendige Gegenwart. [1931]
C 3 IV	'Lebendige Gegenwart' und konstitution der Welt. [1931]
C 3 V	Zum Aufbau der lebendige Gegenwart. [1931]
C 3 VI	Rückfrage zur Hyle. [1931]
C 5	Zur Strukturlehre der lebendige Gegenwart, von der Weltepoché rückfragend. [1930]
C 6	Erste Anfang eines methodishen Abbaus der urphänomenalen Gegenwart. [1930]
C 7 I	Von der Epoché aus Reduktion auf das primordiale Sein des Ego als urtümliches Strömen. [1932]
C 7 II	Uber Reduktion auf lebendige Gegenwart. [1932]
C 8 I	Zur Konstitution der intersubjectiven Welt. [1929]
C 10	'Das gehörte zum komplex der urtümlichen Gegenwart!'
C 11 V	Konstiutionsweg von der elementaren Struktur der lebendigen Gegenwart. [1931]
C 16 I	Die ichlichen Strukturen der lebendigen Gegenwart. [1931/2]

C 16 II Die Actmodification der Epoché. [1931]
C 16 IV Gefühl und Urkonsitution. [1932]
C 16 V Zum Studium der Ichlichen Struckturen der lebendige Gegenwart. [1931]
C 16 VI Phänomenologishe Archäologie: Rückfrage auf das Ich. [1932]
C 17 III Zur Gegebenheitsstrucktur der Welt als Phänomen.
C 17 IV Zur lebendige Gegenwart. [1930]
C 17 V Wie konsitutiert sich einheit einer realen Zeiträumlichkeit. [1931]
C 17 VI Geburt–Tod–Schlaf. [1931/2]
E III 4 Teleologie. [1930]
E III 9 Instinkt, Wert, Gut, Teleologie, Normstruktur der Persönlichkeit. [1931]

Ingraffia, Brian, *Postmodern Theory and Biblical Theology*, Cambridge University Press, Cambridge, 1995.

Janicaud, Dominique, *Le tournant théologique de la phénomenologie Française*, Editions de l'éclat, Combas, 1991.

Kaufmann, Walter, *Nietzsche: Philosopher, Psychologist, Antichrist*, Princeton University Press, Princeton, 1974.

Kearney, R., ed., *Dialogues with Contemporary Continental Thinkers*, Manchester University Press, Manchester, 1984.

Kellner, Douglas, *Jean Baudrillard: From Marxism to Postmodernism and Beyond*, Polity Press, Cambridge, 1989.

Kermode, Frank, *The Sense of an Ending, Studies in the Theory of Fiction*, Oxford University Press, Oxford, 1966.

———, *The Genesis of Secrecy – On the Interpretation of Narrative*, Harvard University Press, Cambridge, 1979.

Kierkegaard, Søren, 'The Work of Love in Remembering One Dead', *Works of Love*, Collins, London, 1962.

Kisiel, Theodore, *The Genesis of Heidegger's Being and Time*, University of California Press, Berkeley, 1993.

Koestenbaum, P., *The Vitality of Death: Essays in Existential Psychology and Philosophy*, Greenwood Publishing, Westport, 1971.

Kohák, Erazim, ed., *Jan Patočka: Philosophy and Selected Writings*, University of Chicago Press, Chicago, 1989.

Kolokowski, Leszek, *Husserl and the Search for Certitude*, University of Chicago Press, Chicago, 1975.

Kojève, Andre, *Introduction to the Reading of Hegel*, tr. J.H. Nichols, Basic Books, New York, 1960.

Kovacs, G., *The Question of God in Heidegger's Phenomenology*, Northwestern University Press, Evanston, 1990.

Krell, David Farrell, *Infectious Nietzsche*, Indiana University Press, Bloomington, 1996.

———, *Intimations of Mortality: Time, Truth and Finitude in Heidegger's*

Thinking of Being, Pennsylvania State University Press, University Park, 1986.

Lampert, Laurence, *Nietzsche's Teaching*, Yale University Press, New Haven, 1986.

Landgrebe, Ludwig, 'Phenomenology and Metaphysics', *Philosophy and Phenomenological Research*, vol. 10, no. 2, 1949–50.

Laycock, Steven, *Foundations for a Phenomenological Theology,* The Edwin Meller Press, Lewiston, 1988.

Levinas, Emmanuel, *Otherwise than Being or Beyond Essence*, tr. A. Lingis, Martinus Nijhoff, the Hague, 1981.

————, *The Theory of Intuition in Husserl's Phenomenology*, tr. A. Orianne, Northwestern University Press, Evanston, 1973.

————, *Totality and Infinity*, tr. A. Lingis, Martinus Nijhoff, the Hague, 1969.

————, 'Tout Autrement' in *Jacques Derrida, L'ARC,* no. 54, 1973.

Lingis, Alphonso, *Deathbound Subjectivity*, Indiana University Press, Bloomington, 1989.

Lucy, Niall, *Debating Derrida*, Melbourne University Press, Victoria, 1995.

Lyotard, Jean-François, *The Postmodern Condition: A Report on Knowledge*, tr. G. Bennington and B. Massumi, History and Theory of Literature series, vol. 10, Manchester University Press, Manchester, 1984.

Macann, Christopher, ed., *Critical Heidegger*, Routledge, London, 1996.

Mall, R.A., 'Theology and Phenomenology', *Husserl Studies*, vol. 8, 1991.

Marion, Jean-Luc, *God without Being*, tr. Thomas Carlson, University of Chicago Press, Chicago, 1991.

————, 'Le phénomène saturé', in ed. M. Henry et al., eds, *Phénoménologie et Théologie*, Criterion, Paris, 1992.

Matthews, Eric, *Twentieth Century French Philosophy*, Oxford University Press, Oxford, 1996.

McIntyre, Alasdair and Ricoeur, Paul, *The Religious Significance of Atheism*, Columbia University Press, New York, 1969.

McKenna,W. and Claude Evans, J., eds, *Derrida and Phenomenology*, Kluwer, Dordrecht, 1995.

Megill, Alan, *Prophets of Extremity: Nietzsche, Heidegger, Foucault, Derrida*, University of California Press, Berkeley, 1985.

Melville, Stephen, *Philosophy Besides Itself: On Deconstruction and Modernism*, Minneapolis University Press, Minneapolis, 1986.

Merleau-Ponty, Maurice, *The Visible and the Invisible*, Northwestern University Press, Evanston, 1968.

————, 'What is Phenomenology', in J.D. Bettis, ed., *Phenomenology of Religion*, SCM, London, 1969.

Montefiore, Alan, ed., *Philosophy in France Today*, Cambridge University Press, Cambridge, 1983.

Mohanty, J.N. et al., *Phenomenological Inquiry*, vol. 14, 'Phenomenological Approaches to the Divine', 1990.

Moran, Dermot, *An Introduction to Phenomenology*, Routledge, London, 2000.

Mortley, Raoul, *French Philosophers in Conversation*, Routledge, London, 1991.

Murray, Michael, ed., *Heidegger and Modern Philosophy*, Yale University Press, New Haven, 1978.

Mouffe, Chantal, ed., *Deconstruction and Pragamatism*, Routledge, London, 1996.

Nietzsche, Friedrich, *Beyond Good and Evil*, tr. R. Hollingdale, Penguin Books, London, 1973.

————, *The Birth of Tragedy*, tr. S. Whiteside, Penguin Books, London, 1993.

————, *Daybreak*, tr. R. Hollingdale, Cambridge University Press, Cambridge, 1982.

————, *Ecce Homo*, tr. R. Hollingdale, Penguin Books, London, 1992.

————, *The Gay Science*, tr. W. Kaufmann, Vintage Books, New York, 1974.

————, *The Genealogy of Morals* (published with *The Birth of Tragedy*), tr. F. Golffing, Anchor Books, New York, 1956.

————, *Human All Too Human*, tr. R. Hollingdale, Cambridge University Press, Cambridge, 1986.

————, *Thus Spoke Zarathustra*, tr. R. Hollingdale, Penguin Books, London, 1961.

————, *The Will to Power*, tr. R. Hollingdale and W. Kauffmann, Vintage Books, New York, 1968.

————, *Twilight of the Idols* and *The Antichrist*, tr. R. Hollingdale, Penguin Books, London, 1990.

————, *Untimely Meditations*, tr. R. Hollingdale, Cambridge University Press, Cambridge, 1983.

Norris, Christopher, *Deconstruction: Theory and Practice*, Methuen, London, 1982.

————, *Derrida*, Fontana, London, 1987.

————, *Uncritical Theory: Postmodernism, Intellectuals and the Gulf War*, Lawrence and Wishart, London, 1992.

————, *The Conflict of the Faculties: Philosophy and Theory after Deconstruction*, Methuen, London, 1985.

Ott, Hugo, *Martin Heidegger: A Political Life*, Harper Collins, 1993.

Patočka, Jan, *Heretical Essays in the Philosophy of History*, tr. E. Kohák, Verdier, Lagrasse, 1981.

Perotti, J.L., *Heidegger and the Divine: The Thinker, The Poet and God*, Ohio University Press, Ohio, 1974.

Pickstock, Catherine, *After Writing*, Blackwell, Oxford 1998.

Pivcevic, E., *Husserl and Phenomenology*, Hutchinson, London, 1970.

Plato, *The Collected Dialogues*, eds. E. Hamilton and H. Cairns, Princeton University Press, Princeton, 1961.

Pöggler, Otto, *Martin Heidegger's Path of Thinking*, Humanities Press International, New Jersey, 1987.

Richardson, William, *Heidegger: Through Phenomenology to Thought*, Martinus Nijhoff, The Hague, 1974.

Ricoeur, Paul, 'The Critique of Subjectivity and Cogito in the Philosophy of Heidegger', in M. Frings, ed., *Heidegger and the Quest for Truth*, Quadrangle Books, Chicago, 1968.

———, *History and Truth*, tr. Charles Kelbley, Northwestern University Press, Evanston, 1965.

———, *Husserl: An Analysis of his Phenomenology,* Northwestern University Press, Evanston, 1967.

———, *Time and Narrative*, University of Chicago Press, Chicago, 1984.

———, *The Rule of Metaphor: Multidisciplinary Studies in the Creation of Meaning in Language*, Routledge and Kegan Paul, London, 1986.

Rockmore, Tom, *Heidegger and French Philosophy: Humanism, Antihumanism and Being*, Routledge, London, 1995.

Rorty, Richard, *Contingency, Irony and Solidarity*, Cambridge University Press, Cambridge, 1989.

———, *Essays on Heidegger and Others: Philosophical Papers Volume 2*, Cambridge University Press, Cambridge, 1991.

———, 'Is Derrida a Transcendental Philosopher?', in D. Wood, ed., *Derrida: A Critical Reader*, Blackwell, Oxford, 1992.

———, *Philosophy and the Mirror of Nature*, Princeton University Press, Princeton, 1980.

———, 'Philosophy as a Kind of Writing: An Essay on Derrida', *New Literary History*, 10, 1978.

Rosemann, Philipp, 'Penser L'Autre: théologie négative et postmodernité', *Revue Philosophique de Louvain*, vol. 91, no. 90, 1993.

Rosen, Stanley, *The Question of Being: A Reversal of Heidegger*, Yale University Press, New Haven, 1993.

Sallis, John, ed., *Deconstruction and Philosophy: The Texts of Jacques Derrida*, University of Chicago Press, Chicago, 1987.

Sartre, Jean-Paul, *Being and Nothingness*, tr. H. Barnes, Routledge, London, 1989.

Schultz, William and Fried, Lewis, *Jacques Derrida: An Annotated Primary and Secondary Bibliography*, Garland Publishing, New York, 1992.

Searle, John, *Speech Acts: An Essay in the Philosophy of Language*, Cambridge University Press, Cambridge, 1969.

———, 'Reiterating the Differences: A reply to Derrida', *Glyph 2*, 1977.

Silverman, Hugh, *Continental Philosophy I: Philosophy and Non-Philosophy since Merleau-Ponty*, Routledge, London, 1988.

———, *Continental Philosophy II: Derrida and Deconstruction*, Routledge, London, 1989.

Smith, B. and Smith, D., eds., *The Cambridge Companion to Husserl*, Cambridge University Press, Cambridge, 1995.

Sokolowski, Robert, *Husserlian Meditations*, Northwestern University Press, Evanston, 1974.

Spielberg, H., *The Phenomenological Movement: An Historical Introduction*, Martinus Nijhoff, The Hague, 1971.

Stapleton, Timothy, *Husserl and Heidegger: The Question of a Phenomenological Beginning*, State University of New York Press, Albany, 1963.

Steiner, George, *Heidegger*, Fontana, London, 1978.

Stern, J.P., *Nietzsche*, Fontana, London, 1978.

Strasser, S., 'Das Gottesproblem in der Spätphilosophie Edmund Husserls, *Philosophisches Jahrbuch*, 67, 1958.

———, 'History, teleology and God in the Philosophy of Husserl', *Analecta Husserliana*, vol. 9, Kluwer, Dordrecht, 1976.

Tavor Bannet, Eve, *Structuralism and the Logic of Dissent*, Macmillan, Basingstoke, 1989.

Taylor, Mark, ed., *Deconstruction in Context: Literature and Philosophy*, University of Chicago Press, Chicago, 1986.

Taylor, Mark, *Altarity*, University of Chicago Press, Chicago, 1987.

———, *De-constructing Theology*, Crossroad Publishing, New York, 1982.

———, *Erring: A Postmodern A/theology*, University of Chicago Press, Chicago, 1984.

———, 'Non-negative Negative Theology', *Diacritics*, vol. 20, no. 4, 1990.

Thao, Tran Duc, 'Dialectical Logic as the General Logic of Temporalization', in *The Logic of the Living Present, Analecta Husserliana*, vol. 46, ed. Anna Teresa Tynieniecka, Kluwer, Dordrecht, 1995.

———, *Phenomenology and Dialectical Materialism*, Kluwer, Dordrecht, 1986.

Tilley, T.W., et al., *Postmodern Theologies: The Challenge of Religious Diversity*, Orbis Books, New York, 1995.

Van Buren, John, *The Young Heidegger, Rumour of the Hidden King*, Indiana University Press, Bloomington, 1994.

Vanhoozer, Kevin, *Is there a Meaning in this Text?*, Apollos, Leicester, 1998.

Vlaisavljevic, Jugoslav, 'Husserl's Legacy in Derrida's Grammatological Opening', *Analecta Husserliana*, vol. 36, Kluwer, Dordrecht, 1991.

Vogel, Lawrence, *The Fragile 'we': Ethical Implications of Heidegger's 'Being and Time'*, Northwestern University Press, Evanston, 1994.

Völkner, Peter, *Derrida und Husserl: zur Dekonstruktion einer Philosophie der Präsenz*, Passagen Verlag, Vienna, 1993.

Ward, Graham, *Barth, Derrida and the Language of Theology*, Cambridge University Press, Cambridge, 1995.

Williams, J. R., *Martin Heidegger's Philosophy of Religion*, Canadian Corporation for Studies in Religion Supplements 2, Wilfred Laurier University Press, Ontario, Canada, 1977.

Wittgenstein, Ludwig, *Philosophical Investigations,* Blackwell, Oxford, 1968.

Wolin, Richard, ed., *The Heidegger Controversy: A Critical Reader*, MIT Press, Cambridge, 1993.

Wood, David, 'Derrida and the Paradoxes of Reflection', *Journal of the British Society of Phenomenology*, vol. 2, no. 3, 1980.

————, 'Style and Strategy at the Limits of Philosophy: Heidegger and Derrida', *The Monist*, 63, no. 4, 1980.

Wood, David, ed., *Derrida: A Critical Reader*, Blackwell, Oxford, 1992.

————, *Heidegger and Language*, Parousia Press, Warwick, 1981.

Wyschogrod, E., *Spirit in Ashes: Hegel, Heidegger and Man-made Mass Death*, Yale University Press, New Haven, 1985.

Index